T0313703

WHITHER RURAL INDIA?

Political Economy of Agrarian Transformation in Contemporary India

A FESTSCHRIFT FOR VENKATESH B. ATHREYA

WHITHER RURAL INDIA?

Political Economy of
Agrarian Transformation
in Contemporary India

A FESTSCHRIFT FOR VENKATESH B. ATHREYA

EDITED BY
A. Narayanamoorthy, R.V. Bhavani and R. Sujatha

 Tulika Books

Published by
Tulika Books
44 (first floor), Shahpur Jat, New Delhi 110 049, India
www.tulikabooks.in

First edition (hardback) 2019

ISBN: 978-81-937329-6-0

Printed at Chaman Offset, Delhi 110 002

Contents

Tables and Figures

Foreword

Professor Venkatesh Athreya, scholar, researcher, teacher and writer, is a widely respected academic in the country. Through his teaching and writing, he has influenced generations of students. He has come to the attention of the public at large through his writings. However, what makes him popular is his innate ability to make friends. He is a charming conversationalist and has the rare capacity to put at ease those with whom he engages. I have known him from the mid-1970s. In the 1980s, we were colleagues for a while in the Madras Institute of Development Studies. When I was working on one of my early writings, *Poverty, Planning and Social Transformation* (1978), he was one of those who helped me in articulating that poverty was essentially the result and reflection of the socio-economic order and hence its eradication would call for much more than economic growth, and that some forms of growth would indeed generate and increase poverty. More recently, Professor Athreya played a major role in bringing out the Tamil translation of my book, *Wealth and Illfare* (2015).

This volume in his honour by his former students and colleagues is a fitting tribute to him. Professor Athreya has paid special attention, by himself and along with his friends, on the major theme of the book, agriculture and rural transformation. Agriculture had been the major sector of the economy till Independence and the focus of planned development was to build up the industrial base of the economy. The 'reforms' initiated in 1991 have been giving further thrust in that direction. It can be claimed that these efforts have been successful to some extent because the share of agriculture and allied activities has come down drastically to about one-seventh of the gross domestic product. Other changes have also taken place, such as the introduction of modern technology, increased use of fertilizers and better use of water.

However, if the focus shifts from the physical aspects of agriculture to the people engaged in it, the picture that emerges is very different. At the aggregate level, more than half of the workforce is still in agriculture and many who are engaged in it do not find it a viable occupation. The large number of suicides among farmers and the increasing protest marches by farmers from different parts of the country to the national capital have brought agriculture to the attention of the public at large.

A critical analysis of this phenomenon at the aggregate level as well as through field studies has been undertaken by the contributors to this volume. There is, naturally, concentration of attention on the landless agricultural labourers and the small peasants, who together constitute the vast majority. However, the attempt has not been to project a particular point of view. Indeed, the field studies reported come to almost opposite conclusions, as for instance on the impact of the 'reforms' on the landless. There are different perspectives about the future of peasant farming. In other words, one of the major contributions of the book is that it opens a debate about the present and future of Indian agriculture. And I hope that, consequently, it will be widely read and discussed.

January 2019

C.T. KURIEN
Former Chairman and Director,
Madras Institute of Development Studies,
Chennai

Preface

This volume is the outcome of an international seminar, 'Agriculture and Rural India after Economic Reforms', organized in honour of Professor Venkatesh B. Athreya, at the M.S. Swaminathan Research Foundation (MSSRF), Chennai, during 29–30 January 2016. It was organized by Professor Athreya's research students as a token of their tribute to his significant contribution to teaching, research and training. With an MS and a PhD from Wisconsin University, USA, Athreya returned to India and worked with different leading institutes and universities. Over the years, he has extensively published research papers and books with reputed publishers on agriculture and rural development, with the main focus on improving the living standards of rural poor. It is not an exaggeration to underline here that the amount of training on research and teaching that we as students have got from him cannot be measured. Most students who completed a PhD under his guidance are from poor and rural backgrounds. All of them are well established today in their chosen fields of endeavour, which itself is a big acknowledgement of Professor Athreya's contribution to teaching, research and training.

This volume has thirteen chapters in all, including an Introduction, which covers various topical themes pertaining to agriculture and rural development. A snapshot of the papers included in the volume is presented in the introductory chapter. While organizing the seminar and preparing to bring out this volume, we have immensely benefited from various quarters. First of all, we would like to profusely thank all the authors who accepted our invitation and presented papers in the seminar, which form the chapters of this volume. We are equally thankful to all the scholars who acted as chairpersons of different sessions in the seminar.

The seminar was inaugurated by N. Ram, well-known journalist and Chairman, Kasturi and Sons, which publishes *The Hindu* and other dailies and magazines. R.S. Deshpande, former Director, Institute for Social and Economic Change, Bangalore and ICSSR Rajiv Gandhi National Professor, chaired the inaugural session. The valedictory address was delivered by Sheela Rani Chunkath, IAS officer (retd). We profusely thank all of them.

The gracious presence and participation of A. Vaidyanathan, former Member of the Planning Commission, Government of India and a pioneer in the field of agricultural economics, is gratefully acknowledged. Likewise, we are grateful to other senior economists, social scientists, persons in public life, teachers and students of economics, and others who participated in the seminar.

Besides the editors of this volume, Professor Athreya's students, viz. N. Ganga Vidya, K. Sivasubramanian, R. Gopinath, R. Rajkumar, V. Sivaprakasam, M. Nageswaran and R. Vidyasagar, not only financially contributed to organize the seminar, but have also supported us in our endeavour to bring out this volume. Friends and close associates of Athreya, viz. A. Rajagopal and Kasim Sait, also contributed financially. We are grateful to all of them, without whose support it would not have been possible to organize the seminar. We would also like to thank the students of A. Narayanamoorthy, viz. P. Alli, R. Suresh, N. Gayathri Devi, P. Jothi, N. Devika and C. Renuka, for helping us during the time of the seminar.

The co-sponsor of this seminar was the Rajiv Gandhi National Institute of Youth Development (RGNIYD), Sriperumbudur. We would like to thank particularly Dr Latha Pillai, the then Director of RGNIYD, for supporting the seminar and also sending their faculty members and students to participate in it. We will be failing in our duty if we do not acknowledge the great support of MSSRF where the event was held and many of the participants accommodated.

We wholeheartedly thank Indira Chandrasekhar and the entire editorial team of Tulika Books for patiently responding to our repeated queries in the course of bringing out this volume. We are hopeful that the papers included in the volume will be useful to teachers, researchers, students, policy makers and others concerned with agriculture and rural development. It is needless to add that the views expressed in the papers included in the book are those of the respective authors, and should not be attributed to the editors and the institutions with which they are affiliated.

A. NARAYANAMOORTHY, R.V. BHAVANI and R. SUJATHA

Introduction: Agriculture and Rural India after Economic Reforms

R.V. Bhavani, R. Sujatha and A. Narayanamoorthy

Indian agriculture is in crisis. India has a large percentage of its population still living in rural areas: 68.8 per cent as per the 2011 Census. Agriculture and allied sectors engage slightly more than half the workforce and account for about one-seventh of the gross domestic product (GDP).[1] Small and marginal farmers constitute the bulk of cultivators in India. According to the Agriculture Census 2015–16, small and marginal holdings (i.e. holdings less than 2 hectares in size) taken together constitute 86.21 per cent of operational holdings and account for 47.34 per cent of the operated area. Large holdings (10 hectares and above) account for just 0.57 per cent of operational holdings but control 9.04 per cent of the operated area, with semi-medium and medium holdings accounting for the remaining 13.22 per cent of operational holdings and 43.61 per cent of operated area. Prosperity and economic growth in rural areas, therefore, depend to a large extent on the productivity of small farmers and the allied workforce.

The acceleration of economic reforms characterized by deregulation, privatization and globalization from 1991 onwards was accompanied by a fall in public investment in agriculture and allied sectors. Ensuing developments created a situation of agrarian distress, which has been continuing for almost two decades now. More than 3,00,000 farmers' suicides were reported between 1997 and 2015, which indicate the worsening situation. The Situation Assessment Survey of Farmers pertaining to the years 2003–04 and 2012–13 found that farming was not seen as a viable occupation for a majority of the farmers. The period of reform also saw a collapse of rural employment, both between 1993–94 and 1999–2000, and 2004–05 and 2009–10. The apparently rapid growth of rural employment in the interim years, between 2000 and 2004, was primarily in the informal sector.

With neoliberal reforms having been in operation for over a quarter century, it seemed appropriate to take stock of their impact on agriculture and on the agrarian population. It was in this scenario that students of the eminent economist and academic Venkatesh Athreya got together and organized a two-day international seminar on the theme 'Agriculture and Rural India after Economic Reforms', on 29–30 January 2016, in honour of their teacher and as a small token of their gratitude to him.

Venkatesh Athreya has been working on issues of rural transformation in India from a critical political economy standpoint for more than three decades. He has been analysing the developments following the onset of economic reforms, and writing and speaking on them regularly. In particular, he has analysed in depth their impact on agriculture and the rural economy. The seminar brought together eminent academics and researchers from the field, both those who have been friends of Athreya over many years, as well as collaborators and younger academics who have been mentored by him. The volume in your hands contains the papers presented at this international seminar. It also includes a paper contributed subsequently.

In the inaugural session, N. Ram, eminent journalist and Chairman, Kasturi and Sons, who has known Athreya for over four decades, recounted details of Athreya's family and educational background, and his seminal contributions as a scholar, a social activist and a public intellectual. The valedictory session on the concluding day had Sheela Rani Chunkath, IAS (retd), felicitating Athreya. As the Collector of Pudukottai district, she had worked closely with Athreya in the mass literacy campaign in the district in 1991–92. Subsequently, she had worked with him on issues of gender equality, public health and environment. Sheela Rani Chunkath highlighted the aspects of social commitment and activism that were an essential part of Athreya, in addition to his being an academic. She highlighted his gender sensitivity, his amazing memory and ability to substantiate his arguments and present them cogently and diplomatically. V. Sridhar, journalist from the fortnightly *Frontline*, spoke of Athreya's contributions to *Frontline* as a columnist, his perceptive analysis and presentation in a form accessible to the general reader, and his adherence to deadlines.

Besides the contributors to this volume, other eminent academics also participated in the seminar and contributed valuable insights on the themes discussed. These included A. Vaidyanathan, an outstanding analyst of the political economy of Indian development and a former member of the Planning Commission of India; D. Narasimha Reddy who had headed the Department of Economics at Hyderabad Central University for many years;

R.S. Deshpande, former Director of the Institute of Social and Economic Change, Bengaluru; Sashanka Bhide and R. Maria Saleth, both former Directors of the Madras Institute of Development Studies, Chennai; and K.A. Manikumar, formerly Head of the Department of History at M.S. University, Tirunelveli.

The twelve papers in this collection range from micro-level studies that examine the ground reality from economic and sociological perspectives to macro and structural analyses of the larger picture. One paper brings in a historical perspective by examining policies that led to the Bengal Famine of 1943 and sees similarities with the neoliberal policies we are witness to today. Two papers examine issues from a sociological perspective. A paper by Narayanamoorthy, Athreya's first PhD student, has also been included in the volume. Many of the papers begin with the authors reminiscing about their association with Athreya or acknowledging his contributions. The first three papers in the volume look at the historical, structural and theoretical aspects; four papers examine issues from the perspective of policies relating to agriculture and the ecosystem, food, credit and cost of cultivation; and the remaining five papers examine evidence from primary-level studies and analyse the theoretical implications of the developments. The focus of each of the papers is discussed here.

Utsa Patnaik, in her paper, examines the factors that led to the Bengal Famine of 1943–44, referring to it as the forgotten 'Holocaust of Bengal', and discusses the larger context of macroeconomics of extreme demand compression. She discusses how the state's policy induced rapid profit inflation that redistributed incomes away from the mass of the working population towards capitalists and companies, which were then taxed. The paper also discusses at length how J.M. Keynes played a critical role in shaping the history of Indian affairs at different points, and how, through 'forced transferences of purchasing power', war financing was appropriated from the colonies. The paper illustrates how Bengal, a rich state before the British period, had been reduced to impoverishment by the end of the British rule in India, and how the famine was in reality a man-made disaster and not a natural one as perceived. The paper concludes by drawing parallels with the neoliberal policies being followed at present in India, and the failure to recognize the new form of imperialistic control through international financial organizations and transnational corporate interests.

Prabhat Patnaik analyses the appearance versus reality of Indian agriculture in his paper, and elucidates a 'disarticulation' within the economy between different sectors. He succinctly explains how a shift of public expenditure away from agriculture to non-agriculture increases the level of poverty in the economy even when the overall growth rate remains unchanged. The paper highlights that a reduction of public expenditure in the agricultural sector would imply an indirect form of taxation. Patnaik discusses in detail the primitive accumulation of capital in the Marxian context and expenditure in stock and flow form, and the need to look at supply and stock of foodgrains vis-à-vis purchasing power. The paper concludes that the process of 'development' has reduced the role of the agricultural sector, and that the process of 'disarticulation' between sectors is reflected in burgeoning stocks with the government from time to time even while the food intake of substantial segments of the population is declining.

Göran Djurfeldt's paper on agrarian transformation in India examines the issue with a sociological lens by looking at social mobility. He outlines the contours of a forthcoming book indicating an emerging scenario of pluriactive–smallholder pattern of agriculture that is different from models of both capitalist agriculture and cooperative agriculture. An extended presentation of this argument has since been published.[2]

The importance of natural resources in capital formation is widely recognized. U. Shankar's paper discusses agricultural growth vis-à-vis natural resource capital formation and how the latter has shown only minimal growth. It reviews past agricultural policies relating to land, water, fertilizers and pesticides, organic farming, technology development and agriculture's linkage to ecosystem services, and examines their current status. It also assesses the extent to which the full costs and benefits are captured in accounting and prices, and suggests measures to achieve sustainable development. There is discussion on the need for agri-environmental policies that incentivize farmers and public investment in eco-system services. The author argues for revisiting agricultural policies keeping the environment as the third pillar of sustainable development.

Madhura Swaminathan, in her paper, discusses the evolution of food policy in India through three phases, culminating in the National Food Security Act (NFSA). The first was the phase of universal public distribution system (PDS) from the mid-1960s to the mid-1990s; the second phase started in the 1990s with targeted PDS, where being below the poverty line was the criterion for selection of eligible beneficiaries; the third is the phase following the enactment of the NFSA in 2013. The author looks at the issues of errors of inclusion and exclusion in the PDS which have a serious impact on food-insecure households, and their welfare implications. She discusses how recent policies continue to marginalize food-insecure communities, and the need to revisit concepts of estimation of waste and inefficiency. The primary concern expressed by the author is related to cash transfers and the real value of these transfers in the context of rising prices. The paper also explores the likely impact of schemes of cash transfer on both procurement from farmers and the distribution network. The importance of food sovereignty and the need to make a rational choice between self-sufficiency and self-reliance, and dependence on global food markets, in conditions of rising price volatility are discussed in detail. The paper also emphasizes that a shift from kind to cash transfers could weaken the system of public procurement and distribution, and why that is inadvisable given the prevalence of food insecurity in India. It argues that serious implementation of the NFSA is the need of the hour.

The paper on agricultural credit and financial liberalization by R. Ramakumar highlights the slowdown in outflow of formal agricultural credit immediately following the onset of reforms and increase in share of informal credit; this seemed to reverse the trend that followed the nationalization of banks in 1969, and the subsequent phase of social and development banking that lasted till 1991. The period between 1991 and 2004 saw a decline in the availability of formal credit and a rise in its cost. Post 2004, an increase in the quantum of formal sector credit for agriculture was observed. However, an analysis of the direction of credit flows reveals that the beneficiaries were corporate groups, joint stock companies and other organizations indirectly involved in agricultural production, and not the farmers themselves. The author critically analyses the implications of this trend for the agricultural sector and for different segments of the agrarian population.

Farmers cultivating cotton have been among the most affected in the post-liberalization period. Using data from the cost of cultivation survey published by the Commission for Agricultural Costs and Prices (CACP) for the period 1970–71 to 2011–12, Narayanamoorthy analyses the trends in profitability of cotton crop in four major cotton-growing states of the country. The study also compares profit levels between rainfed and irrigated cotton. His analysis reveals that although the profit from cotton cultivation increased across the selected states at constant prices, the farmers struggled to garner a consistent margin of profits through the period of analysis. The value of output from cotton cultivation outstripped cost C2 in almost all the states; however, it moved in close tandem with cost C2 resulting in profit that was merely enough to cover the escalating cost C2.[3] The analysis shows that dwindling profit over cost C2 is not only confined to the less irrigated farms, but is equally seen in the highly irrigated farms as well. The study also found that the cotton farmers reaped less profit in the Agrarian Crisis period (1995–96 to 2011–12) as compared to the Green Revolution period (1970–71 to 1995–96).

V.K. Ramachandran's paper examines the agrarian class question from a Marxist perspective, and explains how the dynamics of engagement have changed for the peasant class in contemporary India. Drawing on village survey data from seven states of India, he shows how the unviable dynamics of cost of cultivation are drawing sections of the peasantry into the market for hired labour while retaining their peasant status. The paper highlights the fact that the agrarian question remains unresolved in India, and that its democratic resolution is the key to eliminating mass deprivation in the countryside.

The paper by Barbara Harriss-White, in collaboration with three others, examines the agrarian question and conditions of labour through a study of the rice supply chain in Tamil Nadu. While the procurement chain for the public distribution system represents a vertically integrated state–corporate model compliant with labour laws, the supply chain controlled by the private sector, the authors find, was characterized by varying forms of unregulated employment. The study shows that the entry of corporate food retail had not integrated labour markets and had instead acutely segmented the market between large and small food outlets. It also found that the private rice supply chain created a large number of jobs on highly differentiated terms both at different points in the provisioning system and within a given firm, very little of which was regulated or unionized.

The paper by Vikas Rawal *et al.* examines the impact of acquisition of land for development projects, and the consequent displacement of local livelihoods, through a case study of a village in Jharkhand in eastern India. The differential impact of land acquisition across classes and social groups in a village characterized by unequal class relations is clearly brought out in the paper. The authors point out that land acquisition efforts have been aligned to the interests of the dominant classes. The negative impact of these processes on the poor and the working classes is highlighted by the authors.

The paper by Staffan Lindberg attempts a sociological history of a Dalit caste – the Madhari in south India. It traces the working of Indian capitalism and its intersection with the persistent caste system being such that improvements in real wages are not marked by enhancement along the social hierarchy. The author examines 'reversed opportunity hoarding' and the 'socially immobile' nature of mobility in the caste group, which has moved them towards better income and higher standards of living. This, combined with state social policy reaching the poor in an era of highly exploitative capitalism, has ensured survival of the labouring class while placating them. The paper outlines the sociological transformation of the Dalit caste over the past half-century or so.

Judith Heyer's paper focuses on the dry belt in the Coimbatore and Tiruppur regions of western Tamil Nadu, and finds that agriculture there, characterized primarily by small-scale farmers and agricultural labourers, is making a positive contribution. It looks at a situation in which agriculture has been performing relatively well and playing the role expected of it during the process of industrialization. Drawing on data from two rounds of survey in 1981–82 and in 2008–09, the paper highlights how in closely linked villages with a dynamic local industrial economy, a small agricultural sector has been supporting a smaller group of people; the earnings from the agriculture sector compete well with the earnings from other sectors. It is cautioned that the account of these villages is in a specific context and not generalizable; however, it gives a glimmer of hope that the agriculture sector can still continue to play a positive role. The probability of coexistence of future generations who will continue to remain in agriculture and those who will work outside agriculture, and the need for policy-level interventions to scale or replicate such experiments elsewhere is also discussed.

The twelve papers together present a diverse collage of the underlying theme of agrarian reform and transformation, and its implications. There are also strong critiques and suggestions based on the analysis and findings on what needs to be done to address the problems we are facing in the aftermath of economic reforms; the dangers of not taking necessary measures are also highlighted. Together, they present a timely compendium that will be a valuable contribution to the contentious debate on the nature of India's agrarian transformation in the period of neoliberal economic reforms.

Notes
[1] Government of India (2014).
[2] Djurfeldt and Sircar (2017).
[3] All actual expenses in cash and kind incurred by the owner + rent for leased land + imputed value of family labour + interest on value of owned capital assets (excluding land) + rental value of owned land net of land revenue.

References

Djurfeldt, G. and Srilata Sircar (2017), *Structural transformation and agrarian change in India*, London and New York: Routledge.
Government of India (2014), *Economic Survey 2013–14*, New Delhi: Ministry of Finance.

1

Provisioning Chennai

Labour in the Supply System for Rice

Mohan Mani, Gautam Mody, Meghna Sukumar and Barbara Harriss-White

Background and Research Questions

This paper has been written to celebrate Venkatesh Athreya both as a pioneer of collective research into agrarian transformations, at the village level and over the *longue durée* of a working lifetime, and as a practical contributor to labour activism and welfare in Tamil Nadu. It expands the concept of 'the agrarian' and extends his field of enquiry in the direction of the state's capital city of Chennai, where he lives and works.

For scholars of the agrarian question, the transition to agrarian capitalism is not confined to the myriad forms taken by this process but involves its relations with the rest of the economy. In generating surplus labour to work in industry and services, in supplying raw materials for relatively labour-intensive agro-industries, in contributing to the formation of a national market for consumption goods while feeding the entire society, and in releasing financial resources for investment elsewhere, even if such resources are now available from many non-agricultural sources, the agrarian question in its original form is as relevant today as it ever was. If the state's policies for agriculture, rural development, hard and soft infrastructure, labour and banking have not taken the social forms and roles of the expanded agrarian transition into account, it is at their peril. It is well established that part of the driving force for such a wide range of forms and roles for agriculture is that there is a ceiling to investment in the forces of production in land-based production itself. After the *transition* to agrarian capitalism has been consolidated, forms of control, production technologies and labour processes continue to *transform* agrarian capitalism; and the latter continues to perform dynamic political and economic roles – there is no final state. These further transformations of agrarian capitalism are not confined to land-based production. Capital takes root, concentrates, centralizes, and also diffuses and multiplies in the wider agrarian system without the limitations of landed property control, both upstream of the land-based stage (in agricultural inputs[1]) as well as downstream (in the post-harvest processes through which most agricultural commodities reach consumers in an edible form). Less attention has been paid to the forms and relations of the post-harvest system, despite its salience for policy and despite the social impact of such policy. Interventions in technologies of storage, transport and processing, in logistics as well as prices and subsidies, in a range of forms of food and social security schemes, and in urban planning – to name but a few – all have to engage with the system of agricultural markets.

In the twenty-first century, the Indian state has bowed to political pressure to permit the entry of domestic corporate firms into food retail, a sector estimated at USD 575 billion in value by 2015 and employing more people than any other sector bar agricultural production (Shenoy *et al.* 2013). Its proponents argue that what value chain analysts call 'buyer-driven power' will have beneficial effects on Indian food supply chains: integrating markets spatially, over time and across stages; lowering consumer prices and/or improving the producer's share of the final price; and reducing the apparently egregious waste in the supply chain. Over the period 2002–03 to 2009–10, supermarket food sales expanded by 49 per cent per annum (Reardon and Minten 2011). Even so, by 2009, the share of 'organized retail' was but 12 per cent of total retail sales in India and its share of total food retail was just 1 per cent (Shenoy *et al.* 2013). India's food supply chain is dominated by relatively small family firms (many of which derived their initial capital, generations back, from agricultural rents or profit) and by informal work. The wholesale and retail food sector is estimated to provide about forty million livelihoods (ibid.), and because so few of them are registered in any way, the deregulation that the post-1991 economic reforms are supposed to have released is actually marked by a great deal of informal continuity. At best, formally organized food-provisioning activity reflects a re-balancing between state and social regulation of the food system.

Organized retail, however, is thought to be an exception to the system's institutional continuity. This is due to the threat of displacing livelihoods in an era of jobless growth, when high-quality jobs were a high-profile demand from the electorate in 2014 and were matched by an electoral promise on the part of the now ruling party. In Chennai, the sales of one corporate outlet equal those of at least 100 small retail shops. The sales of rice in an average metropolitan supermarket match those of at least twenty small retail outlets. The question of livelihoods is controversial.

Retail outlets are thought to be dispensable by proponents of supermarkets. Other analysts see both large and small scales of capital coexisting as long as final urban demand for rice expands. Yet others see the possibility of political antagonism and conflict between petty retail – under threat of displacement – and grand retail – the juggernaut of global modernity. And a fourth tendency questions not the quantity but the quality of the livelihoods that are under threat. Organized retail is a disruptive innovation due to the diffusion of subcontracting, outsourcing, casualization and the removal of work rights and social security rights in the corporate sector generally. It has been estimated that anywhere between 40–80 per cent of workforces, not just in the corporate sector but also in the state, have casual contracts.[2] Field research in Tamil Nadu showed that the wages of workers in recently privatized sectors of the Indian state (e.g., railways, hospitals and municipalities) dropped by factors of one-half to two-thirds, an even greater reduction if the money value of the social security rights were foregone and the cost of the risks of moving from secure to insecure employment were able to be factored in.[3]

So a number of practical questions about the expanded agrarian sector – encompassing downstream provisioning activity – deserve answers:

(i) Remedy of the neglect of public knowledge about employment and work conditions in food supply chains; questions of corporate outsourcing and contractualization.

(ii) Scoping the extent to which new downstream corporate companies have disrupted technology, organization and labour processes 'upstream' in the family businesses and petty productive, trading, finance and service activity of the rice supply chain.

(iii) Exploring the entry of women workers into the labour force (with over 2,00,000 absorbed into the garments sector in the region of Chennai alone).[4, 5] Does a more poorly organized female workforce trigger a deterioration in employers' compliance with laws protecting labour? Or does the legal formalization of retail trigger compliance with labour laws and an improvement of work conditions?

In searching for answers, the system of firms and markets through which provisioning takes place has had to be stylized in order to make a field project tractable. This involves reducing the diversity and complexity of actually existing arrangements and deploying the concept of a supply chain, elements and relations of which can be unravelled. This framework has been criticized for its reductionism: the arbitrariness of its boundaries, the reduced set of activities linked into chains, the further reduction in the definition of the final form of the raw material.[6] The powerful metaphor of 'verticality' – embodied in value chains, commodity chains and supply chains – has come under critical fire[7] because verticality sacrifices knowledge of the roles of 'horizontal' conditions of structure, competition and social regulation attending every commodity transaction.

> Unless one knows what else is happening, then the significance of the commodity in the supply chain of a single commodity is uninterpretable. In developing the knowledge of what else is happening including perturbations caused by events such as changing seasons or the actions of the state, the chain approach has to be abandoned. (Harriss-White 2016b: 482)

The supply chain in question however has been studied in the field over a span of forty-five years (ibid.) (Figure 1.1). The research reported here has completed a hitherto incomplete analysis of the supply chain. It focuses on some of the elements and relations previously neglected, most notably labour.

Method

Our previous research started in villages and fleshed out the complex system by working into the post-harvest markets using stratified samples from combined but flawed lists of intermediaries (wholesalers, millers, local retailers) available with the Commercial Taxes Department, Regulated Agricultural Marketing Directorate, local municipalities, etc. – supplemented by self-made urban functional maps, systematic studies of periodic market systems and limited by resources and time. By contrast, the current research proceeded to explore two stages of the system which escaped capture through that method.

Post-harvest evidence is from owners, managers and workers in milling and bulk wholesaling, researched in 2013–14 through multi-sited case studies in Chennai, on its periphery (including mills on contract to the state's public distribution system [PDS]), and in Kancheepuram and Tiruvannamalai districts. The core field material has been supplemented by interviews with lorry owners and loading–unloading labourers.

Meanwhile, employment in rice retail in Chennai was researched in 2012–13 through a sample of forty workers in Ambattur and Anna Nagar:

   (i) supermarkets (multi-product shops with an average total turnover in 2013–14 of Rs 50 crore, of which rice was Rs 1–2 crore [or 1–5 per cent of the total turnover]);

  (ii) medium-sized multi-product stores (with a total turnover of

Figure 1.1 *Paddy and rice marketing system, northern Tamil Nadu, 1970s to 2010s*

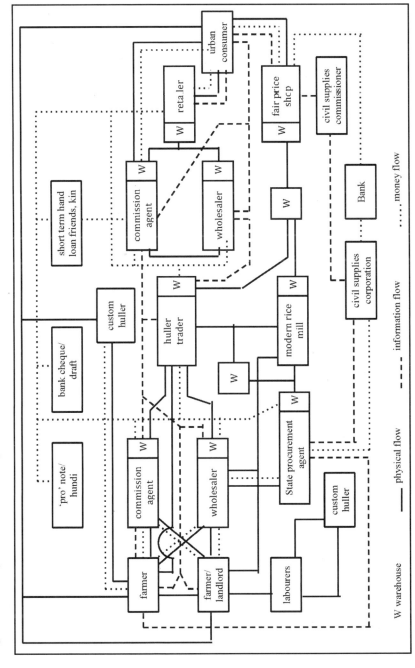

Rs 2 crore, of which rice amounted to Rs 30 lakhs [10–15 per cent of the total]);

(iii) informal small retail groceries (with a combined turnover of Rs 36 lakhs, of which rice was Rs 71,000 [20–25 per cent total]);

(iv) a case study of a fair price shop (FPS) (in an FPS system which sold 3,20,000 tonnes of rice per month).

Some of the urban fieldwork involved training trade union activists working in the informal sector who developed practical ways of countering employers' resistance and employees' fear of adverse reprisals to unionization. Much of the detail of this research, from which the current paper is taken, has been published as two working papers (Mani *et al.* 2013a and 2013b).

First, however, to provide a backcloth to the new material, we update and summarize the social relations of rice production.

Labour in Production and the First Market Transaction

Village-level data on labour has been obtained from a 2013 survey of twenty households growing high-yielding rice, selected to be representative of the distribution of holding sizes published in the Agricultural Census for Tamil Nadu. The sample was drawn from Vinayagapuram, a village that was originally randomly selected as one of a set of ten in the former North Arcot (now Tiruvannamalai) district, whose rice production was studied in 1973–74 and every decade thereafter.[8] Between 2014 and 2016, three focus groups on labour and self-employment and involving around 50 agricultural labourers were also convened. The village supplies the agricultural market town of Arni whose economy has also been studied since 1973 (Harriss-White 2016b and Harriss-White, ed. 2016).

In this region, agrarian property relations have long been dominated by small holder agriculture. While in the 1970s about 35 per cent of village households were landless, by 2009 landlessness had doubled to about 66 per cent and landedness had halved (Arivukkarasi 2016).[9] Over the decades, differentiation has been accompanied by miniaturization. The average holding size declined from 3.4 acres in 1973 to 2.4 acres in 1983 and 1.7 acres in 1993–94. By 1995, though households with over 10 acres had shrunk to 1.2 per cent, they controlled 15 per cent of the land and had captured fertile soil and superior access to water (Harriss-White and Janakarajan 2004: 11–17; Colatei and Harriss-White 2004: 136–39). After the 1980s, production and yields have fluctuated wildly and also stagnated – yields around a mediocre 1.4 tonnes of rice per acre, moving from an inverse relation between size and productivity in the 1980s (Hazell and Ramasamy 1991) to a positive one by the mid-1990s (Harriss-White and Janakarajan 1997). A small minority of labour-employing households have larger (irrigated) landholdings. But limits to land improvement and engrossment led these accumulating households to diversify their assets and occupations in idiosyncratic ways, invest in education and let a new, better educated generation leave agriculture for work in a nearby industrial corridor or in some form of petty commodity production. A new wave of rentier arrangements swept the region including, for the first time, share-cropping. Meanwhile the vast mass (60–80 per cent of agrarian households, varying with the village) formed a class which worked as wage labour. About half of these households also had small land plots.[10]

Despite the key role in production played by purchased chemical inputs, and continual attempts to cheapen or displace it from the 1970s onwards, labour still accounts for just under half the cultivation costs of high-yielding variety (HYV) rice. The incidence of tied labour has declined, and labour-displacing mechanization has proceeded apace alongside the casualization of contracts. Wages for agricultural work have been transformed from payment in kind once a year to daily wages specific to tasks, and then to piece-rates mediated through contractors and work gangs.[11] It was reported that male wages increased by 30 per cent between 2013 and 2016, from Rs 350 a day to Rs 450 ('less because of alcohol deduction'). In 2016, an average, seventeen-day month of agricultural work fetched about Rs 7,000. In the same period, female wages increased by 150 per cent, from Rs 60 to Rs 150: women's take-home pay for a seventeen-day month was Rs 3,000–4,000. In recent times, the absolute wage gap between the genders has intensified. And the gap between women's earnings from agricultural work and that from rice mill, drying yard labour is a factor of two. Agricultural labour unions exist but are unable to gain purchase on work conditions, and so tend to focus instead on claiming redress when labourers are denied their rights to social welfare outside their work.

Paddy Markets, Labour and Livelihoods

It is the first transaction of the marketed surplus that determines returns to production and the division of the surplus between consumption and accumulation. On average, producers obtain 70–80 per cent of the final retail price, but the average hides much variation. Over recent decades, the direction and terms of that transaction have been repeatedly shown to be mediated by finance from many credit institutions. These have changed dramatically over time (Polzin 2016). Constant elements have been the capture of traders' production credit by agricultural capitalists and the class specificity of the terms on which paddy is supplied to market in the repayment for pre-harvest loans. Earlier it was shown that sellers of small consignments of paddy at post-harvest seasonal low prices and at the highest interest rates on credit who repurchased rice for consumption or labour payments at pre-harvest seasonal peak prices effectively faced different terms of trade from the agrarian elite (Harriss *et al.* 1984). But as the marketed surplus of rice has increased both absolutely and as a proportion of output, loans have increasingly been repaid in cash rather than in kind, and the proportion of the marketed surplus that is tied to pre-harvest loans from wholesalers, commission agents and rice millers has declined from about half to about a fifth (Polzin 2016: 242–43).

After decades of neglect, the regulated market yards where open auctions are held are now patronized by all classes of surplus producers, armed with regional price information on their mobile phones. A rule of thumb is that paddy prices per unit weight are roughly half the retail price of rice. From the regulated markets, paddy is transported directly to so-called 'fully automated modern rice mills' (FAMRM). The recent rise in transport costs is also driven by wage rises: over half the costs of transport consist of wages to the driver and his helper/'cleaner'. Local truck drivers take home a basic Rs 500 per day plus Rs 100–500 *mamool*[12] for one to three trips.

A precondition for transport which is much more labour-intensive than lorry-driving itself is loading–unloading.[13] This work is dangerous: heavy loads tear muscles and cause sprains and dislocations; dust from bran and husk enters the lungs; even leathery skin is vulnerable to allergies. Organized if not unionized, the *sangam* in town regulates its activity through strict membership rules (e.g., a Rs 50,000 deposit; compulsory saving of Rs 100 per week, in return for which work is ordered through set twelve-hour shifts averaging Rs 400 per day in 2013 and equally shared among the gang). Two festival bonuses, each of Rs 3,000, are awarded, and medical costs for sickness or accidents are met. Every three years, the *sangam* collectively negotiates piece-rates through the Chamber of Commerce and the Rice Millers Association representing employers. However, the collective organization of loading work is now threatened from several quarters. Larger firms keep a squad of labour construing them as 'permanent' while paying them on daily contracts; and private organizations specializing in (in-migrant, non-local) contract labour are also competing with the *sangam*. 'Transportation, loading and unloading activities are almost all done by contract workers', complained its secretary.

At this local, semi-rural stage in the supply chain (over and above a mass of petty traders which expands through the multiplication of small units), there are actually three accumulating strata. These differ not by their stage or position in the supply chain, but rather by their scale, technology and labour process. One stratum consists of wholesale traders who advance money and whose productive activity is transport. Above them in scale are huller mill owners who lease out their machines to process the local paddy of others. At the apex of scale is an oligopoly of owners of modern rice mills that trades, finances, processes, stores and organizes transport. The complexity of these operations is enhanced by supply volatility from three seasons' production per annum and the need to compensate for local pre-harvest price peaks by long-distance imports of paddy. Further price fluctuations according to rice varieties add to the complexity of transactions.[14] Throughout the system it is the activity of buying and selling that is most profitable, and it is trade-loans that guarantee supplies. The power which this reflects is expressed not just through (more or less disguised) interest rates in interlocked trade contracts, but also through delays in payment. To pay for purchases immediately but be repaid for sales with delays requires more working capital than does a symmetrical payment arrangement, and, like a high interest rate, it detracts from profit.

Rice Milling, Technology, Profits and Labour

Though just 5 per cent of the final retail price is created by milling, rice mill ownership and operating scale have been progressively concentrated and centralized over time. The current technological norm is a series of heavily capitalized (and subsidized), computer-controlled (and thus semi-automatic) and weather-proofed processes involving husk-fired steaming/parboiling and drying, conveyor belts, and silos, rubber roll shellers, imported polishers and stone separators. Whereas northern Tamil Nadu used to mill a sizeable fraction 'raw' (that is, not parboiled), these days the ratio between parboiled or steamed rice to raw rice is 80:20. In making it possible to mill rice during rainy conditions, parboiling and husk-fired drying increase the costs of production over raw milling, but fetch a lower price. The trend towards automation also does not reduce processing costs per unit of output and adds to the pressure of costs on returns. When one rice mill can now mill as much as was milled in an entire town in the 1980s, if capital-intensive machinery is to run at rates of capacity utilization that break even, then, paddy has to be supplied not only locally but also at long distances. Paddy is sourced at long distances through regular wholesalers from southern Tamil Nadu to Telengana and Andhra Pradesh to the north. As a result, the balance between mill capacity and storage quantities and periodicities which used to be regulated – even if only by threat and bribes – by the state has also been disturbed. The new practices (of the 'just in time' kind) minimize the storage periods for both paddy and rice. The most valuable by-product – bran, 6–7 per cent of the out-turn from paddy – is sold onwards as a raw material for capital-intensive solvent oil extraction, adding a crucial 20 per cent to rice mill profits. Over time, all the other waste from milling has been commodified: husk (29–35 per cent outturn) is wholesaled as fuel, while bad and broken grains (2–3 per cent) are wholesaled as poultry feed. This costly and complex set of changes in the dynamics of rice processing has required investment in three kinds of branding in the collective effort to sustain the retail price: (i) the process, (ii) the varieties of rice, and (iii) the towns themselves. Bags of 'Arni Airport Rice' have been found retailed in the inner suburbs of Paris.

Table 1.1, presenting the indicative accounts of a 500 tonne/month rice mill, shows, first, the low contribution of wage labour to the cost structure, and second, the massive bias towards profit of the distributive share – the relation between total wages and profit. It was not always thus, and the distributive share has shifted decisively away from labour over the last four decades.

The recent history of rice milling is one of massive progressive labour displacement, above all – the displacement not of the most costly labour but of the cheapest, least 'skilled' and most compliant labour: that of women. While, in the 1980s, a modern rice mill would have a labour force of 60 (mostly female drying yard workers), by 2014 it had been reduced to ten (mostly men) for the same throughput. Unlike agricultural

Table 1.1 *Variable costs and estimated profits for a 500 tonnes/month capacity rice mill* (Rs per kg rice)

Sale price (fine ponni)	48.00
Purchase price of paddy (per kg rice equivalent)	24.00
Transport cost (range of Rs 0.50 to Rs 0.70 per kg)	0.60
Packaging rice	
– 1 kg pack	0.30
– 20 kg pack	0.70
Processing and milling	1.60
– of which labour cost	0.40
Estimated total cost of processed rice (at very low estimate of 65 per cent out-turn)	39.00
Profit from rice	9.00
Estimated monthly profit (Rs) 45,00,000 = Rs 45 lakh (at 500 MT rice production)	

Source: Field survey evidence in Mani *et al.* (2013b).

production, rice mill labour productivity has increased massively. It has also been masculinized. Displaced female mill workers are hard to trace and are thought to have returned to agriculture.

The skills needed to drive the so-called FAMRM have ramifications for the labour process, which has moved from casual towards discretionary regular contracts, mostly for technically skilled workers. Supervisors earn Rs 7,000–10,000 per month, plus board and lodging. Boilermen earn Rs 6,000 per month plus Rs 300 *batta*[15] per shift (bringing the total to Rs 10,500). Machine operators have a basic income of about Rs 7,000, expanded to Rs 12,000 with the inclusion of Rs 350/ day *batta*). The employer may provide for occupation-related welfare. A machine operator reported he had four off-days per month, an annual bonus, accident costs borne by the mill owner together with loans, but no provident fund: 'With loans we are effectively bonded labour', he commented ruefully. Accountants earn Rs 10,000; security guards Rs 5,000. A new tendency is to outsource specialist services, e.g. machine repair, to self-employed workers.

By contrast, the remaining female casual labour (two to three cleaners) are paid Rs 200–250 per day and Rs 4,000–5,000 per month, which is on a par with earnings from informal self-employment in the waste economy and slightly better than returns to female agricultural labour. But it is hard to compare these estimates with those for unskilled male mill labour because the basis of calculation is different. The ten to fifteen mill machine loaders and bag handlers are considered casual labour, paid piece-rates at Rs 30/tonne plus '*mamool*'. Increasingly, they are long-distance migrants (who were said to 'enjoy working double shifts').

The mill is a prime site for the complexities of the binary concepts of formality and informality – concepts whose enduring traction lies in drawing attention to the limits of state regulation, in practice if not in theory or in law. To the extent that mills are registered, they are formal; but to the extent their organization and labour process do not comply with environmental and labour laws and tax obligations are unfilled, they operate in the informal economy. The terms and conditions of labour, above all, are flexible and subject to the discretion of the employer.

Chennai's Rice Retail Sector: Scale and Labour

While the exact structure of the retail sector is not known, Table 1.2 summarizes the survey data on turnover in 2013 for three strata of retail firms at the 'downstream' end of the supply chain. The total turnover of a large supermarket (where rice accounts for, at the most, 5 per cent of sales) equals that of twenty-five medium-sized department stores and that of 140 small retail/groceries (where rice is 20 per cent of sales). Labour productivity is 50 per cent higher in supermarkets than in the other types of retail outlets. By contrast, the productivity of labour per volume of rice handled is over twice as high in small retail than it is in supermarkets. This is due to the low volumetric importance of rice in the product mix of supermarkets. Rice is even reported to be subsidized on occasion as a 'loss-leading' product to attract supermarket customers.

Rice is sourced in strikingly different degrees of logistical complexity according to the type and scale of retail outlet – see Table 1.3. Large retail tends to purchase from one or a few suppliers either already in the Chennai suburbs or at long distance. By contrast, the wholesaler supplying small groceries deals with two to three brokers apiece in a wide range of market towns throughout the southeast of India. The brokers, in turn, arrange sales from large numbers of mills. The supply chains for large and small retail are already economically segmented by the stage of the penultimate transaction.

In the same way, the retail labour process is highly differentiated. We have field evidence to compare supermarkets and small groceries. An average supermarket will have a labour force of 150–60, while a medium-sized department store will have ten workers. The work is physically demanding

Table 1.2 *Sizes of representative firms (turnover in 2013)*

Large supermarket (e.g., Tata Group–Trent Hypermarket–Star Bazaar)	
Total sales	Rs 50 crore
Rice sales	Rs 1–2 crore (i.e. 2–5 per cent)
Total sales per employee	Rs 30 lakh
Rice sales per employee	Rs 1.3 lakh
Medium department store	
Total sales	Rs 2 crore
Rice sales	Rs 30 lakh (i.e. 15 per cent)
Total sales per employee	Rs 20 lakh
Rice sales per employee	Rs 3 lakh
Small retail	
Total sales	Rs 36 lakh
Rice sales	Rs 7 lakh (i.e. 20 per cent)
Total sales per employee	Rs 20 lakh
Rice sales per employee	Rs 3.5 lakh

Source: Field survey in 2013, Mani *et al.* (2013a).

Table 1.3 *Vertically integrated corporate retail versus neighbourhood wholesale*

Type of outlet	LG-B	LG-E	LG-A	LG-F	Rice WH retail (-> small retail)
Number of outlets	1	6	74	56	1
Supply logistics	One supplier: Red Hills	Centralized rice purchase at Guntur, Chennai, Vabgakire through sister company. Rice for Chennai operations purchased mostly from mandis in Red Hills.	Rice bought from 4–5 mandis in Red Hills in Chennai, Pondicherry and Salem.	Rice bought from ten millers. Boiled rice: Tindivanam, Arani, Kanchipuram, Nellore, Red Hills Nellore Raw rice: Nellore and Naidupettai.	Rice bought from 25 millers through 2–3 brokers in Andhra Pradesh – Guntur, Naidupettai; Karnataka – Raichur, Tumkur; Tamil Nadu – Arani, Tindivanam, Kallakurichi.

Notes: LG: large retail – the letters 'B', 'E', 'A' and 'F' letters identify individual supermarket chains. *WH*: wholesaler.
Source: Field survey in 2013, Mani *et al.* (2013a).

and 95 per cent of the labour force is female, young and educated up to 10th–12th standard.[16] Recruited by hearsay, not through formal procedure, with limited notions of terms, conditions and entitlements, the workforce is commonly driven by household hardship and the sheer proximity of the worksite to their homes. It is marked by high turnover.

By contrast, in small retail, the workforce is overwhelmingly male, drawn from kin in the owner's place of origin: agrarian, migrant, poorly educated but well-apprenticed. There is very low turnover: the experience is understood as a preparation and launching-pad for a lifetime's independent livelihood in retail.

Along with the different structure and social character of the labour forces, the terms and conditions of work are segmented. In 2013, supermarket pay averaged Rs 5,080 per month,[17] some 40 per cent above the state's minimum wage but only slightly above a seventeen-day month of female agricultural labour. Apart from time-keeping, other record-keeping for the workforce was generally lax and workers had low levels of knowledge about their legal rights and bonuses (such as Employees

Provident Fund [EPF], Employees State Insurance [ESI]), their eligibility and the proper procedures for making claims. Vacation and sick leave were 'discretionary' and generally uncompensated.

Workers in small retail earned an average of Rs 6,600, varying with experience up to double the supermarket average. On top of this, they generally received informal cash and kind benefits 'as per need', food and accommodation, overtime pay, clothes and an annual trip to their native places. Small retail is below the threshold for labour laws, which apply to workforces in excess of ten (where electricity is used, and twenty otherwise). Ineligible for formal social security due to their informal status, they got discretionary and ad hoc gratuity payments and contributions from their employer towards (small) costs of medical treatment, payments none of which were got by supermarket labour but for which their loyalty to the owner was a vital condition.

Work intensity and control also differed. The work requires lifting and carrying and the stamina to stand for hours at a time. Supermarket labour works long shifts of ten to twelve hours, measured on time-card punching systems supplemented by surveillance cameras. A twenty-minute toilet leave and one off-day per week are normally permitted. Problem-solving requires a one-to-one meeting with the supervisor. Labour is not organized or allowed initiative or innovation, let alone the 'enterprise' argued to be key to the neoliberal subjectivity of work (Gooptu 2009). If take-home wages are recomputed in terms of overtime entitlements, big food retail wages emerge as below the statutory minimum.

Small retail work is even more mercilessly strenuous: while there are no surveillance cameras and a longer, thirty-minute toilet leave, there is no off-day and the working day stretches up to thirteen hours. Factoring in the eight-hour formal norm for a day's work plus norms of overtime pay, the hourly wage gap between small and big retail disappears and the apparently larger take-home pay for small retail labour is also below the statutory minimum. The difference in benefits, to the advantage of small informal retail labour, remains.

In past decades, employers have spoken of the gender gap not in terms of supply and demand but in terms of gendered social principles: a household wage for men and 'pin money' for women. But while the wages given to male foodshop assistants were far from being a family wage, those to female supermarket labour are far from being a supplement to a family wage. Half the female labour force was contributing more than half their households' income, while the other half was juggling simultaneous debt and savings. Small retail labour characteristically lived on employers' handouts and frugal personal budgets, remitting more than half their earnings while saving, typically for siblings' education, at the same time.

So, while supermarkets compete with small retail, and while their net hourly cash-pay is similar and lower than the minimum wage, their labour forces are quite different and both economically and socially segmented. Supermarkets are formally registered and bound to comply with the labour laws. However, the workers interviewed received no bonus; the minority who had their provident fund component kept up to date had their employers' contribution paid on net rather than gross wages; wages have not been inflation-proofed and so real take-home pay is declining in value. We see that formal status is not the binary opposite of informality but is a multifaceted process which has to be fought for. Greater formal regulation of supermarkets is, in practice, not inconsistent with widespread ignorance about overtime, the flouting of labour law and the procedures of labour organization and unionization. The supermarket labour force is increasingly feminized, at present compliant with unlawful conditions and fearful of the 'mechanized harassment' from technologies of surveillance.

By way of contrast, small retail, already keenly aware of supermarket competition – and in places mimicking certain practices such as branded packaging (which also removes the need to bargain) – pays not lower but higher wages upfront to its labour. Elsewhere, it has been found that this pay gap is due to gender. Small retail labour is very rarely female. Pay also varies with experience; employers need to trust the male worker with the security of their inventories, with pricing and negotiation about superior and special brands and varieties, with customer credit decisions, with loyalty and responsibility. Relations of patronage compromise freedom but in this case are associated with somewhat better work benefits. These additional roles and relations can be argued to segment the very act of food purchase in a way that protects small stores.

Competition in Scale and Vertical Integration in Chennai's Supply System

Having described capital–labour relations in the rice provisioning system, a major policy question can now be addressed in its social context.

Labour-intensive food retail has three reasons to fear what they refer to as 'walmarting' the food system: first, the existence of financial incentives to upstream vertical integration (lower transactions costs enabling the undercutting of existing rates of return); second, big retail's economies of scale (which could undercut small retail); and third, increased labour productivity and the loss of livelihoods.

But our field survey revealed the extent to which complex, local, specialist knowledge is necessary to the management of the supply chain:

knowledge of cropping patterns; the character of the marketed surplus; varieties; qualities; prices that fluctuate with variety, quality, season and local idiosyncrasies of supply, demand and long-distance trade; the quality of intermediaries; credit and the logistics of by-products. While, in north India, corporate food retail is indeed entering and branding the (super) market for wheat flour, by contrast, in south India and in the paddy–rice supply system, the forms of exchange and local, expert, informal knowledge are formidable entry barriers. Rice is also too small a proportion of total supermarket turnover to justify the high transactions costs of 'local' entry. In addition, a single state-of-the-art FAMRM, with milling capacities of up to 2,500 tonnes per month, far exceeds the current monthly rice purchases for the biggest corporate retail company with 74 branches in Chennai. Upstream vertical integration would then require big retail to undertake branding and sales through other corporates, a transactions-costly invitation to increase direct competition, which currently has no commercial logic.

Actually Existing Vertical Integration

It is not as though a vertically integrated supply chain does not exist. Since the 1960s, the state's own PDS of essential commodities, notably food, has been developed alongside private food markets with a view to addressing national and local food insecurity. It has three integrated institutional components: (i) the central government's Food Corporation of India (FCI), responsible for supply logistics; (ii) Tamil Nadu Civil Supplies Corporation (TNCSC), in charge of planned allocations and procurement; and (iii) the system of fair price shops from which food is retailed at controlled quantities and (subsidized) prices. In Chennai, in 2012–13, 3,20,000 tonnes were retailed per month, a scale one thousand times greater than that of the largest corporate retail outlet.

From field case study evidence, it is possible to compare labour in a high-capacity private FAMRM contracted to TNCSC with that of a mill directly owned by the TNCSC (see Table 1.4).

But first, labour needs inserting into the state's cost structure and distributive margin – these differ from those of the private supply chain. Raw material – paddy – procured for the state's system is 81 per cent of total marketing costs against the private chain's 77 per cent. The costs of PDS milling are 10 per cent of the final retail price against 5 per cent for the private system (where profit is a larger component). Packing and transport are 5 per cent of final retail price in the public system against 2 per cent in the private system. The two are strictly non-comparable for longer distances are involved in the PDS. Rail is used for the PDS rather

Table 1.4 *Labour costs in milling: TNCSC milling and private mill compared*

Category	Private	TNCSC
Capacity (MT*/month)	2,700.00	2,500.00
Assumed production of rice (MT)	1,751.00	1,751.00
Monthly-rated 'regular'		
Staff salaries (Rs/month)		
– 4 admin in pvt	38,000.00	
– 27 technical + 20 admin in TNSC mill		5,94,514.00
– security staff	10,000.00	44,830.00
Total monthly-rated	*48,000.00*	*6,39,344.00*
Piece-rated 'casual'		
Daily-rated (pvt for 1751MT)		
Mill staff (2 women, 1 man, 1 operator	40,127.08	
Casual lb	4,96,975.00	2,53,118.00
Total piece-rated	*5,37,102.08*	*2,53,118.00*
Labour cost per kg rice	*0.33*	*0.51*

Note: * metric tonne.
Source: Field survey evidence in Mani *et al.* (2013b).

than lorry transport, which halves the transport cost for long distances. Conversely, lorry transport reaps economies of scale on roads inside the metropolitan city.[18] The wholesale margins converge in a range of 5–10 per cent of the retail price while retail itself absorbs 5–6 per cent of the final price. The state's trading margin is lower than that of the private sector.

The labour process also differs. In the TNCSC mill supplying the PDS, the labour force is top-heavy with administrative staff: over and above twenty-seven technical staff, there are twenty administrative and clerical workers as compared to four in the private mill. Labour costs per unit output are 50 per cent greater in TNCSC than in the case of private milling, a situation that may be due to better work conditions for labour or may instead simply reflect the costs of more clerical staff. Some operations are more elaborately defined than in the private sector – bag handling has twelve separate payment rates for various tasks in the PDS. The role played by casual labour shows stark differences; the ratio of piece-rate to the total private sector wage bill is 92 per cent, compared with only 28 per cent inside TNCSC. The latter's piece-rate workers are loading–unloading labour (from truck to train to truck): 120 migrant piece-rate workers are hired by TNCSC at Rs 1.50 per 40 kg bag (reaping Rs 375 for an average 10 tonnes a day – a wage that is lower than that of male agricultural labour and lower than the loading/unloading share taken home in the paddy marketing town.

PDS retail work conditions are bureaucratized, fully compliant with the labour laws, and significantly better than their equivalents anywhere in the private sector, involving no overtime. Fair price shop workers earn Rs 10,750 per month with comprehensive benefits.

The question provoked by this comparison is whether there is room for improvement in private sector labour conditions within the existing cost structure. To a limited extent, it seems there is.

> If we factor in the likelihood that administrative staff component in the public establishment might be excessive, and allow for a leaner establishment, a private mill contracted to the PDS could, within its present profitability parameters, absorb the increased cost of a regular workforce employed on better terms and conditions. (Mani *et al.* 2013b: 18–19)

Conclusions

Returning to the agenda of practical questions arising from (i) an expanded conception of the agrarian which encompasses upstream and downstream capital in the circuits of distribution, and (ii) the political pressure to allow new scales of capital in food retail, this research has shown that the entry of corporate food retail has not integrated labour markets. Quite the reverse – retail labour is acutely segmented between large and small food outlets. Further, it is the state's PDS rather than the private sector that is found to increase the producer's share of the consumer's rupee.[19] Meanwhile, the private rice supply chain creates a large number of jobs on highly differentiated terms both at different points in the provisioning system and within a given firm, very little of which is regulated or unionized.

Crude monthly incomes for 2013 can be banded to confirm a heterogeneity in the returns to work within the rice supply system that is only increased when access to benefits and conditions of work are also factored in. The lowest band, at under Rs 6,000 (1.5 x the official minimum wage), includes male security guards, female agricultural labour, female rice mill cleaners and female supermarket retail labour. The next band, Rs 6,100–10,000, includes male labour in agricultural production, loading and unloading, parboiling and small retail. Pay at Rs 10,100 to Rs 15,000 is earned by male mill accountants, machine operators, managers and supermarket supervisors. Lorry drivers earn in excess of Rs 15,000.

At the time of writing, outsourcing is confined to transport and loading, where contractualization is proceeding apace alongside the exact opposite process: the internalization and vertical integration of the movement of goods. Regulated commodity transactions and labour relations are revealed as incomplete and better understood as a slice at one point of time through a set of dynamic processes of struggle for decent work. Some informal firms develop parodies of the formal contract, for example, through payments for occupation-related sickness, or pay related to seniority; while formally registered firms employ labour on incomplete contracts (ignoring rules about overtime or employers' obligations).

In the south Indian case, the new downstream corporate retail companies have not yet disrupted technology, organization and labour processes 'upstream' in the supply chain's family businesses and petty productive activity. The entry of corporate retail does not generate large employment multipliers upstream, nor does it 'net' displace much wage labour at present or even threaten to displace labour. This is for two main reasons: first, urban growth acts as a countervailing force; second, small retail which deploys family labour can currently undercut other forms of capital in retail.

Rather, it is the technological change in family businesses that has acted as a severely disruptive force, exemplified most strikingly in the progressive displacement of the casual rice mill labour force and in the entry of local private loading labour contracting firms.

The final question about the impact of the entry of women workers in the rice supply chain on the terms and conditions of work is hard to answer because the segmentation of the labour force and of the tasks required of retail labour makes supermarket-female and small retail-male conditions non-comparable. While the employment of female labour in big retail uses a few elements of the formal contract, formality is revealed as a process requiring countervailing labour power to achieve. Meanwhile, workers in small family firms have more strenuous physical conditions but generally better economic conditions.

With the notable exception of the PDS, the supply chain for rice does *not* generate high-quality, regulated employment. Concentration (supermarkets) and vertical integration (PDS) coexist with local oligopoly capital and petty commodity production and trade in a set of segmented social relations that is both technologically dynamic and structurally stable. The PDS justifies a case for the vertically integrated corporate entity. This state–corporate model was as cost-effective as private milling and its transport costs were much lower for longer total distances. However, despite the existence of this model, upstream private corporate vertical integration is unlikely because, on the one hand, of the extreme complexity of the information and contacts that would be needed by big retail, and, on the other, the massive entry barriers to vertical integration in retail facing private oligopoly in wholesale trade and milling. Time will tell.

The authors, respectively from Centre for Workers' Management, New Trade Union Initiative and Oxford University, acknowledge the help of the Ponn Tozhilalargal Sangam and the Labour Progressive Front. We also gratefully acknowledge the helpful contributions of Alfred Gathorne-Hardy, Gilbert Rodrigo and C.P. Chandrasekhar. The fieldwork was funded by the United Kingdom's ESRC–DFID (Economic Social Research Council – Department for International Development) through their programme on 'Development in a changing world: the challenge for theory, policy and action', but this paper does not reflect the views of DFID or ESRC, and the research was conducted entirely independently of the donors.

Notes

[1] Field resource constraints prevented us from developing research on the upstream system.

[2] The arguments are critically discussed in Jan and Harriss-White (2012).

[3] See Harriss-White (2016a) for detailed evidence.

[4] Mani *et al.* (2013a): 1.

[5] Ibid.

[6] A supply chain for rubber, for instance, would require a choice between up to 5,000 final forms.

[7] Bernstein and Campling (2006a and 2006b).

[8] See Farmer (1977) and Harriss-White (2016b).

[9] Outright landlessness has expanded in fits and starts, its growth decelerating from 1983 and accelerating again since 2000 (Harriss-White and Janakarajan 2004).

[10] Ibid.

[11] Some of these gangs are composed of migrant labour, which contribute deflationary pressure on agricultural wages (Guerin *et al.* 2015).

[12] *Mamool* may mean a routine supplement or private 'bribe'. In this instance, however, it means a work incentive. 'It is extortion', complained an employer.

[13] Transport, loading and unloading comprise 2 per cent of the final retail price.

[14] In 2013–14 alone, the state's procurement prices for a given purchasing season varied from Rs 1,410 to Rs 1,520 per quintal (8 per cent) according to variety, while open market prices varied from Rs 1,100 for coarse 'bold' paddy to Rs 2,400 per quintal for superfine varieties (more than double).

[15] A daily supplement to cover food, etc.

[16] FPS labour generally has college degrees.

[17] In the department stores, wages were similar: at Rs 5,322.

[18] Long-distance rail transport of rice is charged at Rs 1.6 per km/tonne of paddy as against Rs 3 for road transport; economies of scale for lorries within a metropolis are considerable: Rs 15 per km/tonne for FCI versus Rs 40 for the private sector.

[19] We are unable to comment on the third aspect of the case for corporate retail – that it reduces waste. But Jan and Harriss-White (2012: 40) found that this all-India claim rests on low quality or mythical evidence.

References

Arivukkarasi, N. (2016), 'The Making and Unmaking of Handloom Silk Weaving in the Arni Region', in B. Harriss-White, ed., *Middle India and Urban–Rural Development: Four Decades of Change*, Heidelberg and New Delhi: Springer: 201–28.

Bernstein, H. and L. Campling (2006a), 'Commodity Studies and Commodity Fetishism I: Trading Down', *Journal of Agrarian Change*, 6 (2): 239–64.

—— (2006b), 'Commodity Studies and Commodity Fetishism II: "Profits with Principles"?', *Journal of Agrarian Change*, 6 (3): 414–47.

Colatei, D. and B. Harriss-White (2004), 'Social Stratification and Rural Households', in B. Harriss-White and S. Janakarajan, eds, *Rural India Facing the 21st Century*, London: Anthem: 115–58.

Farmer, B.H., ed. (1977), *Green Revolution? Technology and Change in Rice-Growing Areas of Tamil Nadu and Sri Lanka*, London: Macmillan.

Gooptu, N. (2009), 'Neoliberal Subjectivity, Enterprise Culture and New Workplaces: Organized Retail and Shopping Malls in India', *Economic and Political Weekly*, 44 (22): 45–54.

Guerin, I., G. Venkatasubramanian and S. Michiels (2015), 'Labour in Contemporary South India', in B. Harriss-White and J. Heyer, eds, *Indian Capitalism in Development*, London: Routledge: 108–35.

Harriss, B. with G. Chapman, W. McLean, E. Shears and E. Watson (1984), *Exchange Relations and Poverty in Dryland Agriculture*, New Delhi: Concept.

Harriss-White, B. (2016a), 'Matter in Motion: Work and Livelihoods in India's Economy of Waste', in Ernesto Noronha and Premilla D'Cruz, eds, *Critical Perspectives on Work and Employment in Globalizing India*, Heidelberg and New Delhi: Springer.

—— (2016b), 'From Analysing "filieres vivrieres" to Understanding Capital and Petty Production in Rural South India', *Journal of Agrarian Change*, 16 (3): 478–500.

Harriss-White, B., ed. (2016), *Middle India and Urban–Rural Development: Four Decades of Change*, Heidelberg and New Delhi: Springer.

Harriss-White, B. and S. Janakarajan (1997), 'From Green Revolution to Rural Industrial Revolution in South India', *Economic and Political Weekly*, 31 June: 1469–77.

—— (2004), *Rural India Facing the 21st Century*, London: Anthem.

Hazell, P. and C. Ramasamy (1991), *The Green Revolution Reconsidered: The Impact of High Yielding Varieties in South India*, Baltimore: Johns Hopkins.

Jan, M.A. and B. Harriss-White (2012), 'The Three Roles of Agricultural Markets: A Review of Ideas about Agricultural Commodity Markets in India', *Economic and Political Weekly*, 46 (52): 39–52.

Mani, M., G. Mody and M. Sukumar (2013a), 'Employment and Working Conditions and the Supply Chain for Commodities in Retail – A Case Study of Rice in Chennai', RGJW Working Paper no. 11, School of Interdisciplinary Area Studies , Oxford University, available at http://www.southasia.ox.ac.uk/working-papers-resources-greenhouse-gases-technology-and-jobs-indias-informal-economy-case-rice, accessed 17 November 2016.

—— (2013b), 'Supply Chains for Rice in Chennai', RGJW Working Paper no. 16, School of Interdisciplinary Area Studies, Oxford University, available at http://www.southasia.ox.ac.uk/working-papers-resources-greenhouse-gases-technology-and-jobs-indias-informal-economy-case-rice, accessed 27 November 2016.

Polzin, C. (2016), 'Institutional Change in Informal Credit: Through the Urban–Rural Lens', in B. Harriss-White, ed., *Middle India and Urban–Rural Development: Four Decades of Change*, Heidelberg and New Delhi: Springer: 229–50.

Reardon, T. and B. Minten, (2011), 'Surprised by Supermarkets: Diffusion of Modern Food Retail in India', *Journal of Agribusiness in Developing and Emerging Economies*, 1 (2): 134–61.

Shenoy, S.S., A.H. Sequeira and K. Devaraj (2013), 'The Saga of Indian Retail Avalanche', *International Journal of Development Research*, 3 (6): 26–29.

2

No Place for Family Farms?

Agrarian Transformation in India

Göran Djurfeldt

The first time Venkatesh and I met was in a hotel room in Chennai in the late 1970s. We have been lifelong friends, partners in endless quarrels on politics and social science and on developmental trends in Indian agriculture. We did two rounds of fieldwork, together with other colleagues,[1] in the old Tiruchi (Tiruchirappalli) district in 1979–80 and in 2004. Armed with questionnaires and bookish Marxist theories, we came out of the holy bath differently – Venkatesh still a convinced Marxist; myself less so and more of a Weberian, and like many sociologists, tooled up with middle-range theories. Our differences explain the quarrels but not the friendship, which has been overriding, like the mutually shared conviction that theoretical arguments need to be resolved by confrontation with realities, or what we agree are down-to-earth facts. It follows that lofty abstractions without any kind of empirical anchorage are uninteresting.

In this paper, I present some testable hypotheses about structural transformation and agrarian change, drawing on a recent book (Djurfeldt and Sircar 2017). Our common research is inspiration for the argument (Athreya, Djurfeldt and Lindberg 1990; Djurfeldt *et al.* 2007; Djurfeldt *et al.* 2008). In the first-mentioned work, we used theories of agrarian classes, inspired by Lenin, Patnaik and others (Lenin [1899] 1960; Patnaik 1987). These theories underpin the ubiquitous *proletarianization and pauperization discourse* saying that, with capitalist development in agriculture, peasants will necessarily be immiserized and lose their land. A different source of inspiration was theories of 'merchant-usurious capital', drawing on Banaji (1977) and, to some extent, also on Chayanov ([1966] 1986) – both bodies of theories dealing with peasants' relations to markets and merchants. Many leftist discourses posit that with peasants' engagements with markets and merchants, along with technical change, driven by commercialization and the state, peasants are doomed to loss of land and livelihoods.

As I see it, our most important conclusion from fieldwork in Tiruchi highlighted the misinterpretation of state interventions in agriculture, reducing them to midwifery of capitalism and exploitation. Commercialization and technical change in agriculture do not unavoidably, and independent of state policies, lead to proletarianization and pauperization, as is often taken for granted. Rather than facile assumptions, these hotly contested topics call for rigorous research and evidence.

More open-minded to the effects of state interventions, in our next round of fieldwork we looked into the welfare consequences of a range of policies in rural Tamil Nadu (Lindberg *et al.* 2008; Lindberg *et al.* 2011; Lindberg 2012; Lindberg *et al.* 2014). Another and typically sociological concern was that of social mobility: we showed that peasant households were socially mobile in ways that were poorly predicted by popular theories (Djurfeldt *et al.* 2007; Djurfeldt *et al.* 2008). Since that fieldwork, we have been asking ourselves: to what extent are the mobility patterns detected in Tiruchi representative of trends prevailing in other parts of India, and to what extent are they exceptional? This question is pursued in Djurfeldt and Sircar (forthcoming), and the answer is that the exceptionality of Tiruchi and Tamil Nadu should not be overstated: similar trends can be observed over large parts of rural India – observations that, I claim, contradict some pet theories already alluded to.

Scenarios for Agrarian Transformation

One can imagine three scenarios for the agrarian transformation that is currently going on in India. The first is the evolutionist paradigm common to classical economics and Marxism, according to which the endpoint is capitalist agriculture with factories in the field employing armies of wage labour. This is, of course, the classical Leninist conception, which has inspired the Indian left inside and outside academia. A second scenario is the Chayanovian one,[2] which largely corresponds to the *de facto* trajectory in the west via grassroots cooperative movements to giant agro-industries, owned by member farmers and cooperative in name if nothing more. This plot outline ends in highly mechanized agriculture *dependent on family labour* with limited hiring but with a high degree of cooperation between family farms, especially in sales and procurement of inputs.

There is a yawning black hole in both the above scenarios: they both abstract from *pluriactivity*, a fundamental feature of contemporary agriculture. Pluriactivity is the term rural sociologists use to refer to the tendency of farm families to have multiple sources of income in addition to farming. Pluriactivity is gendered, and often transgenerational as well.

To give an example of gendering, contemporary grain farming in Western Europe often sees a male farmer tending to the grain crops and the machines necessary to plough, sow and reap them, while the farmer's wife works in the nearest town, perhaps as a white-collar worker, whose salary is a much-needed buffer against fluctuations in grain prices. But since grain farming is highly seasonal in temperate climates, the farmer himself may also be pluriactive – holding a position in a nearby agricultural university, for instance.

According to journalistic accounts, Chinese farming today is often transgenerationally pluriactive, with the older generation tending both to the farm and to the grandchildren while their parents are away working full-time in the industrial clusters on the coast and coming home only for New Year's day.

Pluriactivity is a pervasive phenomenon, and it must be brought into any attempt at understanding agrarian transformation. We cannot continue to abstract from what has often been stamped as 'subsidiary activities', and pretend that the 'primary activity' can be understood in isolation. My third scenario is, therefore, that India will be drawn closer to the pluriactive–smallholder pattern that is typical of East and Southeast Asia (outside the plantation sector).

The Concept of Family Farm

The year 2014 was proclaimed the 'Year of Family Farming' by the United Nations' Food and Agriculture Organization (FAO). In its flag-ship report, it was reported that out of an estimated 570 million farms worldwide, more than 90 per cent are family farms; in many countries, close to 100 per cent. The definition used in making this generalization requires that the '*farm be partially or entirely owned, operated and/or managed by an individual and her/his relatives*' (FAO 2014: 8). By this definition, India obviously belongs to the group of countries with close to 100 per cent family farms.

In the book mentioned earlier (Djurfeldt and Sircar 2017), I discuss family farm definitions as well as the history of family farming at length. I arrive at a slightly modified definition where I play down ownership and emphasize *family labour* and *management*, especially the former. The emphasis is on family labour rather than management or ownership because there is a crucial inter-relation between hired and family labour during the structural transformation process.

Being aware that many Indian scholars, especially left-leaning ones, prefer the term 'agrarian transition' to 'agrarian transformation', I would like to defend the latter. The definition of structural transformation is not only clear and straightforward, but also easy to operationalize. Take Timmer's definition:

> The structural transformation is the defining characteristic of the development process, both cause and effect of economic growth. Four quite relentless and inter-related processes define the structural transformation: [i] a declining share of agriculture in GDP and employment . . . [ii] a rural-to-urban migration that stimulates the process of urbanization; [iii] the rise of a modern industrial and service economy; and [iv] a demographic transition from high rates of births and deaths (common in backward rural areas) to low rates of births and deaths (associated with better health standards in urban areas). (Timmer 2009: 5; numbering added)

Being a sociologist, I would take partial exception to the above by underlining that all social (and economic) processes, although they may appear 'relentless', are driven by 'free' actors, constrained by existing institutions and structures. In the aggregate, their actions are the ultimate drivers of the process of economic growth and thereby of structural transformation. At the individual level, I would say that the drivers are not utility maximization, as a neoclassical economist might put it, but dreams of a better and more dignified life for oneself, one's family and children.

I hasten to add, as Timmer does, that structural transformation varies much in pace and form between different countries and historical epochs. A major source of variation is politics and state intervention, which may deform, deflect and detract the process.

From an operational point of view, the core of the above definition is that 'a declining share of agriculture in GDP and employment' (Timmer 2009: 5) characterizes the process. This is easy to operationalize, as Timmer and Akkus have done on a global scale (Timmer and Akkus 2008). Using pooled time-series data for 87 countries from 1965 to 2000, they estimate that globally the share of the agricultural labour force has decreased by about 1 per cent a year during the period. This is incontrovertible evidence that global structural transformation is indeed taking place. A comparison of agriculture's share of gross domestic product (GDP) and agricultural labour's share in the total labour force is easy to do for India as well, as I do in Djurfeldt and Sircar (forthcoming). Without foreclosing the issue, the data show that structural transformation was stagnant not only from 1900 to India's Independence in 1947, during the colonial period, but right up to around 1990. After 1990, the share of agricultural labour in the total work force has shown a consistently downward trend. Thus, structural transformation is also proceeding in India. What are we to expect of the agrarian change that it brings with it: factories in the fields or family farming?

Agrarian Transformation

Competition for labour between the industrial and service sectors and the agricultural sector drives agrarian transformation. As the former sectors grow, their demand for labour does, likewise. Once the labour surplus in the farm sector is exhausted, an upward pressure on wages follows. This in turn creates a 'labour problem' for farmers dependent on hiring, and concurrently generates an advantage for family farmers drawing primarily on family labour. This is the crucial mechanism, I claim, that creates a competitive advantage for family labour farms over farms dependent on hired labour ('capitalist farms'). As long as the latter do not enjoy advantages of scale, which is quite rare outside the plantation sector, or are subsidized by the state, one would expect family labour to grow at the expense of farms dependent on hiring.

Is this mechanism active in India's agrarian transformation, or have countervailing forces – for example, via the state – made it inactive? This is a major question in Djurfeldt and Sircar (2017). I research it by studying the propensities of farming households of various types (family labour farms, large farms dependent on hired labour, etc.) to exit the farm sector; and by studying their mobility in size-class of holding, with the evident hypothesis that family labour farms are more stable or prone to upward movement, while farms dependent on labour-hiring are less stable and more downwardly mobile. Finally, I research the effect of the agrarian transformation on the relative life-chances of different categories of farm households, operationalized as changes in relative income, again with results contradicting the standard narrative.

Micro-level panel data provide powerful instruments for this type of analysis – one can compare them to the electronic microscope, or claim that they are the radiotelescopy of the social sciences. They allow us to use micro-level data on households to understand macro-level social processes.

I use two panel studies: ARIS REDS,[3] the first of which was conducted in 1969–71; and the India Human Development Survey (IHDS), of which I use the first two waves – from 1994–95 to 2004–05. In the conclusion, I also use IHDS-II, covering 2004–05 to 2012–13, which was recently published. These data are analysed by means of statistical models: a binomial logistic regression for entry/exit to the farm sector, and a multinomial logistic regression model for mobility in size-class of holding. For changes in life-chances, I use an Ordinary Least Square Log-Log model, with change in income as the dependent variable. A short chapter on regression for those who feel they need it is included in the book. These models allow us to resolve some of the questions about agrarian transformation that Venkatesh and I have long quarrelled over.

I should mention here that I have written the book mentioned together with a young human geographer, Srilata Sircar, who has contributed a chapter on small-town urbanization and its relation to agrarian transformation.

Sabotaging the sales of the book by disclosing the results would be foolish, but I can whet your appetite by revealing that the classical Leninist hypothesis does not fare well in this test, but neither does the Chayanovian saying that in India family labour farms would supersede capitalist farms. Agrarian transformation is India is leading in yet another direction!

Notes

[1] Together with Staffan Lindberg, R. Vidyasagar, A. Rajagopal and others.
[2] After the Russian economist A.V. Chayanov, whose critique of Lenin's 'Development of Capitalism in Russia' led to his being executed in the early 1930s. See Chayanov (1977): 63–108; Chayanov (1986); Shanin (2009): 83–101.
[3] ARIS stands for Agricultural and Rural Industries Surveys, conducted from 1969 to 1971, and REDS is an acronym for Rural Employment and Development Surveys, fielded in 1982, 1999 and 2006. For data descriptions, see http://adfdell.pstc.brown.edu/arisreds_data/, a site maintained by Andrew Foster at Brown University and as per agreement with the data owners, the National Council of Applied Economic Research, New Delhi (www.ncaer.org). I have also used the Human Development Profile of India (HDPI) collected in 1994–95 and made a panel drawing on the India Human Development Survey in 2004–05. These data-sets are exemplary, reasonably clean, with good data descriptions and good weighting systems (see Desai *et al.* 2016). A follow-up survey, enabling a second panel, IHDS-II, was published in 2015; this was somewhat too late to impinge on modelling, although we occasionally refer to it (see Desai and Vanneman (2016).

References

Athreya, V.B., Göran Djurfeldt and Staffan Lindberg (1990), *Barriers Broken: Production Relations and Agrarian Change in Tamil Nadu*, New Delhi: Sage.
Banaji, J. (1977), 'Capitalist Domination and the Small Peasantry: Deccan District in the Late Nineteenth Century', *Economic and Political Weekly*, 12 (33–34): 1375–1404.
Chayanov, A.V. (1977), 'The Journey of My Brother Aleksei to the Land of Peasant Utopia', in R.E.F. Smith, ed., *The Russian Peasant, 1920 and 1984*, London: Frank Cass: 63–108.
——— ([1966] 1986), *A.V. Chayanov and the Theory of Peasant Economy*, Madison, Wisconsin: The University of Wisconsin Press.
Desai, S. and R. Vanneman (2016), *India Human Development Survey-II* (IHDS-II), 2011–12, Inter-university Consortium for Political and Social Research (ICPSR) [distributor].
Desai, S., R. Vanneman and N.D. National Council of Applied Economic Research (2016), *India Human Development Survey* (IHDS), 2005, Inter-university Consortium for Political and Social Research (ICPSR) [distributor].

Djurfeldt, Göran, V.B. Athreya, N. Jayakumar, S. Lindberg, R. Vidyasagar and A. Rajagopal (2007), 'Agrarian Change and Social Mobility in Tamil Nadu', *Economic and Political Weekly*, 43 (45): 50–61; available at https://lup.lub.lu.se/search/publication/80c27e83-f653-478d-a687-64f8e28d5463

———— (2008), 'Modelling Social Mobility in Rural Tamil Nadu', Lund University Publications, http://luur.lub.lu.se/luur?func=downloadFile&fileOId=1267070.

Djurfeldt, G. and S. Sircar (2017), *Structural Transformation and Agrarian Change In India*, London and New York: Routledge.

Food and Agriculture Organization (FAO) (2014), *The State of Food and Agriculture: Innovation in Family Farming, Food and Agriculture Organization of the United Nations*, Rome: Food and Agriculture Organization of the United Nations.

Lenin, V.I. ([1899] 1960), *The Development of Capitalism in Russia*, Moscow: Foreign Languages Publishing House.

Lindberg, S. (2012), 'Rural India 1970–2005: An Arduous Transition to What?', *The Indian Journal of Labour Economics*, 55 (1): 61–75.

Lindberg, S., R. Vidyasagar, V.B. Athreya, G. Djurfeldt and A. Rajagopal (2008), *Caste and Democratic Decentralization in Rural Tamil Nadu*, Lund: Lund University.

Lindberg, S, V.B. Athreya, R. Vidyasagar, G. Djurfeldt and A. Rajagopal (2011), 'A "Silent Revolution"? Women's Empowerment in Rural Tamil Nadu', *Economic and Political Weekly*, 46 (13): 111–20.

Lindberg, S., V.B. Athreya, G. Djurfeldt, A. Rajagopal and R. Vidyasagar (2014), 'Progress over the Long Haul: Dynamics of Agrarian Change in the Kaveri Delta', in N. Gooptu and J. Parry, eds, *Persistence of Poverty in India*, New Delhi: Social Science Press: 344–69.

Patnaik, U. (1987), *Peasant Class Differentiation: A Study in Method with Reference to Haryana*, Delhi: Oxford University Press.

Shanin, T. (2009), 'Chayanov's Treble Death and Tenuous Resurrection: An Essay about Understanding, about Roots of Plausibility and about Rural Russia', *The Journal of Peasant Studies*, 36 (1): 83–101.

Timmer, C.P. and S. Akkus (2008), 'The Structural Transformation as a Pathway out of Poverty: Analytics, Empirics and Politics', Working Paper no. 50, Washington, D.C.: Center for Global Development.

Timmer, P. (2009), *A World without Agriculture: The Structural Transformation Process in Historical Perspective*, Washington, D.C.: The American Enterprise Institute Press.

3

The Role of Agriculture in the Process of Industrialization

Lessons from a Case Study from Western Tamil Nadu

Judith Heyer

Introduction

Pessimism about the role of agriculture in India extends to Tamil Nadu, one of the most urbanized and industrialized states, in which agriculture has not been performing well (Vijayabaskar 2015). This paper follows the tradition of some of the more seminal work in which Venkatesh Athreya has been involved (Djurfeldt *et al.* 2008, for example) by giving a more positive account of the way in which agriculture developed in a set of villages in western Tamil Nadu as the non-agricultural economy grew. It shows agriculture benefitting from the development of the non-agricultural economy with which it became increasingly involved. The villages were in an area in which the non-agricultural economy grew quite dramatically after the 1980s, as industries spread into small towns and villages, and labour was drawn in from the rest of Tamil Nadu and elsewhere. People from the study villages were also involved in this growth, many starting to work outside agriculture, many commuting to work. The paper shows the impact of the development of the non-agricultural economy on agriculture as agriculture kept pace with the non-agricultural economy with smaller numbers involved.

Agriculturalists faced increases in wages and increased water shortages as well as the more positive effects of expanded markets for agricultural products, improvement in transport and communications, and increased flow of capital and credit. They responded by adopting new irrigation technology and changing crop and livestock mixes, to take advantage of new market opportunities and to economize on labour and water that were becoming scarce.

This paper draws on the experience of western Tamil Nadu villages in the 1980s, 1990s and 2000s, where agriculture has been making a more

positive contribution by playing the sort of role that might be expected
of it during the process of industrialization (Mellor 1995; Narayanan
2012). The agricultural sector has continued to produce food and industrial inputs and increases in its productivity in these villages enabling it
to sustain rising incomes and standards of living for those involved as the
non-agricultural economy has grown.[1] Where it has fallen down is on the
environment. The process has been environmentally damaging for some
time, both in that it has been mining the water table and also it has been
associated with the accumulation of toxic residues in soils exposed to high
levels of chemical inputs (Sivanappan and Aiyasamy 1978; Srinivasan *et
al.* 2014; Heyer 2014).

The study villages on which this paper is based are 50–60 kilometres north of Coimbatore and 25–30 kilometres northwest of Tiruppur.
They became gradually more closely integrated into the local regional
economy over the period under review, as relatively small-scale industrialization spread to the surrounding centres and villages. In 1981–82,
when the first survey was conducted, the villages were predominantly
agricultural. Their agriculture relied on relatively small landholdings,
partly irrigated by wells. A wide range of crops was grown. There was
also a strong livestock sector that was an integral part of agriculture. A
minority of residents in the villages were involved in non-agricultural
activities, mainly services and trade. In 2008–09, when the most recent
survey was conducted, while more than half of the households in the villages still relied on agriculture for most or all of their income, there was
much more non-agricultural income than there had been in 1981–82. The
agricultural sector itself had changed very substantially too. Mechanized
draught power had taken over from bullocks; cropping patterns had
changed; there was new irrigation technology; and labour relations had
been transformed. There were fewer larger landholdings in 2008–09 than
in 1981–82 but holdings in all size-groups produced higher incomes and
standards of living in 2008–09 than their counterparts had in 1981–82.
This was as true of those relying mainly on agricultural wage labour as
of those relying mainly on cultivation.

The Coimbatore/Tiruppur region has a history of strong agricultural and industrial development. Agriculture was already both relatively
commercialized and capital-intensive in the late nineteenth century (Baker
1984; Harriss-White 1996). Moreover, the region was the foremost
industrial region of Tamil Nadu for most of the twentieth century, with
an emphasis on textiles and engineering products. The story of cotton
and the engineering industry that was built on cotton textile machinery

and irrigation pumps in the 1920s and 1930s is well known (Baker 1984; Chari 2004; Mahadevan and Vijayabaskar 2014). Cotton continued to play an important role in the region's agriculture until the 1970s and 1980s. Thereafter it dwindled, driven out primarily by increases in labour costs. By the 2000s, only small areas remained. There were other linkages in the 1990s and 2000s though. The markets for other agricultural products expanded as the regional economy grew. Agriculture also benefited from the development of markets in Kerala and further afield. The dynamism of the regional economy fed into entrepreneurial and managerial capabilities in agriculture and an openness to new technology and markets. Flows of information, expertise and capital were all linked to this. The increasing cost of labour was an important incentive for technical change. The development of the non-agricultural economy has not inhibited the development of a vibrant, though smaller, agricultural sector. Quite the reverse.

The villages are the home of a community of relatively small-scale farmers and agricultural labourers in a dry belt in the Coimbatore/Tiruppur region. The position of those still depending on agriculture as a source of income in this community compares well with those depending on non-agricultural sources of income. The data on which this chapter is based come from surveys in 1981–82 and 2008–09, supplemented by in-depth interviews in those and other years up to and including 2016. This was a period over which the total number of residents in the villages changed much less than might have been expected given the urban and industrial developments that were taking place in the vicinity. The villages were not getting depopulated. Far from it. They were holding their own.

The paper shows the way in which changes in the role of agriculture have affected different landholding groups in the population. The standards of living of members of each landholding group, and of the landless group, improved over time, income from cultivation playing an important role for those with more land and income from agricultural wage labour more important for those with less.

The paper starts with sections on the villages and the data, and on the changing population of the villages. These are followed by a section showing a decline in the population relying mainly or exclusively on agriculture. Next, there is a section that focuses on changes in the distribution of landholdings. After this, there is a section on changes in agricultural and livestock production over the period under review. A section on sources of income in the different landholding groups is followed by sections on medium and large landholders, and on small holders, the main source of agricultural income in both cases being cultivation of their own holdings, and on marginal landholders and landless households, for the majority of whom the main source of agricultural income was agricultural wage labour. There is a concluding section at the end.

Background and Data

The data for this paper come from a long-term study that began with a two-month period of fieldwork in 1980 looking at the SFDA (Small Farmer Development Agency) and MFALDA (Marginal Farmer and Agricultural Labourer Development Agency) promoting and subsidizing the acquisition of productive assets by poorer households. The villages were selected for their relatively strong agriculture and relatively high levels of uptake of SFDA and MFALDA loans. They were relatively remote in 1980. Coimbatore was already a major industrial centre. Tiruppur grew rapidly after 1980. There were a number of smaller urban centres near the study villages that grew after 1980 as well.

The first systematic survey was in 1981–82. It covered 20 per cent of the households in seven hamlets in two revenue villages in an unstratified sample based on population census returns in the case of non-Dalit households and house listings in the case of Dalit households for which the population census returns appeared inaccurate. It was supplemented by in-depth interviews in sample and non-sample households. Data were collected on household composition, land ownership and acquisition, ownership of wells, pump-sets and other irrigation equipment, buildings, farm equipment and livestock, etc., in a population that was predominantly agricultural. Data were not collected on costs, prices and incomes. The focus was on longer-term investment and accumulation rather than shorter-term returns in a particular year.

The next systematic survey was conducted in 1996, covering the descendants of the 1981–82 sample households still resident in the villages. Some information was also obtained on the 15 per cent or so that had left. The 1996 survey focused on similar issues to those covered in 1981–82. There had been dramatic changes though. Fewer people were involved exclusively in agriculture as non-agricultural activities had expanded and there was now a significant amount of commuting associated with non-agricultural employment. Transport and communications had developed significantly. The villages were much more integrated into the regional economy than they had been in 1981–82.

I conducted a third systematic survey in 2008–09 as part of a larger project on the impact of the expansion of the knitwear sector in Tiruppur. This survey, with a new 20 per cent sample, was based on house listings in some villages and school census returns in others, and a questionnaire very similar to those used in 1996 and 1981–82. The fact that the original focus had been on longer-term strategies proved to be a good basis for exploring questions that remained relevant over time. I did short bouts of fieldwork in 2003 and 2004, and in all but one of the years from 2010 to 2016, updating some of the information as well as focusing on new issues that had come up.

Most of the figures used in this paper are derived from the systematic surveys. The data from the first and third surveys, which were both based on randomly selected samples of 20 per cent of the households in the villages, are comparable. The data from the second survey, which was a survey of descendants of the 1981–82 sample households still resident in the villages, are not strictly comparable though they do give a fairly accurate picture of the situation in 1996. The focus in this paper, though, is on 1981–82 and 2008–09.

The account given in this paper of what has happened to agriculture does not rely on the usual data on productivity, prices, costs of production, returns from production and incomes. These were beyond the scope of the data collection exercise. It relies instead on data on crops grown, livestock numbers, occupations, sources of income, assets and demographic variables, and on production processes and labour relations. It has been possible, using such data, to build up an account of changes in agriculture and livestock production, and the relative incomes associated with these and non-agricultural activities, showing how different groups in the population have fared. This is not as detailed an account of agricultural and livestock production as would normally be expected in a study of agricultural development. It includes more elements though.

The study villages were multi-caste villages in which caste played an important role. The major landowning castes were Naidu, Gounder and Chettiar, Gounders being the most numerous of the three. There were two main groups of Dalit agricultural labourers, Arunthathiyars and Pallars, who together made up 30 per cent of the population in 1981–82 and 40 per cent in 2008–09, the majority both at the beginning and at the end of the period being landless. The clearest caste divide was between Dalits and non-Dalits. There were important distinctions between non-Dalit castes as well. Caste differences are not the focus of this paper; I have written on these elsewhere (cf. Heyer 2010; 2012; 2013; 2016a).

Changing Population of the Villages

The population of the villages did not change very much as the surrounding economy grew. Table 3.1 shows a relatively small decrease in the sample population between 1981–82 and 1996 as households migrated

Table 3.1 *Total populations in samples: 1981–82, 1996 and 2008–09*

No. of individuals	1981–82	1996	2008–09
All	1180	1164	1035
Male	652	591	545
Female	528	573	490
% female	45	49	47
No. of households	1981–82	1996	2008–09
All	230	255	257
Individuals/household	5.1	4.6	4

Source: Village surveys.

out of the villages, and a larger decrease between 1996 and 2008–09. This contrasts with population census estimates which show the population of the two revenue villages of which the study villages are a part increasing between 1981 and 2011.[2] Household sizes decreased over time in the study villages as decreases in fertility fed through, and as younger generations moved out. The number of households increased as the total population in sample households fell.

The fact that the total numbers in the villages did not change very much was partly due to the strength of transport and communications networks which enabled commuting. Transport and communication networks developed enormously over the three decades or so under review. In 1981–82 the villages were accessible only on a mud road that was difficult for vehicles to negotiate when it had rained. In 2008–09 there were tarmac roads, bus services and substantial numbers of motor vehicles, many of them two-wheelers.

The composition of the village population changed over time. There were more in-migrants in 2008–09 than in 1981–82, and more older couples whose children had moved out, including couples returning after a working life elsewhere.

Decreasing Role of Agriculture

The proportion of the population dependent on agricultural and livestock income[3] fell over time as the opportunities outside agriculture increased. Table 3.2 shows the number of households depending exclusively on agricultural income, the numbers for which agriculture provided major and minor sources of income, and the numbers with no agricultural income at all, in 1981–82 and 2008–09. It is important to note that both

Table 3.2 *Household income sources in 1981–82 and 2008–09*

No. of hh	1981–82	2008–09
Agric/Lstk/AL only	151	105
Agric/Lstk/AL and other	70	105
Agric major	23	30
Agric minor	47	75
Non-agric	9	45
All	230	255
Col. %	1981–82	2008–09
Agric/Lstk/AL only	66	41
Agric/Lstk/AL & other	30	41
Agric major	10	12
Agric minor	20	29
Non-agric	4	18
All	100	100

Notes: Agric/Lstk/AL: agricultural/livestock/agricultural labour; Agric major/minor: agriculture major/minor source of income.
Source: Village surveys.

income from cultivation as well as income from agricultural wage labour are included in 'agriculture' as a source of income in Table 3.2.

There was a decline in the proportion of households dependent entirely on agricultural sources of income (from 66 per cent in 1981–82 to 41 per cent in 2008–09), an increase in the proportion dependent on both agricultural and non-agricultural sources of income (from 30 per cent in 1981–82 to 41 per cent in 2008–09), and an increase in the proportion dependent entirely on non-agricultural sources of income (from 4 per cent in 1981–82 to 18 per cent in 2008–09). The proportion of households for which agriculture was the main or only source of income was 53 per cent in 2008–09.

Changes in Landholding and the Size Distribution of Landholdings

The decline in the importance of agriculture as a source of income was accompanied by a substantial fall in the acreage of agricultural land owned by residents of the villages. This was particularly noticeable between 1996 and 2008–09. Sample households resident in the villages owned 811 acres in 1981–82 and 823 acres in 1996. In 2008–09 they owned only 554 acres. Some of the decline in land owned by residents could be accounted for by land held on to by people who had moved out of the villages and were no longer classed as residents, some holding on to it for retirement and some for security reasons in case they needed to move back. Some of this land was being cultivated by close relatives remaining in the villages. The rest of the decline could be accounted for by land transferred to outsiders. This included land for a steel mill that was being established in 2008–09. (Land was being developed for horticulture-cum-tourism shortly after 2008–09, and land that had solar panels on it appeared in 2016.) The decline observed in 2008–09 included housing layouts that were as

Table 3.3 *Land distribution in 1981–82, 1996 and 2008–09*

Acres	1981–82	No. hh	% of hh	Acres	% land
0	Landless	93	40	0	0
>0<2.5	Marginal	43	19	52	6
2.5<5	Small	27	12	93	11
5<10	Medium	43	19	286	35
10+	Large	24	10	383	47
	All	230	100	814	100
	Mean holding size 3.54				
Acres	1996	No. hh	% hh	Acres	% land
0	Landless	100	39	0	0
>0<2.5	Marginal	53	21	66	8
2.5<5	Small	39	15	137	17
5<10	Medium	39	15	263	32
10+	Large	24	9	358	43
	All	255	100	823	100
	Mean holding size 3.20				
Acres	2008–09	No. hh	% hh	Acres	% land
0	Landless	133	52	0	0
>0<2.5	Marginal	49	19	74	13
2.5<5	Small	38	15	134	24
5<10	Medium	21	8	139	25
10+	Large	14	5	205	37
	All	255	100	551	100
	Mean holding size 2.14				

Source: Village surveys.

yet unoccupied. There was also a considerable amount of agricultural land that had been bought by outsiders that was lying fallow in 2008–09. There was a substantial amount of speculation around land values going on.

The size distribution of resident households' landholdings changed considerably between 1981–82 and 2008–09 (Table 3.3). The proportion with medium and large holdings fell from 29 per cent in 1981–82 to 13 per cent in 2008–09. The absolute numbers of medium and large landholders in the sample almost halved. There was an increase in both the number and the proportion of households with small landholdings. The number of households with marginal landholdings increased a little but the proportion hardly changed. Finally, there was a substantial increase in both the proportion and the number of landless households. Households were moving down the land distribution, from large to medium, medium to small, small to marginal and marginal to landless. Fewer were moving up. There was more out-migration from the upper reaches than the lower. The numbers of landless were also increasing as landless households subdivided and stayed in the villages after subdivision.

There was very little leasing in this area. There was one exception among the larger landholders, someone leasing the only leased-in temple land. There were a few other people leasing in small quantities of land in the landless group.

The area owned by medium and large landholders in the sample fell from 666 acres in 1981–82 to 344 acres in 2008–09, while the area owned by small and marginal landholders rose. In the case of small holders the sample fell from 93 to 137 acres, and from 52 to 74 acres in the case of marginal landholders. The average sizes of both small holdings and marginal landholdings increased.

Thus, in 2008–09 there were considerably smaller numbers of medium and large holdings, larger numbers of small holdings and slightly larger numbers of marginal holdings, and substantially larger numbers of landless households, than in 1981–82. The decline in numbers of medium and large landholdings was one of the most striking changes in the villages. Large landholders had been so dominant and numerous in 1981–82. The increased numbers of landless was another striking change of course.

Changes in Agriculture and Livestock Production

It was not only land distribution that changed between 1981–82 and 2008–09. There were also very substantial changes in the character of agricultural and livestock production. The changes were driven by factors such as the increasing cost of labour, increasing water scarcity and changing market opportunities. Bullocks were replaced by mechanical power both in transport and in field operations; there were substantial changes in irrigation technology; there were significant changes in employment relations; and there were changes in crop and livestock mixes as well. All of this happened within the context of a reduced role of state R&D (research and development). In 1981–82, and even in 1996, cultivators were looking to the TNAU (Tamil Nadu Agricultural University) in Coimbatore for advice on new crops, new varieties of crops, agronomic practices, irrigation technology, and the control of pests and diseases. Much of the advice was transmitted through local agricultural officers who were greatly sought after when they visited the villages. People from the villages visited the TNAU too. By 2008–09 all of this had stopped. TNAU appeared to be focusing more on marketing and agri-processing, less on production. It was no longer a place to which people from the villages felt they could turn for technical assistance. The visits of local agricultural officers were less frequent, and they focused primarily on subsidies and grants. Agricultural officers were barely noticed when they visited the villages in 2008–09. Instead people relied on input suppliers, equipment suppliers and seed companies who provided them with much less comprehensive services than they had received earlier. People also used the internet.

There was less irrigation and less intensive irrigation in 2008–09 than in 1981–82, but some larger landholders had more elaborate and intensive irrigation systems in 2008–09. The water table fell continuously for much of the period under review.[4] There were many cases of previously irrigated land having reverted to 'dry' land. Irrigation based on large open wells in the early 1980s gave way to borewells with compressors and submersibles which were drawing water from greater depths. Drip irrigation first appeared in 2006 and thereafter spread rapidly. It enabled cultivators to economize on water and also on labour as fertilizers and pesticides were delivered through the water in the process of irrigation. It was notable that a state scheme that provided subsidies for drip irrigation was often not taken up. One cultivator who had adopted drip irrigation reported that he had not known about the subsidy at the time of purchasing the equipment and only later learnt that the subsidy had been pocketed by the equipment supplier rather than being handed over to him. Others said that they had known about the subsidy but gone to a supplier not eligible because they thought the equipment and the services provided by that supplier were of better quality.

The bullock-powered *kavalai* system of irrigation was phased out in the 1960s and 1970s. Irrigation was already fully electrified by 1981–82. Electricity was unreliable though. There were periods of acute shortage and a lot of night irrigation was carried out. In the 2000s there were acute shortages again but there was no longer much night irrigation. By 2015–16 the shortages appeared to be a thing of the past, though it remained to be seen whether this was indeed the case.

There were some signs of a decrease in water scarcity in 2014 or so. Well depths no longer appeared to be increasing. Tanks that had not had water for twenty years were full. Whether this was indeed a sign of a real decrease in water scarcity, and, if so, how far it was the result of the decrease in irrigated area, the increased efficiency of irrigation and/or state investment in minor irrigation works, remains to be investigated. It is an interesting possibility though.

Crop mixes changed significantly over the period. Cotton was grown on most holdings in 1981–82, but by 2008–09 there was very little left. Banana, which had been a minor crop in 1981–82, was one of the major crops in 2008–09 with a ready market in Kerala. Turmeric, which featured in 1981–82, was still a major crop in 2008–09. There were significant areas under sugarcane in 1981–82 but less in 2008–09. There were fewer coconuts although there were now one or two coconut plantations, not just coconuts on the edges of irrigated plots. A variety of vegetables, pulses, fruits and flowers were also grown both in 1981–82 and in 2008–09. New crops being tried out by a few cultivators in 2008–09 included papaya, from which papain was being extracted for industrial use, and a range of fruit trees, fodder crops, and trees grown for wood and forestry. There was also some interest in organic farming which was being promoted by a group in Coimbatore. The area of rainfed land under cultivation had fallen more than the area of irrigated land. More *cholam*, and fewer pulses, oilseeds and groundnuts were being grown on the rainfed land still under cultivation.

Livestock have long played an important role in this region, earlier mainly as a source of draught power for irrigation, and for field operations and transport, and mainly as a source of manure, milk and meat more recently. Bullocks, widely used for transport and field operations in 1981–82,were represented only in small numbers in 2008–09 (Table 3.7). They had been replaced by four-wheel tractors for field operations and some transport, and also by a variety of other means of transport ranging from two-wheelers to trucks. It was surprising that there were not more smaller types of mechanical equipment being used for field operations (cf. Biggs *et al.* 2011).

There was a fall in the numbers of dairy cattle between 1981–82 and 2008–09, when cows had almost completely replaced buffaloes which had dominated dairy production in 1981–82. Many households kept sheep and goats, usually in small numbers, both in 1981–82 and in 2008–09.

There were also a few large holdings of sheep and goats in both the periods. In general, those with more land had more livestock than those with less. Fodder was a major problem. Livestock were not a substitute for those with little or no land.

There were radical changes in employment relations between 1981–82 and 2008–09. Tied labour was widespread in 1981–82; labourers were attached to particular employers and were working on a beck-and-call system throughout the year (Heyer 2010; Carswell and De Neve 2013). Larger farmers with substantial areas of irrigated land employed up to five to six tied labourers each in 1981–82. Tied labourers were gradually replaced by daily wage labourers after 1981–82, and by 'contract labourers' working in gangs of five to ten, negotiating rates for particular pieces of work. By 2008–09 there were very few tied labourers left. Instead large numbers of contract labourers worked under completely changed labour relationships, negotiating pay and exercising considerable bargaining power. Labourers could now choose to turn down work as they had more social security and the option of working elsewhere. Employers found it difficult to accept the shift in the balance of power and complained that they could not easily get the labour they needed. They had to offer reasonable terms and reasonable amounts of flexibility if they were to get labourers in 2008–09. At the same time labourers complained that there was not enough work. It was indeed the case that there was not enough employment in the villages to meet the needs of all relying on agricultural wage labour. One of the more experienced agricultural labourers estimated that only about one-third of the agricultural wage labour undertaken by village residents was in the villages in 2008–09. There was work elsewhere though. This was a big change from 1981–82 when there was always plenty of year-round employment in the villages themselves, except where sugarcane crushers were concerned.

In sum, agriculture in 2008–09 was very different from agriculture in 1981–82, generating higher incomes both for wage labourers and for those cultivating their own land. In what follows, we look at the changes for different landholding groups and get a sense of how this was distributed.

Sources of Income in Different Landholding Groups in 2008–09

Table 3.4 shows the income sources of households in landless, marginal, small and medium/large landholding groups in 2008–09, bringing out the interaction between landholding size groups and agricultural and non-agricultural sources of income. Not surprisingly, non-agricultural sources of income played a more important role in groups with less land. Table 3.4 does not distinguish between income from the cultivation of

Table 3.4 *Land and household income sources, 2008–09*

No. of hh	Landless	Marginal	Small	Medium/Large	All
Agric/Lstk/AL only	56	13	17	19	105
Agric/Lstk/AL and other					
Agric major	19	3	3	5	30
Agric minor	31	21	14	9	75
Non-agric	27	12	4	2	45
All	133	49	38	35	255
Col. % hh	Landless	Marginal	Small	Medium/Large	All
Agric/Lstk/AL only	42	27	45	54	41
Agric/Lstk/AL and other					
Agric major	14	6	8	14	12
Agric minor	23	43	37	26	29
Non-agric	20	24	11	6	18
All	100	100	100	100	100
Row % hhs	Landless	Marginal	Small	Medium/Large	All
Agric/Lstk/AL only	53	12	16	18	100
Agric/Lstk/AL and other					
Agric major	63	10	10	17	100
Agric minor	41	28	19	12	100
Non-agric	60	27	9	4	100
All	52	19	15	14	100

Note: Agric/Lstk/AL: agricultural/livestock/agricultural labour. Agric major/minor: agriculture major/minor source of income.
Source: Village surveys.

own land and income from agricultural wage labour. It should be noted however that for small holding and medium/large holding households, with one or two exceptions, agriculture meant livestock production and/ or cultivation of own land, and for marginal landholders and households without land, with one or two exceptions, agriculture meant agricultural wage labour. There was a very clear divide in this respect in 2008–09.

Although the number of medium/large landholders declined substantially, the majority of those that remained were pursuing agricultural and livestock production single-mindedly. It was only a minority of households that combined this with other activities in 2008–09. The number of small holders increased, the majority pursuing agricultural and livestock production seriously, and only a minority doing so along with other activities. Only one of the small holder households in the sample received any income from agricultural wage labour. The number of marginal landholders changed very little and for them the cultivation of own land and/or livestock production was a supplementary activity. For marginal landholders agricultural wage labour was a significant source of income as was non-agricultural employment. Some were engaged in professions and trade associated with higher incomes too. For the much larger number of landless households, agricultural wage labour remained an important source of income, though both the number and the proportion relying on agricultural wage labour were lower than earlier as the range of non-agricultural alternatives had increased.

Table 3.5 distinguishes those with higher quality sources of non-agricultural income, defined as significant business and/or salaried employment, from those with poorer quality sources of non-agricultural income, defined as non-agricultural wage labour, petty business and petty trade. The bulk of the non-agricultural income was poor quality. Of the 60 per cent of households with non-agricultural sources of income,

Table 3.5 *Land and household non-agricultural income sources, 2008–09*

No. of hh	Landless	Marginal	Small	Medium/Large	All
*High quality non-agric	8	12	5	7	32
**Poorer non-agric	72	24	16	9	121
All	80	36	21	16	153
Col. % hh	Landless	Marginal	Small	Medium/Large	All
High quality non-agric	10	33	24	44	21
Poorer non-agric	90	67	76	56	79
All	100	100	100	100	100
Row % hh	Landless	Marginal	Small	Medium/Large	All
High quality non-agric	25	38	16	22	100
Poorer non-agric	60	20	13	7	100
All	52	24	14	10	100

Notes: * Owners of a spinning mill, a transport business, and two owners of electrical shops; people working as supervisors, managers and administrators in mills, etc.; a contractor, an insurance agent; teachers; salesmen, traders and shopkeepers; bus and car drivers; and someone working in IT.
** Manual wage labour, petty trade and services.
Source: Village surveys.

21 per cent had high quality sources and 79 per cent poorer quality sources. Households with high quality sources of non-agricultural income were strongly over-represented among medium/large landholders and among marginal landholders, slightly over-represented among small holders, and strongly under-represented among landless households, as one might expect. Households with relatively poorer sources of non-agricultural income were under-represented in all the groups with land and over-represented in the landless group.

Medium and Large Landholders

There had been some very large landowners in these villages up to the middle of the twentieth century, with hundreds of acres of land, but by 1981–82 they were all gone. In 1981–82, there was a distinct large farmer elite, consisting of Naidu, Gounder and Chettiar employers of tied labour, including descendants of the large landowners of the past, and they ruled the village as an oligarchy. One or two, none in the sample, had more than 30 acres of land in 1981–82. Most had much less. Large farmers were very confident of the future of agriculture in 1981–82 and only a small minority saw the need to educate their sons for anything else (Heyer 2010). By 2008–09 large landowners were much less dominant in the villages, partly because of the reduction in their numbers and the increased bargaining power of labourers and other smaller landowners, and also because their interests no longer centred so exclusively on the villages. Many now had strong connections outside; many, though not all, were educating children outside; and many were looking outside for the future of their children too.

The fall in the numbers with medium and large holdings in the villages between 1981–82 and 2008–09 came about partly through sub-division. It also came about through sale of land driven by the need to meet 'family' and other expenses, and through out-migration, some of which was associated with the sale of land. There were occasional sales to finance investments in non-agricultural enterprises too.[5] Few of the medium and large landholders bought land in this period. However, a few smaller landholders moved into the group by buying land.

The majority (54 per cent) of households with medium or large landholdings in 2008–09 had no source of income other than agriculture (Table 3.6). For another significant proportion (14 per cent), agriculture was the main source of income. For a minority of medium and large landholders agriculture was a secondary source of income as household heads and/or their sons engaged in non-agricultural activities. The better quality non-agricultural income sources included a spinning mill, an

Table 3.6 *Selected assets and education by landholding group in 2008–09*

	Two-wheelers	House exp. >1 lakh	>XII ed	hhs with children rel age
No. hhs*				
Landless	39	9	5	65
Marginal landholders	21	8	8	30
Small landholders	27	10	9	30
Med/large landholders	30	11	12	20
All	117	38	34	145
Percentages of rel hhs	Two-wheelers	House exp. >1 lakh	>XII ed**	
Landless	30	7	8	
Marginal landholders	43	16	27	
Small landholders	71	26	30	
Med/large landholders	86	31	60	
All	46	15	13	

Notes: * households; ** percentages of hhs with children in the relevant age group.
Source: Village surveys.

electrical shop, and the salaries of people working as supervisors, managers and administrators elsewhere. These were very different from the better quality non-agricultural income sources of large and medium landholders in 1981–82 and 1996, most of which were in trade and agri-processing. Furthermore, the majority of the non-agricultural income sources even of those with medium and large landholdings were low-skill wage-work and/ or petty trade in 2008–09. Only one or two (6 per cent) in the medium and large landholding group did not engage in agriculture. They leased out land.

Very little land owned by medium and large landholders was unused in 2008–09, and slightly more than half (52 per cent) was irrigated. All but two of the landholders in this group had some irrigated land. It was on medium and large landholdings that most of the drip irrigation was being introduced. Crops like papaya and trees of different kinds were being grown for the first time on some of these holdings in 2008–09.

Medium and large landholders were the major employers of hired labour in agriculture in 2008–09 as had been the case in 1981–82. They had a much more distant relationship with their hired labourers in 2008–09 than they had had in 1981–82 though.

Livestock played a substantial role in medium and large landhold-

Table 3.7 *Livestock holdings by land ownership groups, 1981–82 and 2008–09*

	1981–82			2008–09		
	Bullocks	Cows/ buffalos	Sheep/ goats	Bullocks	Cows/ buffalos	Sheep/ goats
No. of hh						
Landless	1	13	29	0	12	26
Marginal	4	22	15	0	16	17
Small	4	19	6	3	28	13
Med/Large	48	58	31	5	31	13
All	57	112	81	8	87	69
% hhs						
Landless	1	14	32	0	9	20
Marginal	9	49	33	0	33	35
Small	15	73	23	8	74	34
Med/Large	72	88	31	15	91	38
All	24	49	35	3	34	27
^av/hh						
Landless	1.0	1.8	4.8	0.0	1.1	5.3*
Marginal	2.0	2.7	3.7	0.0	2.0	5.4*
Small	2.0	3.4	20.0*	2.0	3.0	3.1
Med/Large	2.6	3.7	8.0	2.0	4.1	2.9
All	2.5	3.8	6.9	2.0	3.0	4.4

Notes: ^ average per household with livestock; * one or two large holdings.
Source: Village surveys.

ings. As shown in Table 3.7, the large majority had bullocks in 1981–82 and very few in 2008–09. Most medium and large landholders had dairy cattle both in 1981–82 and in 2008–09, and many had small numbers of sheep and goats (shown as Shgoats in the table). With the exception of bullocks, livestock were playing as important a role as ever on medium and large landholdings in 2008–09, as much for own consumption as anything else.

Large and medium landholders were doing as well as their peers outside agriculture. One of the indicators of the increasing wealth of households in this group was the elaborate and expensive houses they were building. This was a big change from 1981–82 when none of the houses being built by medium and large landholders was more than rudimentary. Further, nearly all the medium and large landholders had two-wheelers in 2008–09. This had been the only group in which there were any two-wheelers at all in 1981–82. The majority of the households in this group with children of relevant ages were putting their children through higher education, sending them to more expensive colleges and for more degrees. They were also spending more in this regard than on households in other landholding groups.

Many with medium and large landholdings in 2008–09 had sons engaged in non-agricultural activities, and many were educating sons (and some daughters) to move into non-agricultural activities (see Heyer 2016b for this on Gounders). Some of their sons would continue in agriculture and some would combine agriculture with non-agricultural activities. Examples of the more enterprising sons in this group continuing in agriculture included Muthusamy[6] whose family had set him up with a knitwear unit, first in Tiruppur then on the family farm, and who was more interested in drip-irrigated agriculture than in the knitwear unit despite the fact that the knitwear unit was doing reasonably well; and Subramaniam, a bank employee with higher education who was investing heavily in agriculture and planning to continue to do so, relying on his speech-impaired brother for its day-to-day management. These were both members of households with relatively large landholdings. Others had pursued non-agricultural occupations until their fathers were no longer dominant, and then moved back into agriculture. Examples included Aiyasamy who had come back from leasing land in Karnataka after his father had died, and who was investing heavily in agriculture, of his sons working with him and the other studying engineering overseas; and Murugasamy, an ex-cutting master who had come back to concentrate exclusively on agriculture as his father was getting old. There was also a designer with an MPhil earning Rs 30,000–40,000 per month in Tiruppur who had just got married when we met in 2016, and who was planning to resign from his position in Tiruppur and devote himself to agriculture now that he was married.[7] In this case it was significant that he did not have a father standing in his way. His father had passed away when he was young. Finally, there were relatively well-placed government officials who had moved back on retirement, investing substantially in agriculture as an activity they intended to pursue until they got too old.

To summarize: there were far fewer medium and large landholders in 2008–09, but those still focusing on and investing in agriculture were doing well. They were no longer relatively isolated cultivators putting all their time and energy into the villages and their labour relations in the villages as they had been in 1981–82. They were much better connected, and much less dependent on and occupied by what was going on in the villages. Some would continue in agriculture. Others would move out. However, it looked as though there was still a future for small numbers of medium and large landholders such as these to do well.

Small Holders

There was a sizeable group of relatively independent Naidu, Gounder, Chettiar and one or two lower-caste small holder households in 1981–82, and a somewhat larger group in 2008–09 (Table 3.3). Only one or two of these were Dalits. They included members of households that had had large or medium holdings earlier who had become small holders as a result of inheritance and subdivision. They included people retiring or returning after working outside agriculture for years. There were also a few in-migrant agriculturalists who had sold land elsewhere and bought land in the study villages instead. Households that had moved out of the group included households that had left the villages, and households that had become marginal landholders or landless households after subdivision and/or the sale of their land. The majority of small holder households were making a reasonable living from cultivating their own land. Very few members of these households worked as agricultural wage labourers.

A smaller proportion (45 per cent) of small holders relied exclusively on agriculture in 2008–09 than of medium and large landholders (Table 3.4). There was also a smaller proportion whose main source of household income was agriculture (8 per cent). Agriculture was the main or only source of income nevertheless for just over one-half of all small holder households in 2008–09. Agriculture was a secondary source of income for nearly all of the rest. Very few small holders had no agricultural income.

Nearly all of the agricultural income in small holder households was self-employment income from agriculture or livestock. Thirteen per cent of small holder households had substantial sources of non-agricultural income (Table 3.5). These included teachers, a contractor and the owner of a transport business. The majority with non-agricultural income were engaged in poorer quality wage-work and/or petty trade.

As in the case of medium and large landholders, very little land owned by small holders was unused in 2008–09. Thirty-six per cent of small holder land was irrigated and a little over half of the small holder households (54 per cent) had some irrigated land. This included all but two of those with agriculture as the main or only source of income. Nearly all with agriculture as a secondary source of income only had rainfed land. Cropping patterns were very similar to those of large/medium landholders.

One or two small holders were experimenting with new crops too. Small holders were significant employers of hired labour though on a smaller scale than larger landholders.

Livestock played a major role on small holdings both in 1981–82 and in 2008–09. Only a few had bullocks, either in 1981–82 or in 2008–09 (Table 3.7). Many had dairy cattle and significant numbers had small holdings of sheep and goats. One or two had large holdings of sheep and goats in 1981–82 but not in 2008–09. Livestock played a similar role on small holdings in 1981–82 and 2008–09.

One of the indicators of the increased well-being of this group was the investment in houses that were more substantial than those in which small holders had been living earlier. There was significant spending on houses in this group. Moreover 75 per cent of small holder households had two-wheelers in 2008–09 (Table 3.6). A number of small holder households were also putting children through higher education, though they were not spending as much on this as households in the medium and large landholding group. Small holders had bank loans as well as relatively low interest loans from relatives and friends. Most appeared to be repaying these without difficulty. There were very few cases of small holders having to sell land or other major assets in order to repay loans. Nearly all the cases involved major medical expenditure preceding death.

Many with small landholdings in 2008–09 had sons engaged in non-agricultural activities and substantial numbers were educating sons (and some daughters) to move into non-agricultural activities. Some of the sons would continue to combine agriculture with non-agricultural activities, with agriculture as a minor rather than a major source of income. Some would move back into agriculture after a working life elsewhere. There were one or two innovative entrepreneurial farmers continuing in agriculture in this group, though not as many as in the medium and large landholding group. The most striking example was Gurusamy who had a Master's degree and was one of the first to introduce drip irrigation on land on which he was growing vegetables in 2008–09. The majority with small landholdings were in the process of moving out of agriculture however, investing in their children's higher education if they could. Whether they could or not depended more on whether their children continued to study well than on whether they could finance the higher education. Larger landholders whose sons were not studying well usually sent them to boarding schools which would ensure their success. The children of small landholders might end up as small holders or something similar simply because they did not study well.

Small holders were a robust and relatively independent intermediate group in the villages in 1981–82. In 2008–09 they continued as such, holding their own in competition with the opportunities that had opened up outside agriculture. The opportunities available to them outside agriculture did not always compete well with agriculture. Agriculture was a good alternative for many of them.

Marginal Landholders

There were households from a wide variety of castes. A number were households from a particular Dalit group many of whom had very small holdings of land. Some were engaged in services or trade. Many of these were members of households for whom this was a caste occupation in 1981–82.

The numbers of marginal landholders had risen only slightly between 1981–82 and 2008–09. The proportion of households in the village population who were marginal landholders had remained the same (Table 3.3). The average size of marginal landholdings had risen since 1981–82 though, from 1.2 acres on average in sample households in 1981–82 to 1.5 acres in 2008–09. Households moved into and out of the marginal landholding group through similar processes to those involved for small holders. There were more relatively well-placed people among marginal landholders than among small holders though, including teachers and shopkeepers who had moved in from elsewhere and bought a little land.

This was a group for virtually all of whom cultivation was a subsidiary occupation. All of them had other sources of income that were more important.[8] For the majority of marginal landholders in 1981–82, the main source of income was agricultural wage labour and some migrant sugarcane crushing, the latter an occupation engaged in mainly by Dalits. Marginal landholders were in a very different situation in 2008–09. One of the changes was that there were now large numbers of non-agricultural wage labourers among them. The other change was that almost one in four had high quality sources of non-agricultural income in 2008–09 (Table 3.5). These included employment in IT, in teaching, trade and shopkeeping, in a debt collection agency, and employment as a salesman. Agricultural wage income was still the main, and for many, the only source of income for one-third of marginal landholding households in 2008–09 however, although there was no longer any sugarcane crushing. There were fewer in services too, particularly services which were caste-related.

A few marginal landholders had bullocks and carts which they hired out in 1981–82 and none in 2008–09. The numbers with dairy cattle were smaller in 2008–09 than in 1981–82, and the numbers of cattle per household had fallen (Table 3.7). A larger proportion had sheep and goats, the numbers of which per household had risen by 2008–09. Both the proportions of households with livestock and the numbers per household with livestock were low compared with those in other landholding groups, however. It was difficult for most households with marginal holdings to feed and care for livestock.

Many marginal landholders valued having a little land in order to grow fodder for livestock, and/or to grow small amounts of crops mainly for their own use. In some cases marginal landholders working in non-agricultural occupations were holding on to land, either leaving it fallow or leaving wives or parents to cultivate it in a minor way. There was considerable underutilization of land in this group both in 1981–82 and in 2008–09.

Fewer marginal landholders than larger landholders had been spending significantly on housing, and fewer had two-wheelers (Table 3.6). Similar proportions of marginal landholders to small holders were putting children through higher education though, and this included poor households as well as better-placed households. This was as much a priority for marginal landholders as for any other group. There were cases of Dalits in the marginal landholding group benefiting from state support for higher education and/or bank education loans. Marginal landholders had loans from banks, and from relatives and friends. A few had more costly loans, from employers and from *kandu*[9] moneylenders. While these were drains on their incomes, in only a few cases were they associated with the sale of land or other major changes in employment or living conditions.

To summarize: whereas in 1981–82, virtually the only occupations of marginal landholders other than cultivating their land were agricultural wage labour and petty trade, in 2008–09, people in this group were engaged in a wide range of occupations, some of them of relatively high quality. Even marginal landholders without higher quality sources of income were much better off in 2008–09 than marginal landholders had been in 1981–82. It should be noted that they were more detached from agricultural labour than landless labourers were. Marginal landholders were the group least dependent on agriculture in 2008–09.

Landless Households

The number of landless households increased very substantially over the period between 1981–82 and 2008–09. The increase in numbers came about mainly as households that had never had land subdivided. Landless households in earlier generations had high fertility rates. This meant that there were a lot of subdivisions in the period between 1981–82 and 2008–09. A much smaller part of the increase in numbers of landless households was associated with subdivided households, with relatively small landholdings selling their land. There were also a few households that lost land through mismanagement or misfortune of one kind or another.

The large majority in landless households in 1981–82 were agricul-tural labourers, many of them tied labourers working for low pay on terms and conditions that were harsh (Heyer 2010). There was also a substantial group of migrant sugarcane crushers working outside the villages. Over 60 per cent of landless households were Dalits in 1981–82. It was from these households that both tied labourers and sugarcane crushers came. Others in landless households worked on a daily basis as casual agricultural labourers. A minority were also engaged in services and petty trade. In 2008–09, just over half of the people in landless households still worked as wage labourers in agriculture. One or two also leased land. There was no migrant sugarcane crushing however in 2008–09. A little less than half the people in landless households now worked as wage labourers outside agriculture, in manufacturing, mainly textiles, and in construction, as well as in services and petty trade. Twenty per cent of landless households had no agricultural income at all in 2008–09, and for 23 per cent agriculture played a minor role. This was a big change. The fact that over half still worked as agricultural wage labourers is significant though. Dalits now represented 70 per cent of the landless households and it was from these that the majority of agricultural wage labourers came. The pay and the terms and conditions of agricultural wage labour were much better than they had been in 1981–82. Agricultural wage labour competed well with other sources of wage income to which members of landless households had access in 2008–09. MGNREGA (Mahatma Gandhi National Rural Employment Guarantee Act) was an additional source of income for agri-cultural labourers after 2008–09. It was not yet established well enough to show up in the 2008–09 figures though. There was not enough agricultural wage-work in the villages. A lot of it was further afield.

It is not always the case that all landless households in villages are poor, but the overwhelming majority here were so. There were only two households in the sample with high quality sources of income who did not have any agricultural land (Table 3.5). One was headed by an insurance agent, and the other an electrician with a shop in a nearby urban centre whose wife was a teacher.

Livestock played a relatively small role in landless households. It was difficult for them to get enough fodder and also to spare enough labour to look after livestock. In the sample, there was one landless household rearing bullocks in 1981–82 and none in 2008–09. A small number (14 per cent) had dairy cattle in 1981–82, and a similar number but smaller proportion (9 per cent) in 2008–09 (Table 3.7). Thirty-two per cent of landless households had small numbers of sheep and goats in 1981–82, and a similar number but smaller proportion (20 per cent) in 2008–09. There were one or two landless households in the sample with larger holdings of sheep and goats both in 1981–82 and in 2008–09.

State support was particularly important for landless households in 2008–09 (Heyer 2012). Significant numbers, mainly Dalits, had acquired better quality housing as a result of state support, much of it involving spending of their own as well. Few landless households had spent substantial sums on housing apart from this. Thirty per cent of landless households had two-wheelers, including a number whose only source of income was agricultural labour. A small number, mainly Dalits, were putting children through higher education in 2008–09, and there were more with children who were not yet old enough who were planning to do so.[10] Many but not all Dalit households putting their children through higher education benefited from state support and/or bank education loans. Some of them were households depending on agricultural wage labour alone. Landless labourers had a lot of high-interest debt, from employers and from *kandu* moneylenders. Levels of debt as a proportion of their income appeared very similar in 2008–09 to what they had been in 1981–82. Dalits had less debt from relatives and friends at relatively lower interest rates than members of any other group.

What kept landless households in the villages in 2008–09 was not land but housing and living conditions, which were generally much better than in urban areas for households such as these. The relative ease of access to the PDS (public distribution system) and other welfare programmes was an important factor. MGNREGA may also have played a part after 2008–09.

To summarize: there were far more landless household residents in the villages in 2008–09 than in 1981–82. However, while landless households were still the poorest in the villages, they were in a far better position in 2008–09 than their counterparts had been in 1981–82. Substantial numbers in landless households worked as agricultural wage labourers with much better terms and conditions than in 1981–82. Nearly as many worked outside agriculture in 2008–09 as well.

Conclusions

This paper has shown that in villages that are closely linked to a relatively dynamic local industrial economy, a slimmed down agriculture has been supporting significant numbers of people at standards of living very similar to those they would be able to achieve outside agriculture.

What is distinctive about this case is that the relative success of agriculture has been due to the way it has interacted with the non-agricultural economy. Agriculture has done well because it is situated in a relatively integrated regional economy in which linkages between agriculture and the rest of the economy are strong. The fact that there has been a dynamic non-agricultural economy has pulled agriculture in the villages up.

While the proximity of the dynamic non-agricultural economy has pulled agriculture in the villages up, the fact that this non-agricultural economy has been a low road economy has limited the extent to which it has been able to do so. Both agricultural and non-agricultural activities are providing relatively low incomes for the majority in this area. If the non-agricultural economy were a higher road economy, agriculture would do better than this through positive linkages that would be stronger.

It is also true that agriculture could do better with more support from the state. It would benefit from more R&D support, more support for water and irrigation infrastructure, and more reliable electricity. It has achieved what it has despite the fact that it has had relatively little support from the state over the past couple of decades or so.

The biggest remaining question is that of the environment. This was an agriculture that had been damaging the environment for a long time, mining the water supply which was not able to recharge itself fully, and degrading the soils through the extensive use of chemicals. There were some indications that the water situation might improve as the cultivated area fell and the efficiency of irrigation increased. There was also growing interest in organic agriculture which might revive the soils, though this needed further encouragement. The environmental damage done by the industrial sector on which agriculture relied for its success was continuing apace too. The damage done by the industrial sector was at least as serious as the damage done by agriculture. Reports of the destruction of the Noyyal river flowing through Tiruppur and Coimbatore hint at the scale of the problem and the ineffectiveness of efforts to tackle it so far (see Srinivasan *et al.* 2014; T.S. Subramaniam 2018). The performance of agriculture in this area is intimately linked to the performance of the non-agricultural economy. It has to be recognized that it is intimately linked to the environmental degradation caused by the non-agricultural economy as well.

The research on which this paper is based was funded by the UK Department of International Development (DFID, formerly ODA), the Oxford University Webb Medley Fund, the Leverhulme Trust and the Queen Elizabeth House Oppenheimer Fund, at various stages. The 2008–09 research was funded as part of a project on the effects of the expansion of the knitwear industry in the Tiruppur region funded by a DFID-ESRC Research Award, a project in which Grace Carswell, Geert De Neve and M. Vijayabaskar were also involved. The research could not have been done without the support of Dr V. Mohanasundaram, my interpreter and co-researcher for most of the fieldwork since 1981–82, and without the contributions of M.V. Srinivasan, Paul Pandian, Selva Murugan, Arul Maran, Gowri Shankar, S. Saravanan and Jagan Subi who acted as research assistants at different stages in the field. The research has also benefited from discussions particularly with K. Nagaraj, J. Jeyaranjan and Barbara Harriss-White.

Notes
[1] Djurfelt *et al.* (2008) provide another example of such.

[2] In the case of the revenue village all of which was included in the study, the 1981 to 2011 increase recorded in the population census was 15 per cent. However, the Dalit population in that village was seriously underestimated in 1981. In the revenue village only part of which was included in the study, the 1981 to 2011 increase was larger. Some of the hamlets in this village were near a main road and centre with a larger population. Hamlets that were further away were included in the study, not hamlets that were nearer the main road.

[3] Agricultural and livestock income is referred to as 'agricultural income' in much of what follows. It is important not to lose sight of the fact that livestock were integral to agricultural production and income.

[4] The water table had been falling for some time. The deepest wells in sample households in the study villages were 200 feet in 1981–82, 600 feet in 1996 and 1200 feet in 2008–09.

[5] Chari (2004) and Vijayabaskar (2005) report that land sales were significant sources of investment in textile units in Tiruppur. There were only one or two cases of such in the study villages.

[6] All names are pseudonyms.

[7] Two years later, we found that this is what he had done.

[8] There were two exceptional cases in the marginal landholder sample whose main sources of income were own account agricultural and livestock production. These were: a household with 2 acres of land all of which was irrigated, and a household with large numbers of sheep.

[9] *Kandu* is the colloquial term used in Tamil Nadu for professional moneylenders charging usurious rates of interest, *kandu vatti* – typically, in this case, Rs 10 per Rs 100 per month.

[10] There had been a substantial increase in young Dalits going to college by 2016, the latest year of fieldwork at the time of writing, most planning to become teachers.

References
Baker, C.J. (1984), *An Indian Rural Economy 1880–1995: The Tamilnad Countryside*, Oxford: Clarendon Press.

Biggs, S., S. Justice and D. Lewis (2011), 'Patterns of Rural Mechanisation, Energy and Employment in South Asia: Reopening the Debate', *Economic and Political Weekly*, 46 (9): 78–82.

Carswell, G. and G. De Neve (2013), 'From Field to Factory: Tracing Transformations in Bonded Labour in the Tiruppur Region, Tamil Nadu', *Economy and Society*, 42 (3): 430–53.

Chari, S. (2004), *Fraternal Capital, Peasant-Workers, Self-Made Men, and Globalization in Provincial India*, New Delhi: Permanent Black.

Djurfeldt, G., Venkatesh Athreya, N. Jayakumar, Staffan Lindberg, A. Rajagopal and

R. Vidyasagar (2008), 'Agrarian Change and Social Mobility in Tamil Nadu', *Economic and Political Weekly*, 43 (45): 50–61.

Harriss-White, B. (1996), *A Political Economy of Agricultural Markets in South India: Masters of the Countryside*, New Delhi and London: Sage.

Heyer, J. (2010), 'The Marginalization of Dalits in a Modernizing Economy', in B. Harriss-White and J. Heyer, eds, *The Comparative Political Economy of Development, Africa and South Asia*, London: Routledge: 252–74.

————— (2012), 'Labour Standards and Social Policy: A South Indian Case Study', *Global Labour Journal*, 3 (1): 91–117.

————— (2013), 'Integration into a Global Production Network: Impacts on labour in Tiruppur's rural hinterlands', *Oxford Development Studies*, 41 (3), September: 307–21.

————— (2014), 'Dalit Households in Industrializing Villages in Coimbatore and Tiruppur, Tamil Nadu: A Comparison across Three Decades', in V.K. Ramachandran and Madhura Swaminathan, eds, *Dalit Households in Village Economies*, New Delhi: Tulika Books: 133–69.

————— (2016a), 'Rural Gounders on the Move in Western Tamil Nadu: 1981/2 to 2008/9', in Himanshu, Praveen Jha and Gerry Rodgers, eds, *Longitudinal Research in Village India: Methods and Findings*, New Delhi: Oxford University Press: 327–56.

————— (2016b), 'Loosening the Ties of Patriarchy with Agrarian Transition in Coimbatore Villages: 1981/2–2008/9', in Bibhuti Mohanty, ed., *Critical Perspectives in Agrarian Transition: India in the Global Debate*, London, New York and New Delhi: Routledge: 199–221.

Mahadevan, R. and M. Vijayabaskar (2014), 'The Making of Non-Corporate Capital: Some historical and contemporary entrepreneurial narratives from Tiruppur, Tamil Nadu', Occasional Paper Perspectives in Indian Development, New Series 33, New Delhi: Nehru Memorial Museum and Library: 1–43.

Mellor, J.W. (1995), *Agriculture on the Road to Industrialization*, Baltimore: Johns Hopkins University Press.

Narayanan, Sudha (2012), 'Inflections in Agricultural Evolution: Contemporary Commodity Complexes and Transactional Forms in Interior Tamil Nadu', *Economic and Political Weekly*, 52 (47): 84–94.

Sivanappan, R.K. and P.K. Aiyasamy (1978), *Land and Water Resources of Coimbatore District*, Coimbatore: Tamil Nadu Agricultural University.

Srinivasan, V., D. Suresh Kumar, P. Chinnasamy, S. Sulagna, D. Sakthivel, P. Paramasivam and S. Lele (2014), 'Water Management in the Noyyal River Basin: A Situation Analysis', Environment and Development Discussion Paper No. 2, Bengaluru: Ashoka Trust for Research in Ecology and the Environment.

Subramaniam, T.S. (2018), 'Wastelands of the Noyyal', *Frontline*, 35 (3), 16 February: 90–8.

Vijayabaskar, M. (2005), 'Labour and Flexible Accumulation: The Case of Tiruppur Knitwear Cluster', in K. Das, ed., *Industrial Clusters: Cases and Perspectives*, Aldershot: Ashgate: 37–53.

————— (2017), 'The Agrarian Question amidst popular welfare, interpreting Tamil Nadu's emerging rural economy', *Economic and Political Weekly*, 52 (46).

4

Rationale for the Continuation of a Food-Based System of Public Distribution

Madhura Swaminathan

Policies to ensure food security in India have traversed a long distance from the 1940s, when rationing was started as a wartime measure, to the enactment of a Food Security Act in 2013. In this paper, I argue that a move to shift to cash transfers and eventually to close down the public distribution system (PDS) will be disastrous for ensuring food security at the current stage of development.

Looking back at food policy over the last 60 years, three major phases can be distinguished.

First Phase: Towards a Universal Public Distribution System

The first phase, from the mid-1960s onwards up to the mid-1990s, was that of universalization of the public distribution system.

The public distribution system (PDS) for food in India was started as a wartime rationing scheme in the 1940s in six cities. The rationing scheme was established in this context in mainly urban areas. Rural areas were left largely unserviced, an exception being the Malabar region (Swaminathan 2000). Rationing was abolished in 1947, but with crop failures and the Korean War boom the prices of foodgrain skyrocketed and the government reintroduced rationing in 1951. This was a stopgap arrangement, however, and during the 1950s and early 1960s, a very small amount of grain was distributed mainly in the urban areas. Most of this distribution depended on imports under the PL (Public Law) 480 schemes, since domestic production was low in relation to demand.

It was only in the mid-1960s that it was decided to introduce a system of permanent and universal food subsidy. A Foodgrains Policy Committee was established in 1966, which 'envisaged a vital role for the Food Corporation of India' (Chopra 1981: 126) in preparing a National

Food Budget for procurement at reasonable prices, a buffer stock, and supply and distribution through the PDS. Food policy in this phase involved the setting up of institutional structures, including the Agricultural Prices Commission (now Commission on Agricultural Costs and Prices [CACP]), the Food Corporation of India (FCI) and a large network of fair price shops (FPS).

The PDS was established alongside the FCI and the Agricultural Prices Commission in 1965, and foodgrain distributed under the PDS increased to more than 10 million tonnes. As agricultural production grew and the PDS achieved countrywide spread, there was an emphasis on maintenance of adequate buffer stocks and domestic self-sufficiency of foodgrain. From the Second Five Year Plan (1956–61) onwards, the concept of buffer stocking and price control assumed importance. In the Third Plan period (1961–66), emphasis was placed on providing incentives to the farmers along with protecting the interests of the consumers. From the Third Plan onwards, the areas of debate were the size of buffer stocks; buffer stocking and control of the foodgrain market by the government were accepted in principle. From the late 1970s, the size of buffer stocks was quite comfortable, with a large network of fair price shops (FPS). The understanding during the 1970s and 1980s was that food security was an essential precondition for poverty alleviation, and subsidized foodgrain distribution was considered a cornerstone of food security.

In this phase, food security was viewed from the twin angles of production and distribution, and policies covered the entire gamut of actors – from producers to consumers.

The objectives of the PDS as spelt out in Swaminathan (2000) were:

(i) maintaining price stability;
(ii) increasing the welfare facilities for the poor (by providing access to basic foods at reasonable prices to the vulnerable population);
(iii) rationing during situations of scarcity; and
(iv) keeping a check on private trade.

Second Phase: Targeted Public Distribution System

The second phase began in the 1990s with a shift from universal to targeted distribution. In the early 1990s, geographical targeting, called the revamped public distribution system, was introduced. Then, in 1996–97, the targeted public distribution system was introduced, which distinguished households on the basis of the poverty line.

During the late 1980s and 1990s, neoliberal economists argued that the subsidy bill was costing the exchequer too much, and that therefore subsidized food should be made available only to the poor. In response to this, the government introduced the targeted PDS in 1997.

The distinguishing features of targeted PDS was that it targeted the BPL (below poverty line) category of households, while the APL (above poverty line) category of households was to be excluded or treated differentially. Subsidy was to be provided only to BPL households and APL households were to be sold foodgrain at the full economic cost – i.e. the sum of the procurement price given to the farmers, and costs of storage and distribution incurred by the FCI.[1] Moreover, the decision-making on targeted PDS allocation was shifted from state governments to the central government. Under the earlier universal public distribution system, it was the state governments that demanded allocation of foodgrain from the central pool. Allocation was done by the central government based on past utilization and statutory requirements. This was a more efficient system, since the state governments were better at understanding local requirements and the required allocation per household. After the introduction of targeted PDS, the central government (based on the Planning Commission's estimates of poverty) started deciding the size of the BPL population and the amount to be allocated per household. This introduced an element of arbitrariness into the earlier process.

In 2000, in my book titled *Weakening Welfare*, I challenged the rationale of 'targeting' in India, pointing out the consequences for the food-insecure (Swaminathan 2000). The biggest problem with targeting, as is now well established, is errors of wrong exclusion. Targeting errors are classified into two types – errors of wrong inclusion and errors of wrong exclusion. While a universal PDS has higher risk of erroneous inclusion, the targeted PDS has higher risk of erroneous exclusion. There is, of course, a trade-off between the two types of errors. In my view, priority should be given to elimination of errors of wrong exclusion since such mistakes have serious welfare consequences (such as continued undernutrition and its effects on people, economy and society), while errors of wrong inclusion result only in additional expenditure to the government.

Since the publication of *Weakening Welfare*, the literature on problems of targeting has grown. An evaluation of the PDS by the Planning Commission (GoI 2005) recognized the problems of targeting. The Evaluation Report states that only about 57 per cent of BPL households are covered by the targeted PDS, and that there are large errors of both exclusion and inclusion. In fact, according to the Report, 'transition from UPDS to TPDS has neither led to a reduction of budgetary food subsidies, nor has it been able to benefit the large majority of the food-insecure households in the desired manner' (ibid.: xi).[2]

Apart from the issue of prioritizing exclusion errors over inclusion errors, another argument against targeting is that the measurement of incomes is notoriously difficult, especially in a country like India where most of the poor are located within large agricultural and informal sectors. There is also a large amount of fluctuations in incomes. While some of the poor can, through an increase in their incomes, join the ranks of the non-poor, the reverse is also possible, and indeed, does happen (Krishna *et al.* 2003). This implies that one-time identification of BPL and APL households runs contrary to welfare. A policy for food security must consider not only the chronically hungry, but also those who are vulnerable to food poverty, and the only possible way to ensure this is through a universal PDS.

After the introduction of the targeted PDS, a lot of discussion was generated regarding its effectiveness and the extent to which the poor were truly covered by its benefits. Implementation of the targeted PDS required identification of the poor – of the so-called BPL households. The manner in which these households were identified included, apart from income, a number of non-income measures. These measures came under heavy criticism for their arbitrariness, because of which they were changed in each round of the BPL surveys. The BPL census method and estimates based on this have been criticized by a number of authors (Hirway 2003, Usami *et al.* 2010, among others) as having a number of flaws and for not being precisely defined. Moreover, based on results from a field survey in Maharashtra, Swaminathan and Misra (2001) argued that non-income measures of poverty used at the field level are both unjust and arbitrary, and that the results underestimate the numbers of the poor. For all these reasons, there are several errors in the calculation of the BPL population.

The scale of targeting errors has now been established with data from the 61st round of the National Sample Survey (NSS) (GoI 2007). These data show that in rural India, targeting has led to high rates of exclusion of needy households from the system, and a clear deterioration of coverage in states like Kerala where the universal PDS was most effective (Swaminathan 2009). To illustrate, excluding the states of North East India,[3] the proportion of households with 'no card' was highest in Orissa – 33 per cent of rural households here did not possess any type of ration card. Thus, in a state that is characterized as 'severely food insecure' (MSSRF 2001), one-third of rural households were outside the purview of the PDS. In another ten states, more than 20 per cent of rural households did not possess a ration card. In an overwhelming majority of states, 60 per cent or more of the population either had no ration card or had an APL card, and were thus effectively excluded from the PDS. This includes the BIMARU states – the relatively backward states of Bihar, Madhya Pradesh, Rajasthan and Uttar

Pradesh. It also includes states like Kerala, which was a model for the rest of the country before targeted PDS was introduced. The exceptions were Andhra Pradesh and Karnataka – the only two states in which a majority of rural households possessed BPL or Antyodaya cards.

It is important to understand the implication of this large-scale exclusion of households from the PDS by identifying characteristics of households that are excluded from the PDS. It has been noted, for instance, that exclusion is very high among agricultural labour households (ibid.). There were only four states (Tamil Nadu excluded) in which two-thirds or more of agricultural labour households held Antyodaya or BPL cards: Andhra Pradesh, Karnataka, Jammu and Kashmir, Tripura. The all-India average indicates that 18.5 per cent of agricultural labour households had no card and another 33.6 per cent had an APL card.

Using the official poverty line as the cut-off, Swaminathan (2009) found that the error of wrong exclusion was 28.3 per cent, while the error of wrong inclusion (of the so-called non-poor) was 12.3 per cent. Targeting has come at a high cost – high exclusion of households living below the official poverty line.

Third Phase: National Food Security Act and Beyond
The third phase of food policy can be dated to 2013 when the National Food Security Act (NFSA) was passed.

After being approved by Parliament, the government notified the National Food Security Act on 10 September 2013 with the objective 'to provide for food and nutritional security in a life cycle approach, by ensuring access to adequate quantity of quality food at affordable prices to people to live a life with dignity'. The Act provides for coverage of up to 75 per cent of the rural population and up to 50 per cent of the urban population for receiving subsidized foodgrain under targeted PDS, thus covering about two-thirds of the population. As of April 2016, the NFSA was being implemented in all parts of the country with the exception of three states (Tamil Nadu, Kerala and Nagaland).

The PDS today is probably the world's largest food security programme (not in terms of financial outlay but in terms of persons covered and quantities distributed). Here are some summary statistics.

- The number of people covered as of May 2016 was 731 million (based on 237 million ration cards).
- The number of fair price shops in the country was 5,32,102 or 0.53 million.
- The quantity of grain distributed through the PDS was 47.4 mil-

lion tonnes in 2014–15, and 51.7 million tonnes in 2015–16. The quantity goes up to 51.7 and 56 million tonnes respectively if other food schemes are included.

- The financial outlay on the PDS was Rs 11,31,710 million in 2014–15 and Rs 13,49,190 million in 2015–16. By contrast, the US food stamp programme reached 46.5 million people in 2014 at an outlay of 74.1 billion dollars.

I now turn to three issues concerning the PDS.

Three Key Issues
Is the PDS Affordable?

Over the last two decades, the main criticism of the PDS has been that of the growing burden on the exchequer. The question is wrongly posed, in my view, as that of a fiscal burden and the need to reduce subsidies to meet a fiscal target. It should rather be posed in terms of the number of people to be reached and the resources required to reach them effectively.

Given the scale of chronic hunger and malnutrition, and food insecurity in India, the population in need of a programme of food security is in the range of 800 million to 1 billion. There are three possible ways of identifying the food-insecure population (as distinct from the BPL population).

(i) First, taking only those already suffering from malnutrition (about 29.4 per cent of young children are moderately or severely underweight according to UNICEF, and about 33 per cent of adults have a BMI below the norm), approximately 30 per cent of India's population (363 million) is malnourished. This is the lower limit of food-insecure people – those who already suffer from malnutrition.

(ii) The second method is based on the NFSA definition of the eligible or priority population, comprising 75 per cent of the rural population and 50 per cent of the urban population. This amounts to 813 million persons (two-thirds of the all-India population).

(iii) Thirdly, taking a food share criterion (the one used by the USA for its food stamp programme), households that spend more than one-third of their monthly budget on food are eligible for food stamps.[4] By this criterion, only 5 per cent of rural households and 10 per cent of urban households in India are food-secure (see Table 4.1). In other words, 95 per cent of rural households and 90 per cent of urban households, or 1,130 million persons, are food-insecure, that is, at the risk of food insecurity though not necessarily malnourished today.[5] This estimate is based on the consumption expenditure data for 2011–12.

Table 4.1 *Share of food expenditure in total household (monthly) expenditure, (uniform reference period), 2011–12* (per cent)

MPCE fractile	Rural	Urban
0–5	62.4	59.3
5–10	61.0	57.4
10–20	60.3	55.4
20–30	59.2	53.2
30–40	57.8	50.7
40–50	56.5	48.3
50–60	54.6	46.1
60–70	53.5	43.5
70–80	51.3	40.9
80–90	47.4	36.8
90–95	43.4	31.4
95–100	28.1	20.9

Note: MPCE is monthly per capita expenditure.
Source: GoI (2013).

Table 4.2 *Food subsidy in India as share of budget and GDP, 2012–17*

Year	Total food subsidy (Rs in crores)	Total food subsidy as % of Union budget	Total food subsidy as % of GDP
2012–13	85,000	6.03	0.85
2013–14	92,000	5.90	0.82
2014–15	1,17,671	7.07	0.94
2015–16 RE*	1,39,419	7.81	1.03
2016–17 BE**	1,34,835	6.82	0.90

Notes: * Revised estimate; ** Budget estimate.

Using the internationally recognized third criterion, the number of food-insecure persons in India is as high as 1,130 million, or 90 per cent of the population.

The budgetary outlay of the central government on food subsidies (or the operational deficit of the FCI) was just about 1 per cent of India's GDP (0.91 in 2014–15 and 0.99 in 2015–16). Table 4.2 shows the share of food subsidy in GDP in recent years. Even eliminating the subsidy entirely would not solve the country's fiscal problems. More importantly, is it too much to spend 1 per cent of our GDP to provide minimal food security to 67 per cent of the population (as per the NFSA)? *The financial outlay on the PDS is minuscule as compared to the scale of the problem of hunger and malnutrition in India. We need to raise outlays in order to improve and expand the PDS.*

Let me digress briefly on an oft-made argument against the PDS: that it is wasteful and 'inefficient', and that the same expenditure could be used better to ensure the goal of food and nutrition security. I have two points to make here. First, the magic figure cited in almost all writings on the PDS, that 'for every rupee spent, only a quarter reaches the consumer', was given by Rajiv Gandhi in the mid-1980s. I have not found any study or source in the two decades since that substantiates this figure.

Second, in terms of quantities, the methodology for estimating leakages is flawed. To take an example, Khera (2011) shows that 67 per cent of the wheat meant to be delivered to the poor misses the target by taking the difference between wheat and rice as reported by the FCI and actual wheat and rice purchased from the PDS, as reported in the NSS on consumer expenditure, as diversion. On this basis, she argues that diversion was 18 per cent for rice and 67 per cent for wheat in 2001–02. This is an unsatisfactory calculation since it has been long established that the total figures for consumption obtained from NSS consumer expenditure surveys are significantly lower than estimates of consumption obtained from the national accounts. In other words, NSS estimates of total consumption are underestimates. To illustrate, if we take cereals and pulses consumption in 1999–2000, NSS estimates of total consumption were only 75 per cent of that reported by national accounts. So, comparing actual annual distribution through the PDS, as reported by the FCI, with an estimated consumption from a sample survey in order to gauge leakages is highly error-prone, and results in an exaggerated estimate of diversion.[6]

To take a hypothetical example, if 150 kg were distributed through the PDS and actual consumption from the corresponding NSS survey was 100 kg, we would argue that leakages amounted to 50 kg or 33 per cent of total distribution. However, if consumption from the NSS survey is adjusted for underestimation (using the assumption of NSS consumption being 75 per cent of actual consumption), then estimated diversion is only 15 kg or 11 per cent.

Inefficiency is a tricky concept. An example of the so-called inefficiency of the FCI is the higher cost of packaging relative to private traders. This is because it is mandatory for the FCI to use jute packaging (to support the jute farmers of eastern India). Similarly, labour costs are higher because FCI conforms to the new International Labour Organization

(ILO) norm that the maximum weight a human can bear on his back is 50 kg and not 60 kg.

While making all efforts to reduce waste and inefficiency in the PDS, I argue that better estimates of waste and inefficiency are required.

Should Transfers Be in Cash Instead of Kind?

An argument is often made that the same benefits can be transferred to a household or individual through a cash subsidy instead of actual distribution of food (in-kind transfer). There are a lot of studies on this question in India and elsewhere, and there are mixed opinions.

In my view, the first and the biggest concern with cash transfers is control over the real value of the transfer, given inflation in food prices. This shortcoming is not easy to overcome as it requires regular revaluation of the cash transfer, control over food price inflation and ensuring that local food outlets charge the stated price. Also, most studies show that the marginal propensity to consume food out of kind transfers is higher than the marginal propensity to consume food from an equivalent cash income. A shift from kind to cash implies doing away with goals in terms of consumption of food.

Secondly, cash transfers can work where the level of achievement is already high and, as a consequence, where the specific social policy has to address a relatively small target group. In Latin American countries, Mexico and Brazil in particular, where cash transfers have taken off, the scale of deprivation is much smaller than it is in India.

To take the case of malnutrition among young children, in 2009, the proportion of children aged 5 and below with weight below normal was less than 2 per cent in Mexico, 5 per cent in Brazil and 42 per cent in India (Table 4.3). To put it differently, a programme for nutritional supplements for young children has to deal with 5 per cent of children in Brazil and 42 per cent of all children in India.

Thirdly, while cash transfers, like kind transfers, can be universal in coverage, most of the proposal for cash transfers are in the context of narrow targeting. In short, the objective of introducing cash transfers is often a fiscal one, that is, one of reducing subsidies to the poor by means of targeted cash transfers. As shown in Swaminathan (2000), in almost all developing countries that introduced food stamps in the 1980s and 1990s under pressure of structural adjustment, there was an overall decline in the size of the food subsidy programme.

The exception to this pattern has been the recent experience of Brazil:

Table 4.3 *Selected indicators of human development, Mexico, Brazil and India*

Country	Adult literacy rate	GDP per capita (PPP$)* 2007	Proportion of children below 5 with weight for age below normal	Proportion of persons with less than $1.25 a day
Mexico	92.8	14,104	5	<2
Brazil	96.7	9,567	6	5
India	61.0	2,753	46	42

Note: * PPP: purchasing power parity.
Source: *Human Development Report* 2009.

> Unlike targeted social programmes elsewhere in the world, which are associated with immediate and steep reductions in government expenditure, spending on the Bolsa Familia increased threefold between 2003 and 2008 (from USD 1.9 billion to USD 6.1 billion). The total expenditure of the federal government departments that undertook the various programmes doubled, and, in addition, there was a trebling of funds for rural credit. Also, unlike most cash transfers, where the real value of the subsidy is quickly eroded by inflation, using a price index based on staples, the real value of the transfers through Bolsa Familia remained constant over the years, despite food prices rising more rapidly than the overall rate of inflation. (Swaminathan 2012)

An often ignored but critical impact of the PDS has been on market prices and overall inflation. The PDS implies a huge intervention in foodgrain markets. There is no doubt that the FCI, through the PDS and other market operations, has held food prices and inflation relatively low in India (as compared to many other developing countries). Price stability in India relative to the world is well established. This, again, is an argument against cash transfers. An important counterfactual here is, what would happen to inflation in basic food commodities in the absence of a PDS? To put it another way, the macro effect of distribution through the PDS, in addition to open market operations by the government, keeps a check on food prices.

The system of procurement (support to our farmers) and system of distribution (support to our consumers) in India is like walking on two legs (to borrow a Chinese phrase). Historically, as I have mentioned, the concerns of both producers and consumers were taken into account in setting up the system of food security in India. Today, while designing or altering the PDS, the concerns of producers have to be kept in mind. A shift to cash transfers and subsequent closing down of the system of procurement and distribution will obviously affect producers. Procurement cannot continue if there is to be no transfer in kind.

Food Sovereignty

The last point I wish to make is that for a country of more than 1.2 billion people, we have to ensure a degree of self-sufficiency in food production. The country has to decide between self-sufficiency in food, and reliance on a thin and increasingly price-volatile world food market. Chand (2001) has shown convincingly that prices go up in the world market when India imports grain, and prices fall when India exports grain (India is a large country and not a small country in terms of trade theory).

Projections for cereal demand in India in 2020 range from 237 million tonnes to 296 million tonnes, with 269 million tonnes as the accepted moderate figure. Production levels in 2014–15 were of the order of 252 million tonnes, of which cereals constituted 225 million tonnes. In other words, there is no place for complacency and efforts have to be made to increase foodgrain productivity and production. One of the most effective means of achieving this increase is the system of support prices and procurement. As M.S. Swaminathan recently noted, 'Public procurement at a remunerative price has been a key factor in stimulating and sustaining the green revolution' (M.S. Swaminathan 2016).

While there is a need for more crops to be brought into the net of price support and procurement in a planned way so as to meet the demands for more nutritious food (e.g., pulses and millets), there is no doubt that shifting to cash transfers and stopping procurement at an assured price will have deleterious effects on foodgrain production in India.

Concluding Remarks

Given the prevalence of food insecurity on a mass scale in India, a system of kind transfers as has been developed historically in the form of the PDS needs not only to be continued, but to be expanded in scale and strengthened. The expenditure on food subsidy is minuscule in relation to the problem of food insecurity in India. Serious implementation of the National Food Security Act requires greater expenditure (to be accompanied, of course, by reductions in loss and waste). Lastly, a shift to cash transfers will make food-insecure households vulnerable to inflation, and also undermine production of foodgrain in the country by weakening the system of public procurement and price support.

The topic of this paper is close to the concerns of Venkatesh B. Athreya, and one I have discussed with him often. I am happy to contribute this paper to the volume in honour of Venkatesh.

Notes

[1] An additional subsidy is given to the 'poorest of the poor' under the Antyodaya Yojana.

[2] The Evaluation Report also highlights the leakages in terms of inclusion errors, and the additional 'unintended subsidy' necessitated by these leakages and diversions – the central government had to issue 2.4 kg of foodgrain per kg of foodgrain actually delivered to the poor. It finds that the government spends Rs 3.65 to transfer Re 1 to the poor through food subsidies. Underscoring the difference between local market prices and the economic cost of the PDS, the Evaluation Report concludes that the market is a more efficient way of transferring income to the poor than public agencies. This argument, of course, finds its answer in the earlier discussion on 'efficiency of the FCI'.

[3] There are some serious problems of data quality in the data for Northeast India.

[4] The logic behind the food share criterion is that as income rises, the share of expenditure on food declines. So, households with greater share of food expenditure in total expenditure are relatively poorer (Anand and Harris 1980).

[5] If we take the cut-off in terms of food share that was used in China during the period of rationing, namely a food share of 50 per cent, then 80 per cent of the rural population and 40 per cent of the urban population will be eligible for food security (see Swaminathan 2000). In absolute terms, this amounts to 854 million persons (close to the NFSA number).

[6] The same flawed methodology is used by Dutta and Ramaswami (2001) and others. The methodology used by the oft-cited TECS (Tata Economic Consultancy Services) Report is unclear.

References

Anand, S. and C. Harris (1980), 'Food and Standard of Living: An Analysis Based on Sri Lankan Data', in J. Dreze and A. Sen, eds, *The Political Economy of Hunger*, Vol. 1, Oxford: Clarendon Press.

Chand, Ramesh (2001), 'Wheat Exports: Little Gain', *Economic and Political Weekly*, 36 (25), 11–17 August: 2226–28.

Chopra, R.N. (1981), *Evolution of Food Policy in India*, Delhi: Macmillan.

Dutta, B. and B. Ramaswami (2001), 'Targeting and Efficiency in the Public Distribution System', *Economic and Political Weekly*, 36 (18): 1524–32.

Government of India (GoI) (2005), 'Performance Evaluation of the Targeted Public Distribution System (TPDS)', *Programme Evaluation Organization*, New Delhi: Planning Commission.

——— (2007), *Public Distribution System and Other Sources of Household Consumption 2004–2005*, New Delhi: National Sample Survey Office.

——— (2013), *Key Indicators of Household Consumer Expenditure in India 2011–12*, New Delhi: National Sample Survey Office.

Hirway, Indira (2003), 'Identification of BPL Households for Poverty Alleviation Programs', *Economic and Political Weekly*, 38 (45), 8 November: 4803–08.

Khera, R. (2011), 'India's Public Distribution System: Utilization and Impact', *Journal of Development Studies*, 47 (7).

Krishna, Anirudh, Mahesh Kapila, Mahendra Porwal and Virpal Singh (2003), 'Falling into Poverty in a High-Growth State: Escaping Poverty and Becoming Poor in Gujarat Villages', *Economic and Political Weekly*, 38 (49), 6–12 December: 5171–79.

M.S. Swaminathan Research Foundation (MSSRF) (2001), *Food Insecurity Atlas of Rural India*, Chennai: World Food Programme and M.S. Swaminathan Research Foundation.

Swaminathan, Madhura (2000), *Weakening Welfare: The Public Provisioning of Food in India,* New Delhi: LeftWord Books.

———— (2009), 'Programmes to Protect the Hungry: Lessons from India', United Nations, Economic and Social Affairs, DESA Working Paper No. ST/ESA/DWP/October 2008, available at http://www.un.org/esa/desa/papers/2008/wp70_2008.pdf, viewed on 31 July 2016.

———— (2012), 'Food Policy and Public Action in Brazil', *Review of Agrarian Studies*, 2 (2), July–December, http://www.ras.org.in/food_policy_and_public_action_in_brazil.

Swaminathan, Madhura and Neeta Misra (2001), 'Errors of Targeting: Public Distribution of Food in a Maharashtra Village 1995–2000', *Economic and Political Weekly*, 36 (28), 30 June: 2447–54.

Swaminathan, M.S. (2016), 'National Policy for Farmers: Ten Years Later', *Review of Agrarian Studies*, 6 (1), January–June, http://www.ras.org.in/national_policy_for_farmers_ten_years_later.

Tata Economic Consultancy Services (TECS) (1998), *Study to Ascertain the Extent of Diversion of PDS Commodities*, New Delhi: TECS.

Usami, Y., B. Sarkar and V.K. Ramachandran (2010), 'Are the Results of the BPL Census of 2002 Reliable?', unpublished manuscript, Foundation for Agrarian Studies, Bengaluru.

5

Aspects of the Proletarianization of the Peasantry in India

V.K. Ramachandran

The agrarian question is, in general, the key national question confronting social movements in the less-developed world. It is concerned, *inter alia*, with the nature and pattern of the development of capitalism in agriculture (and the countryside), the socio-economic characteristics of the classes that arise on the basis of the development of capitalism in the countryside, and the political alliances that are necessary for carrying forward progressive social transformation.

A great deal of Marxist effort in the study of agrarian relations in India has focused on formulating criteria for identifying classes in the countryside (Ramachandran 2012a; Communist Party of India [Marxist] 2016). One of the main historical influences on Indian Marxist work in this regard is the work of P. Sundarayya (1913–85) (Ramachandran 2012b). The main influences on Sundarayya's work were the writings of Marx and Engels, and Lenin's *Development of Capitalism in Russia* and *To the Rural Poor*, but more particularly Mao Zedong's writings on the peasantry, particularly *Report on an Investigation of the Peasant Movement in Hunan* and *Analysis of the Classes in Chinese Society*, and the documents and formulations of land reform legislation in post-liberation China (including Liu Shaoqi's speech titled 'On the Agrarian Reform Law'). The actual classifications attempted by Sundarayya were, of course, specific to the basic conditions that obtained in India (see ibid.).

The three main socio-economic class strata engaged in crop production in a village are landlords and big capitalist farmers, agricultural workers, and a differentiated peasantry. There are also classes in the village that are not directly engaged in crop production (though they may be associated with the agrarian economy in different degrees), and these are to be analysed and classified separately.

The analysis of class formation in rural India requires field-based study. Data in this paper come from the surveys of households conducted in villages located in different agro-ecological zones of India as part of the Project on Agrarian Relations in India (PARI). This project, organized by the Foundation for Agrarian Studies and planned for the period 2006–16, involved detailed census-type household surveys in villages across diverse agro-ecological regions of India. The number of villages surveyed as part of PARI is now twenty-five, and data for sixteen villages have been analysed in this paper. While no aggregation of case studies can claim to be representative of the country as a whole, these, we believe, do give us an insight into methods of study and into on-the-ground developments in different regions of village India.[1]

This paper is concerned specifically with aspects of the peasantry in contemporary India. Peasant households, whose members work on all or some of the major manual operations on the land, constitute the sector of petty producers that lies between landlords and big capitalist farmers on the one hand, and manual workers on the other. The peasantry is a tenacious and enduring social category, having existed continuously under different historical social formations. The transition from a peasantry that was essentially engaged in subsistence cultivation, in pre-capitalist and early capitalist epochs, to one whose chief characteristic is its subjugation to the market (and indeed both types exist concurrently in different parts of the world) is a process that has spanned centuries and historical epochs.

In the *Eighteenth Brumaire*, Marx wrote of the small-holding French peasantry that

> their field of production, the small holding, permits no division of labour in its cultivation, no application of science, and therefore no multi-fariousness of development, no diversity of talent, no wealth of social relationships. Each individual peasant family is almost self-suffi-cient, directly produces most of its consumer needs, *and thus acquires its means of life more through an exchange with nature than in inter-course with society.* (Marx 1852; emphasis added)

It is clear that such a definition is not true of the modern peasantry, both with regard to the productive forces (and, in particular, the application of science and technology to agriculture) as well as to the relations of production (in particular, the subjugation of the peasantry to the capitalist market).

As commodity production and the development of capitalism in agriculture proceed, so does the differentiation of the peasantry. The most complete definition of differentiation is Lenin's classic formulation, which is at the end of Chapter 2 of *The Development of Capitalism in Russia*: 'The

sum total of all the economic contradictions among the peasantry constitutes what we call the differentiation of the peasantry.' The differentiation
of the peasantry is not restricted to squeezing out the middle tiers of the
peasantry, or the consequent exacerbation of inequality, nor is it restricted
to the process by which the peasantry, particularly the poor peasantry, is
proletarianized, but encompasses the whole range of contradictions that

> are inherent in every commodity economy and every order of capital-
> ism: competition, the struggle for economic independence, the grabbing
> of land (purchasable and rentable), the concentration of production in
> the hands of a minority, the forcing of the majority into the ranks of
> the proletariat, their exploitation by a minority through the medium of
> merchant's capital and the hiring of farm labourers. There is not a single
> economic phenomenon among the peasantry that does not bear this
> contradictory form, one specifically peculiar to the capitalist system,
> i.e., that does not express a struggle and antagonism of interests, that
> does not imply advantage for some and disadvantage for others. (Lenin
> 1899 [1972])

This paper examines an aspect of the process of differentiation of the
peasantry – that is, 'the concentration of production in the hands of a
minority [and] the forcing of the majority into the ranks of the proletariat'.

Landlessness

Proletarianization can take the form of the absolute loss of land
by cultivating peasants. A rough measure of proletarianization in this
regard (that is, in the absence of long-term time-series data for specific
locations) is the proportion of landless households in a village. The class
of landless workers in rural India comprises those whose households have
historically been part of the landless labour force in the village, as well
as households that, having lost land, which was the primary means and
instrument of production in agriculture, now sell their labour power to
others for a livelihood.

A substantial proportion of households in our study villages have
no ownership holdings of land, and all the villages are characterized by
high levels of inequality in the distribution of ownership holdings of land
(Table 5.1). The Gini coefficient, a summary measure of inequality ranging from 0 (no inequality) to 1 (perfect inequality), was 0.7 or higher in
fourteen of the study villages. In nine of the twenty villages in Table 5.1,
more than 40 per cent of households resident in the village were without
any ownership holdings of land. And in no village other than one (Rewasi,
Sikar district in Rajasthan) was the proportion of landless households less

Table 5.1 *Households without ownership holdings of land as a proportion of all households, and Gini coefficients of the distribution of household ownership holdings of land, selected villages*

State/village	Households without ownership holdings of land as a proportion of all households	Gini coefficients of the distribution of household ownership holdings of land
Andhra Pradesh		
Ananthavaram	65	0.9
Bukkacherla	15	0.6
Kothapalle	47	0.8
Bihar		
Katkuian	54	0.9
Nayanagar	53	0.9
Karnataka		
Alabujanahalli	18	0.6
Siresandra	11	0.5
Zhapur	45	0.8
Madhya Pradesh		
Gharsondi	19	0.7
Maharashtra		
Nimshirgaon	41	0.8
Warwat Khanderao	24	0.6
Punjab		
Hakamwala	36	0.9
Tehang	76	0.8
Rajasthan		
25F Gulabewala	64	0.8
Rewasi	5	0.5
Uttar Pradesh		
Harevli	37	0.8
Mahatwar	19	0.7
West Bengal		
Amarsinghi	35	0.6
Kalmandasguri	22	0.7
Panahar	43	0.8

Source: PARI data.

than 10 per cent of all households of a village. By this measure, the extent of proletarianization was high in two villages of North West India (Tehang in Punjab and 25F Gulabewala in Rajasthan) and Ananthavaram village in coastal Andhra Pradesh. All these three villages were characterized by a relatively advanced level of development of the productive forces.

Deployment of Labour Time

There is another aspect of proletarianization that is observed but less analysed because of lack of data. This is the extent to which *all* sections of the working poor, including poor and middle peasants, have to employ wage labour, and the extent to which peasants have to work as hired workers on and off the farm in order to achieve subsistence levels of income.

In Lenin's classification of proletarian and peasant farms in the *Capitalist System of Modern Agriculture*, for instance, 'peasant farms' are defined thus: 'We have put under the heading peasant farms those groups in which, on the one hand, the majority of cultivators are independent farmers and, on the other hand, the number of family workers is greater than the number of wage-workers' (Lenin 1910). Thus, a predominance of family labour is intrinsic not only to the so-called 'proletarian farms', but also to all *peasant* farms. It thus goes without saying that 'proletarian farms' are not characterized by a predominance of labour hired in by the peasant owner or farmer, but they 'include groups in which the minority of farmers regard the conduct of independent agriculture as their chief occupation, groups in which the majority are wage-workers, and so on' (ibid., second article).

In P. Sundarayya's definition, family labour predominated over hired labour even on the middle-peasant farm: 'In no case should he be considered a middle peasant if family labour does not predominate over wage labour or when his income from family labour is less than earned from exploitation, irrespective of whether this would be enough to meet his needs or not' (see the citation in Ramachandran 2012b).

However, the extent of participation of working members of peasant households in the labour process in agriculture in India depends on the nature of land use and cropping pattern in each village, and on their economic and social status. In every village, cropping pattern and technological processes are such that there are substantial variations in labour absorption per crop, and in the relative ratios in which family labour, exchange labour (if it exists at all) and different types of hired labour are deployed. In particular, the wetland cultivation of rice and of certain other crops in India are characterized by substantial employment of hired labour by *all* sections of the peasantry. Patterns of labour deployment may also vary with caste and religious community, and with traditional gender roles. It is clear also that as capitalism in agriculture and the differentiation of the peasantry advance, (i) agricultural mechanization advances and covers more and more crop operations, (ii) occupational diversity within households becomes greater, and (iii) agricultural tasks themselves become specialized or based on specialized skills. In each of these circumstances, a narrow labour participation criterion becomes less and less a robust criterion for differentiating classes. Each of these conditions has profound implications for the labour ratio on the farm, that is, the extent of family labour actually expended on the farm, and the relationship between family labour, labour hired on the farm and labouring out (agricultural and non-agricultural) by the farm family itself.

Empirical Evidence

We have examined aspects of the deployment of labour time by households, particularly the poorer sections of the peasantry (broadly speaking, the poor and middle sections of the peasantry, with respect to ownership of the means of production, incomes and the extent to which family members labour out), in the villages we have studied.[2] Annexure Table 5.1 gives the list of villages examined in this paper with their physical location and agro-ecological features. Annexure Table 5.2 shows the number of manual worker, small peasant and middle peasant households in each of these villages.

Certain salient features emerge from our analysis of data on deployment of labour time.

First, the ratio of family labour to all labour varies widely across regions (Table 5.2). In the eastern Uttar Pradesh village of Mahatwar (Ballia district), 94 per cent of labour deployed on a farm by small peasant households was family labour. By contrast, in the three villages of Andhra Pradesh, the share of family labour in total labour deployed (family labour plus hired labour) was only around one-quarter to one-third.

Secondly, in all regions, small and middle peasants had to hire in workers for various agricultural operations. In fourteen out of sixteen villages, the ratio of family labour to total labour deployed by middle peasant households was 55 per cent or less, implying that the balance of labour deployed was hired labour (Table 5.2).

Table 5.3 presents the following ratio in percentage terms. The numerator is the aggregate number of days of family labour that members of peasant households work on their own farms. The denominator is the number of days that they work the whole year, that is, the total of the

Table 5.2 *Days of family labour on farm as a proportion of days of all types of labour (family + hired) on farm, middle and small peasant households, selected villages*

State/village	Small peasant (family/family labour+hired labour)	Middle peasant (Family/family labour+hired labour)
Andhra Pradesh		
Ananthavaram	32	21
Bukkacherla	26	27
Kothapalle	27	52
Karnataka		
Alabujanahalli	63	52
Siresandra	56	49
Zhapur	48	48
Madhya Pradesh		
Gharsondi	75	53
Maharashtra		
Nimshirgaon	60	38
Warwat Khanderao	45	23
Rajasthan		
25F Gulabewala	47	24
Rewasi	77	71
Uttar Pradesh		
Harevli	87	56
Mahatwar	94	82
West Bengal		
Amarsinghi	56	15
Kalmandasguri	71	43
Panahar	78	32

Source: PARI data.

number of days of labour on their own farms, the number of days worked as hired farm workers and the number of days worked as hired non-farm workers. In almost all the villages, the share of family labour on the farm was 50 per cent or less for small peasants. The two exceptions were 25F Gulabewala, where there were very few small peasant households, and Alabujanahalli in Mandya district, Karnataka.

Tables 5.4 and 5.5 give an idea of the spread of the labour market

Table 5.3 *Days of family labour as a proportion of days of all labour (i.e.*
family labour + manual labour) by small and middle peasants, selected villages
(per cent)

State/village	Small peasant	Middle peasant
Andhra Pradesh		
Ananthavaram	23.2	45.1
Bukkacherla	47.1	64.3
Kothapalle	37.6	66.2
Karnataka		
Alabujanahalli	70.3	94.5
Siresandra	34.9	76.6
Zhapur	33.3	99.7
Madhya Pradesh		
Gharsondi	33.3	66.4
Maharashtra		
Nimshirgaon	44.1	85.3
Warwat Khanderao	33.8	92.4
Rajasthan		
25F Gulabewala	90.9	100.0
Rewasi	66.1	72.3
Uttar Pradesh		
Harevli	28.2	96.4
Mahatwar	35.2	58.6
West Bengal		
Amarsinghi	49.0	44.7
Kalmandasguri	53.5	78.5
Panahar	28.7	79.5

Source: PARI data.

beyond the class of manual workers. We took the total number of days of
employment in wage-work (time-rated and piece-rated) in each village in
the reference year. From that aggregate, we separated the number of days
of wage-work performed by workers who belonged to households whose
major source of income was wages from manual work (that is, manual
worker households). The data show that the market for hired labour
has spread well beyond the class of manual worker households to other
households (of whom a substantial part are, in fact, peasant households).

Table 5.4 *Total number of days of manual employment obtained by members of households of the class of manual workers as a proportion of the total number of days of manual employment obtained by members of all households, selected villages* (per cent)

Village	Manual workers	Small and middle peasants	All other classes
Andhra Pradesh			
Ananthavaram	41.9	46.1	12.0
Bukkacherla	58.3	39.9	1.8
Kothapalle	83.8	11.2	5.0
Karnataka			
Alabujanahalli	81.5	11.3	7.2
Siresandra	27.7	70.3	2.0
Zhapur	73.9	18.6	7.5
Madhya Pradesh			
Gharsondi	68.9	19.9	11.3
Maharashtra			
Nimshirgaon	76.0	12.4	11.7
Warwat Khanderao	56.6	29.5	13.9
Rajasthan			
25F Gulabewala	90.2	0.4	9.4
Rewasi	47.8	44.6	7.6
Uttar Pradesh			
Harevli	42.3	56.7	1.0
Mahatwar	40.8	44.4	14.8
West Bengal			
Amarsinghi	65.4	21.6	12.9
Kalmandasguri	58.3	34.3	7.4
Panahar	45.7	52.6	1.7

Source: PARI data.

As Table 5.4 shows, the class of manual workers contributed between 28 and 90 per cent of the days of manual employment in a village across the villages studied. The share of manual workers was less than 50 per cent of wage employment in a village in six of the sixteen villages. Conversely, members of small and middle peasant households contributed up to 70 per cent of total wage employment in a village. In Ananthavaram

Table 5.5 *Days of farm labouring out by households of selected classes as proportion of days of farm labouring out by all village households, selected villages* (per cent)

State/village	Manual workers	Small and middle peasants	All other classes
Andhra Pradesh			
Ananthavaram	42.5	51.9	5.6
Bukkacherla	55.2	43.4	1.4
Kothapalle	83.7	8.0	8.3
Karnataka		0.0	
Alabujanahalli	82.0	10.9	7.1
Siresandra	27.7	70.3	2.0
Zhapur	57.2	37.9	5.0
Madhya Pradesh		0.0	
Gharsondi	73.8	18.2	8.0
Maharashtra		0.0	
Nimshirgaon	83.4	11.2	5.4
Warwat Khanderao	59.4	30.8	9.8
Rajasthan		0.0	
25F Gulabewala	94.7	0.7	4.6
Rewasi	53.8	42.5	3.7
Uttar Pradesh		0.0	
Harevli	39.3	60.4	0.3
Mahatwar	55.8	34.4	9.8
West Bengal		0.0	
Amarsinghi	81.5	9.8	8.7
Kalmandasguri	58.3	34.3	7.4
Panahar	43.5	55.0	1.4

Source: PARI data.

village, Guntur district, Andhra Pradesh, for instance, small and middle peasants accounted for 46 per cent of manual employment recorded in the village.

Table 5.5 shows a similar picture when we consider labouring out in agriculture alone. To illustrate, in Panahar village of Bankura district, West Bengal, small and middle peasants (classes other than manual workers) accounted for 55 per cent of days of labouring out in agriculture recorded in our survey. The market for hired labour thus covers a very large section of the village population.

Discussion and Conclusions

An important aspect of the differentiation of the peasantry is proletarianization, particularly of the poor and middle sections of the peasantry. Loss of land by the peasantry and complete depeasantization is widespread, and is, justifiably, the most widely discussed form of proletarianization. In addition, however, is a phenomenon that is well known but, for the want of quantitative data, has been less analysed statistically in India – that is, the extent to which sections of the peasantry are drawn into the market for hired labour while preserving their peasant status. This latter phenomenon is the subject matter of this paper.

In respect of deployment of labour time, first, we showed that even on the farms of small and medium peasants, the share of family labour expended on the farm was, in many cases, less than the share of hired labour employed on the farm. In any case, in every village, large sections (and often the majority of workers) of small peasant households worked as hired workers on the farms of others and at non-farm tasks. It is no longer possible to use the absence of labouring out as a criterion for distinguishing the middle sections of the peasantry from the poor.

In general, the costs of cultivation rise to levels that make it impossible for peasants to earn a livelihood without labouring out, often heavily. We note here also that mechanization has had a very big impact on the volume and pattern of the seasonal deployment of family labour. Other than in very backward areas, tractor-based operations predominate in land preparation, and motor-pump technology predominates in groundwater irrigation. In most parts of the country, some form of mechanization predominates in threshing, and harvesters have come to play an important role in wheat harvesting. The combined effect of these has been that inputs of family labour have widely been reduced in specific operations in cereal production in many (though not all) parts of the country. Further, when mechanization occurs, agricultural operations are less staggered than previously, and the demand for labour peaks too steeply to be met by the deployment of family labour alone (for example, if harvesting on a field can be done over a week or more, a family can do it; if it is to be done over two days, it requires hired labour).

Secondly, if the labour power deployed by a peasant household in a year is divided into three parts – family labour on the farm, farm work for wages, non-farm work for wages – the share of the first element in the total is low, and, in many villages, less than 50 per cent.

Thirdly, the market for hired labour has broadened; more sections than before are participating in it. A particularly telling statistic is the following. In 2005–06, we resurveyed Ananthavaram, a village surveyed by P. Sundarayya in 1974. We computed the aggregate number of days of hired labour employed on all agricultural land owned and operated by households resident in the village. Of this, no less than 47 per cent was actually hired labour performed by households that were primarily *peasant* households, thus showing that hired labour extended well beyond the class of manual workers in the village. Forty-seven per cent is admittedly a very high figure; nevertheless, the general situation is that (except in very technologically backward, particularly tribal, villages) the proportion of the aggregate number of days of hired labour in agriculture performed by members of households that are primarily peasant households was, in many villages, greater than 50 per cent.

Fourthly, small and middle peasants, taken together with manual workers, generally constitute 72 per cent or more of all households in the study villages (Annexure Table 5.2).

In a discussion of the 'significance of these masses of proletarian "farmers" in the general system of agriculture', Lenin notes that, in the first place, they represent historical continuity (or 'kinship') between pre-capitalist and capitalist systems of social economy. In the second place,

> the bulk of the 'farmers' owning such insignificant plots of land that it is impossible to make a living from them, and which represent merely an 'auxiliary occupation', form part of the *reserve army of unemployed* in the capitalist system as a whole. It is, to use Marx's term, the *hidden* form of this army. It would be wrong to imagine that this reserve army of unemployed consists only of workers who are out of work. It includes also 'peasants' or 'petty farmers' who are unable to exist on what they get from their minute farm, who *have to* try to obtain their means of subsistence mainly by hiring out their labour. (Lenin 1910, second article)

In India, although there are continuities between the era of globalization and liberalization and preceding periods, it is clear that, since 1991, state intervention and the part played by imperialism in the countryside – that is, the class policies of the state in rural India – have taken qualitatively new forms. The rural poor, particularly manual workers and poor and middle peasants, continue to be, however, the great reserve army of labour of capitalism in India. If the agrarian question in India is to be resolved in a progressive and democratic way, these sections of the rural working people must also be the vanguard of social change in the countryside.

This paper is for Venkatesh Athreya, comrade and friend for more than forty years. I am grateful to the Foundation for Agrarian Studies team, particularly Arindam Das, Aditi Dixit and T. Sivamurugan, for helping me with the research for this paper.

Notes
1 The list of the sixteen villages for which data have been used for this chapter are in Annexure Table 5.1.
2 Although the definition is village-specific, see Ramachandran (2011) on the broad criteria used to classify the peasantry.

References
Communist Party of India (Marxist) (2016), 'Report of Study Group on Agrarian Classes', *The Marxist*, 32 (2), April–June, available at http://cpim.org/sites/default/files/marxist/201602-marxist-studynotes-agrarian-classes.pdf, accessed on 19 January 2019.

Lenin, V.I. (1899 [1972]), *Collected Works, Volume 3: The Development of Capitalism in Russia*, Progress Publishers: Moscow.

——— (1910), *The Capitalist System of Modern Agriculture*: first article, available at http://www.marxists.org/archive/lenin/works/1910/csma/i.htm#v16pp74-437; second article, 'The Real Nature of the Majority of Modern Agricultural "Farms" (Proletarian "Farms")', available at http://www.marxists.org/archive/lenin/works/1910/csma/ii.htm#v16pp74-434; third article, 'Peasant Farms Under Capitalism', available at http://www.marxists.org/archive/lenin/works/1910/csma/iii.htm#v16pp74-434 – all accessed on 17 January 2019.

Marx, Karl (1852), *The Eighteenth Brumaire of Louis Bonaparte*, Chapter 7, available at http://www.marxists.org/archive/marx/works/1852/18th-brumaire/ch07.htm, accessed on 15 May 2014.

Ramachandran, V.K. (2011), 'The State of Agrarian Relations in India Today', *The Marxist*, 27 (1–2), January–June.

——— (2012a) 'Classes and Class Differentiation in India's Countryside', *World Review of Political Economy*, 2 (2): 646–70.

——— (2012b), 'P. Sundarayya on the Agrarian Question', *The Marxist*, 28 (3), July–September.

Annexure Table 5.1 *Agro-ecological features of sixteen villages studied between 2005 and 2010 as part of the Project on Agrarian Relations in India (PARI)*

Name of village	Sub-district, district, state	Agro-ecological features
Ananthavaram	Kollur, Guntur, Andhra Pradesh	Paddy-dominated area
Bukkacherla	Raptadu, Ananthapur, Andhra Pradesh	Dry and drought-prone
Kothapalle	Thimmapur, Karimnagar, Andhra Pradesh	Groundwater-irrigated, multi-crop
Harevli	Najibabad, Bijnor, Uttar Pradesh	100 per cent canal-irrigated, plus groundwater, wheat and sugarcane cultivation
Mahatwar	Rasra, Ballia, Uttar Pradesh	Groundwater-irrigated, wheat-paddy rotation
Nimshirgaon	Shirol, Kolhapur, Maharashtra	Irrigated sugarcane and multi-crop system
Warwat Khanderao	Sangrampur, Buldhana, Maharashtra	Unirrigated, cotton region
25F Gulabewala	Karanpur, Sriganganagar, Rajasthan	Canal and groundwater irrigation, with cotton, wheat and mustard cultivation
Rewasi	Sikar, Sikar, Rajasthan	
Gharsondi	Bhitarwar, Gwalior, Madhya Pradesh	Limited canal and groundwater irrigation, cultivation of soyabean, wheat and mustard
Alabujanhalli	Maddur, Mandya, Karnataka	Canal-irrigated, sugarcane, paddy and ragi cultivation, sericulture
Siresandra	Kolar, Kolar, Karnataka	Groundwater-irrigated, cultivation of ragi and a large number of vegetables, sericulture
Zhapur	Gulbarga, Gulbarga, Karnataka	Unirrigated, cultivation of millets and oilseeds, non-agricultural employment in stone quarries
Amarsinghi	Ratua I Block, Malda, West Bengal	Groundwater-irrigated, cultivation of aman paddy, boro paddy and jute
Kalmandasguri	Cooch Behar, Cooch Behar, West Bengal	Unirrigated, jute, paddy and potato cultivation
Panahar	Kotulpur, Bankura, West Bengal	Groundwater irrigation, paddy (aman and boro), potato and sesame cultivation

Source: Survey data.

Annexure Table 5.2 *Number of manual worker and small and lower middle peasant households as a proportion of number of all households, sixteen PARI villages, 2005–10* (per cent)

Village	Middle and small peasant and hired manual worker households	Other classes	All classes
Andhra Pradesh			
Ananthavaram	55.0	45.0	100
Bukkacherla	61.6	38.4	100
Kothapalle	58.4	41.6	100
Karnataka			
Alabujanahalli	82.3	17.7	100
Siresandra	87.3	12.7	100
Zhapur	78.0	22.0	100
Madhya Pradesh			
Gharsondi	73.8	26.2	100
Maharashtra			
Nimshirgaon	72.3	27.7	100
Warwat Khanderao	73.6	26.4	100
Rajasthan			
25F Gulabewala	74.5	25.5	100
Rewasi	80.8	19.2	100
Uttar Pradesh			
Harevli	75.2	24.8	100
Mahatwar	66.7	33.3	100
West Bengal			
Amarsinghi	80.3	19.7	100
Kalmandasguri	83.7	16.3	100
Panahar	83.9	16.1	100
All (pooled)	**75.0**	**25.0**	**100**

6

Indian Agriculture

Appearance versus Reality

Prabhat Patnaik

The appearance of phenomena under capitalism is often vastly different from, indeed the very opposite of, the reality. The classic example of this, which Marx had given in *Capital*, relates to the 'reification' associated with the 'commodity' form that products take under this system. But it is not just in this fundamental sense that appearance and reality differ. There are innumerable instances of this difference in our perception of the economic reality around us in particular spheres. A telling instance, which I shall discuss in this paper, relates to Indian agriculture in the period of neoliberalism.

While the growth rate of Indian economy has been on the whole more rapid in the post-liberalization era than in the pre-liberalization era, that of the agricultural sector, including of foodgrains in particular, has been much lower on average than before. And yet in the case of foodgrains, in which the government engages in procurement and stock-holding operations, the level of stocks has been on average much larger as a proportion of output than before. In fact, in all but six years since the introduction of neoliberal policies in 1991, the level of foodgrain stocks has been above what the government considers 'normal'. As on July 2012 this level had reached a massive 82 million tonnes, and even though exports on a significant scale have been resorted to since then, this level still remains to this day much higher than 'normal'.

This fact of excessively high stocks, indeed relatively higher than the level in earlier years, despite a slowing down of agricultural growth, has led many to conclusions that can be summed up in two propositions. The first is that there has been a 'disarticulation' within the economy between the different sectors, whereby the overall growth rate of the gross domestic product (GDP), unlike in the earlier period of *dirigisme* and unlike what many authors, including Michael Kalecki, had theorized, is no longer tied to that of the agricultural sector. And the second proposition is that this 'disarticulation' has been the result of the increasing 'maturity' of the economy, whereby the very growth of the GDP, which has, no matter how unevenly, been shared by all, has led to a diversification of demand away from agricultural goods towards manufacturing and service sector products.

From this perception in turn, *which so closely corresponds to the appearance of things that these propositions are normally taken to be self-evident,* it is concluded that any further emphasis on agriculture is unnecessary: with 'unwanted' stocks piling up, any attempt to boost agricultural production, especially foodgrain production, would merely compound the problem of excess supply. It is suggested therefore that those who argue in favour of enlarging government expenditure for boosting agricultural output, or of providing larger subsidies to this sector, or even of raising procurement prices to induce farmers to increase output, are barking up the wrong tree.

What I wish to argue in this paper is that the reality is just the opposite of this assertion, which appears almost self-evident at first sight. The piling up of foodgrain stocks is not because of an all-round increase in real incomes and purchasing power, but because of a *decrease* in the real purchasing power of large sections of the people. The build-up of stocks is not a phenomenon that justifies a curtailment of government expenditure earmarked for boosting agricultural production, but itself arises because of the curtailment of government expenditure towards agricultural production. The apparent excess supply of foodgrains is caused not by the fact that the agricultural sector is receiving more attention than is warranted, but because it is receiving less attention than is warranted.

Indeed, the persistence of this misconception, viz., that it is receiving more attention than warranted, induces action on the part of the government that actually worsens the state of excess supply, and thereby results in a dangerous self-perpetuation of this mistaken belief.

II

The basic reason why appearances relating to the agricultural sector are so illusory and in sharp contrast to the reality is that while the effect of cutbacks of government development expenditure on agricultural, and hence foodgrain, *production* is well known, and is generally taken into account, their effect on the *demand* for foodgrains is not. To put it differently, the fact that the non-maintenance of canals or a reduction of the fertilizer subsidy causes a decline in agricultural output is so obvious that it is perceived by all. But the fact that the same measures also have a demand-side effect on the output of the same sector is not so obvious, since the demand-side effect is indirect and a mediated one: it operates through a reduced injection of purchasing power into the hands of people; and the identity of the people in whose hands this purchasing power is reduced is not even immediately clear.

All this is also in addition to the fact that a demand-side effect is in any case not recognized in the kind of economic theory that acquires hegemony in the era of neoliberalism. This theory which believes in Say's Law, namely that there can never be any deficiency of aggregate demand, is in conformity with the ideology of international finance capital that acquires hegemony in this period *at the social level*. This ideology holds that the 'unfettered' working of markets, i.e. the removal of all restrictions on the capacity of finance capital to move across national frontiers, is the socially optimal policy. The claim that 'markets know best', that they are not afflicted by any problem of deficiency of aggregate demand, is therefore a necessary concomitant of this ideology.

Paradoxically, however, the demand-side effect, which is very real, is both *immediate* and *pronounced*, while the effect on the supply side takes time. Because of this, any curtailment in government development expenditure on agriculture or on rural infrastructure shows itself immediately as a reduction in the off-take of foodgrains, and hence as an addition to 'unwanted' foodgrain stocks. Such 'unwanted' stocks in turn are taken as a signal for a further curtailment of public expenditure, on the grounds that there is an excess supply of agricultural products; any such secondary curtailment further reduces demand, and so on. Even when the delayed effect of curtailed public expenditure on the supply side does make an appearance, it still may not be, and actually is not, enough to prevent repeated rounds of curtailment of expenditure that becomes self-justifying.

The logic of my argument can be given through a simple illustration. Let me start from some 'comparison path' along which there is an equality between demand and supply of foodgrains and of other products in every period, and discuss only deviations from this path arising from specific government action that entails a shift of public expenditure away from rural infrastructure and the agricultural sector towards the non-agricultural sector. Such a shift always occurs within a neoliberal regime for the following reason.

The government, in order to attract direct foreign investment in the non-agricultural sector, feels obliged to build up infrastructure in the latter. But 'fiscal responsibility' legislation ties its hands in the matter of the size of the fiscal deficit, and it cannot raise higher taxes at the expense of the rich, who are the ones best able to pay higher taxes, for fear that it would discourage private investment. Hence it perforce cuts down expenditure, especially on agriculture and rural infrastructure.

Let us assume that Rs 100 less is spent on rural infrastructure by the government and that this amount is spent instead on infrastructure, in other, non-agricultural, sectors. This latter expenditure typically generates incomes for persons who are on average better off than those whose incomes are curtailed because of lower government expenditure on rural infrastructure. The shift in government expenditure, in other words, typically entails a shift in private incomes, and hence of purchasing power, from poorer persons to somewhat better-off persons. Now, the latter absorb a higher amount of foodgrains per capita than the former on average, if we take not just direct consumption but also indirect absorption through processed foods and animal products (into which foodgrains enter as an input in the form of feedgrains) together. But the marginal absorption of foodgrains of the better-off segments of the population is lower than that of the poorer segments in terms of the per unit expenditure in rupees. If we assume, for simplicity, that the shift in purchasing power from the poorer segments to better-off ones makes no difference to the sum total of the private consumption expenditure on *all commodities*, it nonetheless reduces the expenditure on *foodgrains*, and hence, at the given prices (which I assume always prevail), the physical demand for foodgrains.

There is an additional factor working in the same direction and this has to do with the greater health consciousness among the better-off segments of the population. This has the effect of lowering parametrically the foodgrain absorption of the better-off segments (though such absorption continues to remain higher on average than the absorption of the poorer segments). For the time being, however, let us ignore this aspect, which in any case would strengthen our argument presented below.

If the switch of Rs 100 of public expenditure away from rural development and agriculture towards other sectors has the effect of reducing the net demand for foodgrains by, say, Rs 20, then Rs 20 worth of foodgrain stocks will accumulate with the government at the end of the period in question. The foodgrain output in the next period, however, will go down, and let us assume that the drop will be Rs 15. This drop will mean in addition that the incomes of those engaged in foodgrain production, whether as peasants or as agricultural labourers, will get reduced, and hence their demand for foodgrains too will fall, say, by Rs 10. By the end of the next period, therefore, the magnitude of stocks will be worth Rs 15.

But there is an additional factor here. The very fact that unwanted stocks worth Rs 20 would be with the government at the end of the first period would make the government cut back public expenditure on agriculture and rural development further in the second period too, in order to get rid of this apparent 'excess supply' of foodgrains. But this would mean that the stocks at the end of the second period would not be just Rs 15 but of a larger magnitude. And so the process will go on.

Hence an autonomous curtailment of public expenditure results in an excess supply of foodgrains, and consequently a further, induced, curtailment of public expenditure on this sector occurring over several rounds. And all this curtailment has the effect of reducing not only output but also the level of consumption of the population dependent upon this sector (owing to a shortage of purchasing power in its hands) relative to the comparison path.

The belief that an improvement in income leads to a reduced absorption of foodgrains is in any case a completely erroneous one to start with. This is because, whether we take cross-section data or time-series data, the marginal propensity to consume foodgrains, *taking both direct and indirect consumption together* (the latter in the form of processed foods and animal products), is positive. Hence the claim that a shift of consumption pattern away from foodgrains is indicative of an improvement in living standards is in any case unsustainable. My contention is that such a shift, on the contrary, is a reflection of *a worsening of living standards* caused *inter alia* by a shift in the direction of public expenditure.

III

Let us carry this analysis a little further. Again, we measure everything in terms of deviations from a 'comparison path', which is a sort of benchmark and along which the demand and supply of agricultural goods, and of foodgrains in particular, are equal. Likewise, the demand and supply of non-agricultural goods along this path are also equal. We assume too, throughout our discussion of the deviation from the comparison path, that prices remain unchanged and, for simplicity, that deviations take the form of stock adjustment and output adjustment in the case of all sectors.

Again for simplicity, we assume that the 'public expenditure' movements we would be talking about refer exclusively to investment movements; that the effect of such investment movements are the same for all sectors, i.e. that the capital–output ratios are identical everywhere, and that total private investment remains unchanged relative to the comparison path throughout the periods over which the deviations occur. In other words, the effect of the movements we shall be discussing are symmetrical between agriculture and non-agriculture, though our focus will be only on agriculture, which, again for simplicity, we assume to be producing only foodgrains.

If for autonomous reasons, having to do with the pressure of international finance capital, x is the amount of investment that is shifted by the government from agriculture to the non-agricultural sector, then, denoting by c the marginal propensity to consume foodgrains by those whose incomes would fall by this, and by c' the marginal propensity to consume foodgrains by those whose incomes would rise, the reduction in demand for foodgrains in rupee terms during this period is x.(c–c').

If the output–capital ratio is denoted by b, then the reduction in agricultural output *in the next period* is b.x, and the reduction in consumption on account of this fall in output by those engaged in its production is bxc. The increase in consumption of foodgrains from elsewhere because of the rise in output *there* is bxc'. Hence the net reduction in consumption owing to output changes is bx(c–c'), *arising exclusively from the initial shift in public expenditure of x from agriculture to the non-agricultural sector*. The stocks at the end of the second period therefore would be [x(c–c') (1+b) – x.b].

But meanwhile, the fact of higher stocks at the end of the first period makes the government curtail public expenditure in the second period too and shift this amount to the non-agriculture sector. If the curtailment is some fraction a of the level of excess stocks then, in the second period, there would be *an additional amount of stocks arising from this reason* of a.x.(c–c') (c–c').

At the end of the second period, therefore, the level of total additional stocks would be

$$x(c-c')\ (1+b) + a.x(c-c')^2 - b.x$$

This level would be positive if

$$[(c-c') + a.(c-c')^2] > b[1-(c-c')]$$

For this to happen, a *sufficient* condition is that

$$(c-c') > b$$

The level of stocks at the end of the second period would be *higher* than the level at the end of the first period if

$$b.(c-c') + a.(c-c')^2 > b$$

This condition is unlikely to be satisfied unless the value of a is very large, i.e. unless the government responds very strongly to extra stock holding of foodgrains by way of curtailing public expenditure. But even if the level of additional stocks relative to the comparison path declines over time, following the initial shift of public expenditure away from agriculture to non-agriculture, by the time the level of additional stocks relative to the comparison path has declined to zero, the economy would have witnessed *a shift of position, though not of overall growth rate, in relation to the original comparison path. The essence of this shift would have been a decrease in the relative size of the agricultural sector and an increase in the relative scale of poverty among the agriculture-dependent population.*

In other words, even if a shift of public expenditure away from the agricultural to the non-agricultural sector leaves the growth rate unchanged relative to the comparison path, both ultimately and by our assumptions *even in the traverse*, there would nonetheless be a shift of the path in the new equilibrium. The new equilibrium path where the level of stocks would be no different compared to the comparison path, will nonetheless be a different path. This difference would be visible through an exercise in comparative statics; and the comparative statics between the two paths, the original one and the eventual one, would show the latter to have a lower level of agricultural output, a lower level of income and hence a higher level of poverty among the agriculture-dependent population.

Moreover, since poverty *in the economy as a whole* is defined with respect to a calorie norm whose satisfaction depends fundamentally upon the magnitude of foodgrain intake, the new path would entail a higher level of poverty *in the economy as a whole* than the original path.

A shift of public expenditure away from agriculture to non-agriculture, in other words, even when it leaves the overall growth rate unchanged, increases the level of poverty in the economy. What appears at first sight as 'disarticulation' between sectors turns out in reality to have been a poverty-aggravating switch of public expenditure away from sectors like agriculture and rural development. It constitutes what has been called an imposition of 'income deflation' on the working population in rural areas.

Every such autonomous act of expenditure switch entails an aggravation of poverty and an atrophy of agriculture when we compare the 'equilibrium growth paths' before and after the switch. But if such autonomous acts are repeated, then there would be a series of such shifts in the position of the equilibrium growth path. Though each shift would be followed by a dwindling over time of the extra stocks down to zero, the series of shifts would entail a continuous tendency towards an aggravation of poverty over time, and also towards an atrophy of agriculture, with its growth rate not just continuing to fall behind that of other sectors but decelerating as well, while that of other sectors accelerates. This, incidentally, is exactly what we find in the case of the Indian economy.

IV

Such a shift of expenditure from the agricultural sector to the non-agricultural sector is analytically exactly analogous to a larger taxation of the agricultural sector for financing a larger expenditure on the non-agricultural sector. And while we have been talking so far of *sectors*, the issue really relates to *classes*. The shift of expenditure from the agricultural to the non-agricultural sector is in effect a shift from peasants and petty producers, who predominantly people the former sector, to capitalists belonging to the corporate-financial oligarchy, who dominate the latter. *It follows, therefore, that this shift constitutes in effect an instance of primitive accumulation of capital.*

The process of primitive accumulation of capital is not confined only to the pre-history of capitalism as is commonly supposed, but characterizes the system throughout its entire history. This is because the system continues to remain ensconced within a setting of pre-capitalist producers throughout its history and continues to encroach upon the latter. This is a phenomenon that is not confined only to the colonial period, during which such encroachment was obvious, but continues to occur even after the end of formal colonial rule. The difference between then and now consists in the fact that now domestic big capitalists also engage in this process of primitive accumulation of capital, in addition to capitalists from metropolis, while earlier it was only the latter who were its beneficiaries.

This primitive accumulation of capital however has a 'stock' and a 'flow' form. The 'stock' form is when petty producers are displaced from their means of production through expropriation by the capitalists, such as, for instance, peasants' land being taken over either entirely *gratis* or merely 'for a song' by the capitalists. (The mere fact of payment of compensation, in other words, does not amount to a negation of primitive accumulation of capital.) The Narendra Modi government's Land Acquisition Bill, whose enactment has so far been successfully resisted, is meant to facilitate such a process of primitive accumulation of capital in the 'stock' sense.

There is, however, a 'flow' sense in which primitive accumulation of capital also occurs, which is when a transfer takes place from the incomes of the peasants and petty producers to those of the capitalists. If peasants are taxed and the proceeds are handed over as subsidies to the capitalists, or if peasants are squeezed through a lower price being paid for their products by the capitalists, then we have primitive accumulation of capital in a 'flow' form. Yevgeny Preobrazhensky, who had advocated 'primitive socialist accumulation' at the expense of the peasantry in the 1920s for financing socialist industrialization in the Soviet Union, was talking about this 'flow' form of primitive accumulation (though, of course, in an altogether different social setting).

This process of primitive accumulation of capital gets greatly enhanced in the period of neoliberalism as compared to the *dirigiste* period that immediately followed the end of colonial rule. This is because the *dirigiste regime* had, to an extent, provided protection to the peasants and petty producers (though not all segments of the peasantry were equal beneficiaries of such measures of protection). Such protection was given both in partial fulfilment of the promises of the anti-colonial struggle and as a requisite step for the domestic bourgeoisie's project of pursuing a capitalist path *in relative autonomy from imperialism* (for which the development of the public sector as a counter to metropolitan capital was another requisite step).

With the big capitalists' abandonment of this project of a relatively autonomous development trajectory and their closer integration with international finance capital, of which the adoption of neoliberal policies is an expression, such protection to peasants and petty producers is no longer offered, which unleashes once more a virulent process of primitive accumulation of capital. Indeed, the agrarian crisis we witness today is nothing else but the consequence of this process of primitive accumulation of capital.

The neoliberal state not only opens the way for primitive accumulation of capital at the expense of peasants and petty producers, but also privatizes public sector assets 'for a song'. I have elsewhere used the term 'accumulation through encroachment' as distinct from 'accumulation through expansion' (which consists of the investment of surplus value generated within the capitalist sector) to cover both these forms in which capitalist property expands at the expense of non-capitalist property.

While all this has been much discussed, what has received less attention is the ideological justification that is usually provided for such primitive accumulation of capital. The promise of a better life to the peasants and petty producers who are the victims of this process through greater employment in the capitalist sector, compared to the miserable conditions in which they subsist (or do not even succeed in doing so, as the mass suicides of peasants suggest), constitutes one strategy of winning them over. This argument, however, is utterly disingenuous. Its disingenuousness lies as much in the fact that such promised employment never materializes, since capitalist development scarcely generates too many additional jobs, as in the fact that the cause of their miserable conditions itself lies *inter alia* in this very process of 'flow' of primitive accumulation of capital.

But there is an additional ideological argument, and that consists in the claim that the process of 'disarticulation' between sectors has proceeded so far that agriculture itself is no longer as necessary as it used to be, that the very process of development of the economy has reduced its role, of which the burgeoning stocks with the government are an indication. *The burgeoning stocks too, however, are nothing else but a reflection of the process of primitive accumulation of capital in the 'flow' form.* The objective of this paper has been to underscore and elucidate this point.

7

Agricultural Credit and Financial Liberalization in India

R. Ramakumar

Introduction

Consider the following two sets of results, both from official sources of secondary data in India.

Result 1

Here, let us consider three sets of numbers from the All India Debt and Investment Survey (AIDIS) reports of 1992 and 2013. These surveys provide data on household-level indebtedness for two groups of households: all 'rural households' and 'cultivator households'. Rural households operating at least 0.002 hectare of land were treated as 'cultivator households'.

First, a higher share of rural and cultivator households were indebted in 2013 than in 1992. The share of indebted rural households rose from 23.4 per cent in 1992 to 31.4 per cent in 2013; the share of indebted cultivator households rose from 25.9 per cent in 1992 to 45.9 per cent in 2013.

Secondly, while a rise in the share of indebted households need not be an adverse phenomenon in itself, what was striking was that the rise in incidence of indebtedness occurred alongside a rise in the debt–asset ratios (which shows the extent to which debt is a drain on the value of owned assets) of households. In 1992, the debt–asset ratio for rural households was 1.78, and this rose phenomenally to 3.23 in 2013. Thus the data point not just to a higher share of indebted households, but also to an intensification of the debt burden.

Thirdly, from where did households borrow? Between 1992 and 2013, the share of debt outstanding from *informal* credit sources increased sharply. For all rural households, the share of debt outstanding from the formal sector fell from 64 per cent in 1992 to 56 per cent in 2013. Similarly, for cultivator households, the share of debt outstanding from the formal sector fell from 66.3 per cent in 1992 to 64 per cent in 2013. The most important reason for this was the withdrawal of commercial banks from lending to farmers and rural areas. Between 1992 and 2013, the share of debt outstanding from commercial banks fell from 33.7 per cent to 25.1 per cent for rural households, and from 35.2 per cent to 30.7 per cent for cultivator households.

Concurrently, informal sources of credit became increasingly important in the 1990s and 2000s. If only 32.7 per cent of the debt outstanding of rural households was from the informal sector in 1992, the corresponding share rose to 44 per cent in 2013. If we consider cultivator households, the share of debt outstanding from the informal sector rose from 30.6 per cent in 1992 to 36 per cent in 2013. Within the informal sector, it was the share of debt from moneylenders that rose most sharply. For all rural households, the share of debt outstanding from moneylenders rose from 17.5 per cent in 1992 to 33.2 per cent in 2013. For cultivator households, the share of debt outstanding from moneylenders rose from 17.5 per cent in 1992 to 29.6 per cent in 2013.

The results from the AIDIS reports of 1992 and 2013 lead us to the conclusion that about twenty-five years of financial liberalization have left the rural and cultivator households worse off.

Result 2

Now, let us contrast the above findings from the AIDIS with the secondary data on commercial bank credit released by the Reserve Bank of India (RBI) till 2012. The figures released by the RBI lead us to a very different conclusion regarding changes in the supply of rural credit in India, particularly in the decade of the 2000s.

First, there was an increase in the number of rural bank branches after 2005. If 922 rural bank branches were closed down between 1995 and 2005, more than 5,800 new rural bank branches were opened between 2005 and 2012 (see Table 7.1). The period after 2005 also saw the opening of 10,902 semi-urban bank branches.[1]

Secondly, the increase in the number of bank branches was accompanied by a sharp rise in the growth of credit flow to agriculture. Between 2001 and 2012, agricultural credit grew by 17.7 per cent per annum, which was significantly higher than the growth rate recorded for the 1990s (Table 7.2). The growth rate of agricultural credit in the 2000s and 2010s was higher than the growth rate of total bank credit. In Figure 7.1, we have normalized the growth of agricultural credit with population growth; the

Table 7.1 *Changes in the number of bank branches in India, by population group, 1991 to 2012*

Quarter ending	Number of bank offices located in regions				
	Rural	Semi-urban	Urban	Metropolitan	Total
March 1991	35,206	11,344	8,046	5,624	60,220
March 1994	35,329	11,890	8,745	5,839	61,803
Change, 1991–94	*123*	*546*	*699*	*215*	*1,583*
March 1995	33,004	13,341	8,868	7,154	62,367
March 2005	32,082	15,403	11,500	9,370	68,355
Change, 1995–2005	*–922*	*2,062*	*2,632*	*2,216*	*5,988*
March 2005 (corrected)	30,646	15,253	12,315	11,685	69,899
March 2012	36,517	26,155	20,661	19,079	1,02,412
Change, 2005–12	*5,871*	*10,902*	*8,346*	*7,394*	*32,513*

Notes: (i) The number of branches/offices in this table excludes administrative offices.
(ii) The periods shown in the table are the ones for which the number of branches are comparable. Data on branches/credit by population groups are not strictly comparable across time. This is because the RBI periodically updates the classification of centres using the latest available census figures. Till 1994, the centres were classified using the Census of 1981. From 1995, the RBI began to apply the Census of 1991. From 2006, data from the 2001 Census were used to classify the centres. However, for one year – 2005– the RBI has also published comparable data after reclassification of centres as per 2001 Census. For a detailed discussion, see Ramakumar and Chavan (2011).
Source: Reserve Bank of India, 'Basic Statistical Returns of Scheduled Commercial Banks in India', various issues.

Table 7.2 *Rate of growth of credit to agriculture, total bank credit, at constant prices, India, 1972 to 2012* (per cent per annum)

Period	Annual growth rates	
	Credit to agriculture	Total bank credit
1972–81	16.1	8.4
1981–91	6.8	8.0
1991–2001	2.6	7.3
2001–12	17.7	15.7

Source: Reserve Bank of India (RBI), 'Basic Statistical Returns of Scheduled Commercial Banks in India', various issues; Central Statistical Organization (CSO), 'National Accounts Statistics', various issues.

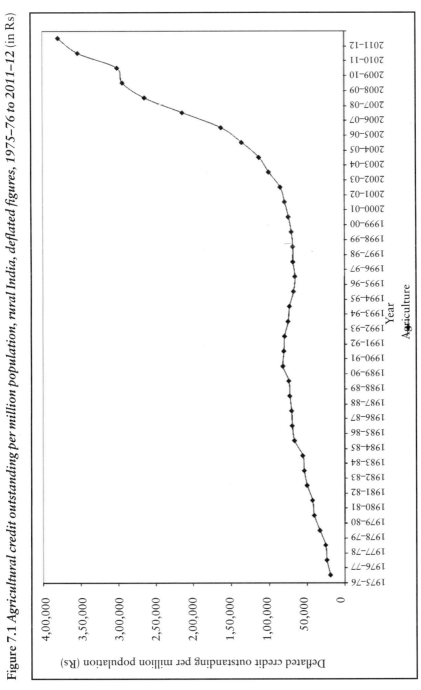

Figure 7.1 *Agricultural credit outstanding per million population, rural India, deflated figures, 1975–76 to 2011–12 (in Rs)*

Source: Reserve Bank of India, 'Basic Statistical Returns of Scheduled Commercial Banks in India', various issues.

plot of agricultural credit outstanding per million rural population fell in the 1990s and rose sharply in the 2000s.

In sum, the number of rural bank branches and credit flow to agriculture picked up significantly in the decade of the 2000s. These results from the RBI reports sharply contradict the findings from the AIDIS. If indeed the supply of rural credit had expanded till 2012, as the RBI reports show, why might it be that the AIDIS reports show a very different picture of change between 1992 and 2013? This paper is an attempt to examine why the AIDIS and RBI reports show apparently paradoxical results with regard to the supply of agricultural credit in India between the early 2000s and the mid-2010s. Dealing only with credit from commercial banks, it argues that the reasons lie in the changes in the pattern of distribution of agricultural credit after the early 2000s, which was backed by conscious official policy.

The paper is divided into four sections, including the introductory section. The second section provides a background to the evolution of agricultural credit policy in India after 1969. The third section analyses the pattern and distribution of agricultural credit in India in the 2000s. The fourth and last section is a concluding section.

A Background to Agricultural Credit Policy in India

Since the nationalization of commercial banks in 1969, India had strongly pursued a policy of 'social and development banking' in the rural areas. As a result, formal institutions of credit provision, mainly commercial banks, emerged as important sources of finance to agriculture, displacing usurious moneylenders and landlords. The policy of social and development banking was a supply-led policy; it aimed at augmenting the supply of credit to rural areas, and that too at affordable interest rates (see Ramachandran and Swaminathan 2005; Shetty 2006; Chavan 2002 and 2005).

Three aspects of the post-1969 policy of social and development banking stand out. First, according to the new branch licensing policy, commercial banks were required to open four branches in unbanked rural areas for every branch opened in metropolitan or port areas. As a result, if there were only 1,443 rural branches of banks in 1969, there were 35,134 rural branches by 1991. Secondly, according to the policy of priority sector lending, 40 per cent of net bank credit was to be provided to those sectors of the economy (or sections of the society) that would not get timely and adequate credit in the absence of binding targets. Loans to these sectors were typically loans to farmers for agriculture and allied activities (18 per cent), to micro and small enterprises, to poor people for housing, to students for education and other low-income groups and weaker sections (10 per cent). As a result, the share of credit from rural branches in total bank credit increased from 5.9 per cent in 1975 to 15 per cent in 1990. Thirdly, according to the differential interest rate scheme of 1974, loans were provided at concessional interest rates on advances made by public banks to selected low-income groups to engage in productive and gainful activities. The differential rate of interest was fixed uniformly at 4 per cent per annum, i.e. 2 per cent below the bank rate.

There is little quarrel among economists on the effect that the increased flow of bank credit after 1969 had on agricultural growth in India. The regulations on banking and the promotional role of the government were premised on the recognition that rural credit markets are deeply imperfect. The social and developing banking policy consciously mopped up surplus savings as deposits from richer rural areas and diverted them as loans to savings-deficient areas (Ramachandran and Swaminathan 2005). Increased availability of credit from public banks helped small and marginal farmers adopt the costlier new technologies and farming practices that were a part of the strategy of the green revolution.

Yet, in the early 1990s, the policy of social and development banking came to be severely criticized. First, the Committee on the Financial System (Narasimham Committee) made a sharp pitch for delinking monetary policy from the objective of redistribution (RBI 1991). It argued that banks should function on a commercial basis, and that profitability should be the prime concern in their activities. Thus, the 4:1 norm for opening new branches under the branch licensing policy was removed and banks were permitted to rationalize their branch network in rural areas. Secondly, the norms related to the definition of priority sector lending were considerably broadened. Thirdly, it was argued that banks should be given a free hand to charge rates of interest because administering interest rates would lead to 'financial repression'. Financial repression is defined as a situation where the degree of financial intermediation is weak due to negative real rates of interest on deposits and a large spread between borrowing and lending rates. As a result, it was argued, private savings and investments are discouraged in the economy.

The recommendations of the Narasimham Committee, except for a few, were implemented to a large extent in the 1990s and 2000s. Consequently, the period of financial liberalization after 1991 was a period of reversal of the achievements of social and development banking. It is by now well documented that the trends that emerged in India in the 1990s with respect to the supply of rural credit in general, and agricultural credit in particular, were deeply disturbing. In the 1990s, there was (i) large-scale closure of commercial bank branches in rural areas; (ii) a widening of inter-state inequalities in credit provision and a fall in the proportion of bank credit directed towards regions where banking was historically underdeveloped; (iii) a sharp fall in the growth of credit flow to agriculture; (iv) increased sidelining of small and marginal farmers in the supply of agricultural credit; (v) increased exclusion of disadvantaged and dispossessed sections of the population from the formal financial system; and (vi) strengthening of the hold of moneylenders on rural debt portfolios. (For details, see the collected papers in Ramachandran and Swaminathan 2005; Shetty 2006; Chavan 2005 and 2007.)

In 2004, the central government announced its intent to double the flow of credit to agriculture over a period of three years. Increase in credit flow was an integral part of the so-called 'New Deal for Rural India' promised by the United Progressive Alliance (UPA) government. A 'comprehensive credit policy' was announced in June 2004, which included a commitment to raise agricultural credit flow by 30 per cent every year; financing of 100 farmers per branch (thus, 50 lakh farmers in a year); two to three new investments in agricultural projects per branch every year; and a host of debt relief measures, such as debt restructuring, one-time settlement and financial assistance to redeem loans from moneylenders (see Ministry of Agriculture 2007).

From 2004 onwards, it was regularly claimed in official circles that the flow of credit to agriculture has been increasing at a rapid rate, even surpassing its annual targets (Ministry of Finance 2007; NABARD 2013). These claims were largely based on data from RBI reports, cited in the last section. This paper largely concerns itself with a disaggregated analysis of the last phase.

Agricultural Credit Growth in the 2000s

Six distinct features of the growth in agricultural credit have had a major role in determining the *extent* of increase in credit supply as well as its *distribution* within the agricultural sector. In our view, these features are at the root of the variance noted earlier across the results of AIDIS and RBI reports. These features are discussed separately in the sub-sections below.[2]

Rural Population per Branch

An important indicator of the geographical spread of rural banking is the figure for rural population per bank branch. In 1969, there were more than 76,100 rural persons per (rural) branch, which came down to 13,900 rural persons per branch in 1990 (see Table 7.3). Between 1995 and 2005, due to the closing down of rural bank branches, rural persons

Table 7.3 *Population per bank branch, rural and total, India, 1969–2011*

Year	Rural population per rural branch	Total population per branch
1969	76,100	62,200
1990	13,900	14,000
1995	14,700	14,800
2005	17,100	16,400
2006	17,900	16,500
2011	16,100	13,900

Note: For the periodization adopted in this table, see notes under Table 7.1.
Source: Reserve Bank of India (RBI), 'Basic Statistical Returns of Scheduled Commercial Banks in India', various issues.

per branch rose from 14,700 to 17,100. The number of rural persons per branch improved from 17,900 in 2006 to 16,100 in 2011, but remained considerably higher than the corresponding figures for 1990 or 1995. Thus, one of the reasons for the variance between the AIDIS and the RBI reports is clearly the fact that the number of rural persons per branch did not adequately decline till 2011.

The Rise of Indirect Credit

A significant proportion of the increase in total bank credit to agriculture in the 2000s was accounted for by *indirect credit* to agriculture. Of the total increase in agricultural credit between 2002 and 2010, more than one-fourth (26 per cent) was contributed by indirect credit.

Historically, agricultural credit has comprised mainly of credit provided directly to cultivators, which is called 'direct credit to agriculture'. Direct credit to agriculture comprises of short-term credit or credit for seasonal agricultural operations, and long-term credit towards investments in agriculture. Short-term loans to agriculture are also referred to as 'crop loans', as they are advanced for crop cultivation against the hypotheca-tion of the crop to be cultivated by the farmer. Crop loans are provided as cash or in kind, such as the supply of fertilizers and seeds. The second component of agricultural credit is called 'indirect credit', which does not go directly to cultivators but to institutions that support agricultural pro-duction in rural areas. The typical forms of indirect credit to agriculture were loans to input dealers for their role in the provision of agricultural inputs and loans to electricity boards for supplying power to cultivators.

In the decade of the 1990s and after, the share of indirect credit in total agricultural credit rose consistently (see Table 7.4). Between 1985

Table 7.4 *Shares of direct and indirect credit to agriculture in total credit to agriculture from scheduled commercial banks, India, 1985–2012* (per cent)

Year	Share in total agricultural credit (per cent)		
	Direct credit	Indirect credit	Total
1985	83.2	16.8	100.0
1990	86.8	13.2	100.0
2000	84.5	15.5	100.0
2005	76.1	23.9	100.0
2006	72.1	27.9	100.0
2007	74.5	25.5	100.0
2008	77.5	22.5	100.0
2009	77.1	22.9	100.0
2010	76.1	23.9	100.0
2011	82.0	18.0	100.0
2012	83.4	16.6	100.0

Source: Reserve Bank of India (RBI), 'Basic Statistical Returns of Scheduled Commercial Banks in India', various issues.

and 1990, there was actually a fall in the share of indirect credit in total agricultural credit; the share began to rise in the 1990s – particularly after 1998 – to reach 23.9 per cent in 2005 and 27.9 per cent in 2006. Even in 2010, the share of indirect credit in total agricultural credit stood at 23.9 per cent. Thus, while the share of indirect credit in total agricultural credit had begun to rise in the 1990s, its increase in the 2000s was considerably rapid. While the share of indirect credit has registered a fall after 2010, the fact remains that it contributed a large part of what was provided as agricultural credit till 2010.

The most important reason for the rise of indirect credit was the broadening of the definition of what constitutes indirect credit to agriculture.[3] The major changes introduced in the definition of indirect credit are as given below.[4]

- Till 1993, only direct credit to agriculture was considered as a part of the priority sector target of 18 per cent for agriculture and allied activities. From 1993 onwards, direct and indirect credit were considered together for meeting the priority sector target.
- In 1993, it was stipulated that indirect credit to agriculture only up to one-fourth of total agricultural advances would be considered while meeting the priority sector target of 18 per cent for agricul-

ture. However, indirect credit over and above one-fourth of total agricultural advances was allowed to be reckoned while meeting the overall target of 40 per cent for priority sector advances.

- From 1994 onwards, loans up to Rs 5 lakh for financing distribution of inputs for allied activities in agriculture, such as cattle feed and poultry feed, were considered as indirect credit to agriculture. The upper limits were revised and fixed at Rs 15 lakh in 2000, Rs 25 lakh in 2002, Rs 40 lakh in 2004, Rs 1 crore in 2012 and Rs 5 crore in 2013.

- From 1996 onwards, loans to dealers in drip irrigation systems, sprinkler irrigation systems and agricultural machinery were considered as indirect credit to agriculture. From 2002 onwards, the credit limit to these dealers was raised from Rs 10 lakh to Rs 20 lakh; it was further raised to Rs 30 lakh in 2004 and Rs 5 crore in 2013. Till 2003, only loans to those dealers *located in rural or semi-urban areas* were under the ambit of indirect credit. However, from 2003 onwards, all dealers, *irrespective of their location*, were treated as eligible for such advances.

- Loans extended to State Electricity Boards (SEBs) for reimbursement of expenditure towards providing low-tension connections to individual farmers from step-down points for energizing wells were historically classified as indirect credit to agriculture. From 2001 onwards, loans to SEBs for systems improvement under the Special Project Agriculture (SI-SPA) were also considered as indirect credit to agriculture. From 2005 onwards, loans to power distribution corporations or companies emerging out of the bifurcation or restructuring of SEBs as part of power sector reforms were also considered as indirect credit to agriculture. From 2010 onwards, however, these loans were removed from the list of eligible categories under indirect credit to agriculture.

- From 2001 onwards, loans extended under the scheme for financing 'agri-clinics' and 'agribusiness centres' were considered as indirect credit to agriculture.

- From 2001 onwards, subscriptions to bonds issued by the Rural Electrification Corporation (REC) exclusively for financing the pump-set energization programme in rural and semi-urban areas were considered as indirect credit to agriculture.[5]

- From 2000 onwards, loans from banks to Non-Banking Financial Companies (NBFCs) for on-lending to agriculture were considered as indirect credit to agriculture.

- From 2002 onwards, loans for the construction and running of storage facilities (warehouses, market yards, godowns, silos and cold storages) *in the producing areas* and loans to cold storage units *located in rural areas*, which were used for hiring and/or storing mainly agricultural produce, were considered as indirect credit to agriculture. However, from 2004 onwards, loans to storage units, including cold storage units, that were *designed to* store agricultural produce, *irrespective of their location*, were treated as indirect credit to agriculture.

- From 2004 onwards, if the securitized assets of a bank represented indirect credit to agriculture, investment by banks in such assets was considered as indirect credit to agriculture.
- From 2007 onwards, loans to food- and agro-based processing units with investments in plant and machinery up to Rs 10 crore (other than units run by individuals, self-help groups and cooperatives in rural areas) were considered as indirect credit to agriculture.
- From 2007 onwards, two-thirds of loans given to *corporates, partnership firms* and *institutions* for agricultural and allied activities (such as beekeeping, piggery, poultry, fishery and dairy) in excess of Rs 1 crore in aggregate per borrower were considered as indirect credit to agriculture. The remaining one-third was treated as direct credit.
- From 2012 onwards, all the loans given to *corporates, partnership firms* and *institutions* for agricultural and allied activities in excess of Rs 2 crore in aggregate per borrower were treated as indirect credit. All such loans below Rs 2 crore were to be treated as direct credit.

Indirect credit was traditionally understood as loans that would not go directly to farmers, but to activities undertaken by individuals/ institutions that aided farmers in undertaking cultivation. Loans given for the provision of agricultural inputs (to dealers), power (to electricity boards) and formal credit (to primary agricultural credit societies) were such typical indirect activities. With the definitional changes introduced in the late 1990s, the meaning of indirect credit itself has undergone a major change. In Figure 7.2, we have presented the trends in different types of indirect credit to agriculture between 1971 and 2012. The plots show that the traditional components of indirect credit to agriculture did not exhibit any notable recovery in the 2000s. Instead, loans under the category 'other types of indirect credit' began to increase from 1996 onwards, and recorded a phenomenal rise in levels after 1999. From 1999 onwards, except after

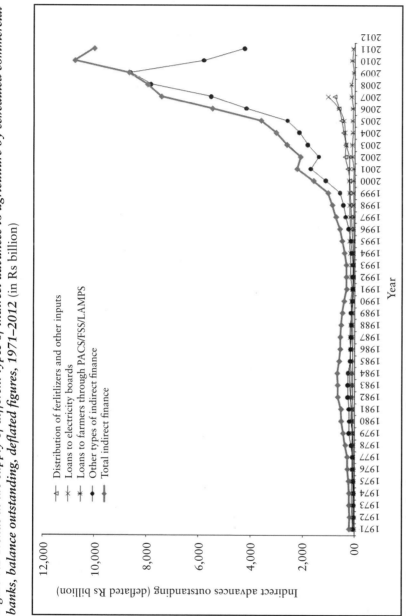

Figure 7.2 Trends in the supply of different types of indirect advances to agriculture by scheduled commercial banks, balance outstanding, deflated figures, 1971–2012 (in Rs billion)

Source: Reserve Bank of India (RBI), 'Handbook of Statistics on Indian Economy 2005–06'.

2009, 'total indirect credit' and 'other types of indirect credit' have also moved in close tandem. Our estimates show that the share in total indirect credit of 'other types of indirect credit', which was 56.6 per cent in 1999, increased to 74.3 per cent in 2007.[6]

In sum, indirect credit to agriculture expanded rapidly since the late 1990s, thus aiding significantly the growth of total agricultural credit. Most of the definitional changes (that either expanded the ambit of indirect credit or steeply raised ceilings on loan sizes) also took place after the late 1990s. In other words, the task of banks to follow the government's directive in 2004 to double agricultural credit became considerably easier given the major changes in the definition of indirect credit.

The promotion of indirect credit by banks also reflects the changing pattern of demand for credit as well as shifts in public policy on agriculture. In essence, most of the new forms of indirect credit are related to investments in the agricultural value chain, such as financing the construction of warehouses, against warehouse receipts, cold storage chains, large-scale dairy farms, contract farming, start-up entrepreneurs, private agricultural extension services, drip irrigation projects, food parks and so on. The Indian Banks Association (IBA) released a document in 2008 with recommendations to increase credit flow to agriculture (IBA 2008). It recommended that banks should increasingly fund private participation or joint ventures in irrigation projects, extend credit to corporate houses in order to process and export agricultural products, on-lend to farmers in contract farming agreements and commercial horticulture. It noted that 'contract farming has the potential for expanding credit outreach, especially to the small/marginal farmers and oral lessees' (ibid.: 39). In other words, banks expressed a major interest in funding projects outside the traditional sphere of agricultural credit.

Increase in indirect credit is necessary to improve the capacity of farmers to absorb more direct credit. However, the promotion of indirect credit should not lead to an undermining of direct credit. The RBI's 'Advisory Committee on Flow of Credit to Agriculture and Related Activities' in 2004 noted the demand made by banks to relax the stipulation that indirect credit to agriculture should not exceed 4.5 per cent of the net bank credit.[7] This stipulation had been earlier put in place in order to channel bank credit directly to farmers. The Advisory Committee rejected this demand by banks, noting that 'indirect lending needs to be subject to certain limitations, lest banks neglect direct credit for agricultural production, which may jeopardize the goal of achieving annual growth of 4 per cent in agricultural production' (RBI 2004: 32).[8]

Increase in Agricultural Loans of Large Sizes

Much of the increase in total advances to agriculture in the 2000s was on account of a sharp increase in the number of loans of size above Rs 10 crore, and particularly above Rs 25 crore. In Table 7.5, we have provided the distribution of the amount of total agricultural advances (direct *plus* indirect) by size-classes of credit limits between 1990 and 2011. A comparison of figures for 1990 with those of 2011 shows that the share in total amount of advances of advances of size less than Rs 25,000 shrank significantly: from 58.7 per cent in 1990 to 5.8 per cent in 2011. Taken together, the amount of loans of size less than Rs 2 lakh constituted 82.6 per cent of all loans in 1990, 51.9 per cent of all loans in 2005 and 41.4 per cent of all loans in 2011. On the other hand, the share in total advances of advances of size above Rs 10 crore increased from 1.3 per cent in 1990 to 20.4 per cent in 2011. If we consider the amount of loans of size above Rs 25 crore, the corresponding shares were 5.7 per cent in 2000 and 17.7 per cent in 2011.

All agricultural loans are not loans to farmers; only direct credit can be considered as loans to farmers. In Table 7.6, we have provided the distribution of the amount of *direct* agricultural advances alone by credit limit size-classes. The results are equally striking. Even under direct credit, only 6.7 per cent of the total advances comprised loans of size less than Rs 25,000. Another 41.3 per cent of the total direct advances comprised of loans of sizes between Rs 25,000 and Rs 2 lakh. About 17 per cent of direct advances comprised of loans of size more than Rs 1 crore.

Table 7.5 *Distribution of amount outstanding under total agricultural advances by scheduled commercial banks, by credit limit size-classes of loans, 1990–2011* (per cent)

Credit limit size-class of loans (Rs)	Share of amount outstanding in total amount outstanding (%)			
	1990	2000	2005	2011
Less than 25,000	58.7	35.2	17.8	5.8
25,000 to 2 lakh	23.9	32.4	34.1	35.6
2 lakh to 10 lakh	4.3	11.7	17.9	22.6
10 lakh to 1 crore	7.6	6.6	6.4	6.4
1 crore to 10 crore	4.2	6.7	8.0	6.3
10 crore to 25 crore	1.3	1.7	3.3	2.7
Above 25 crore		5.7	12.6	17.7
Total advances	100.0	100.0	100.0	100.0

Source: Reserve Bank of India (RBI), 'Basic Statistical Returns of Scheduled Commercial Banks in India', various issues.

Table 7.6 *Distribution of amount outstanding under direct agricultural advances by scheduled commercial banks, by credit limit size-classes of loans, 1990–2011* (per cent)

Credit limit size-class of loans (Rs)	Share of amount outstanding in total amount outstanding (%)			
	1990	2000	2005	2011
Less than 25,000	66.1	41.1	22.9	6.7
25,000 to 2 lakh	26.1	37.4	43.8	41.3
2 lakh to 10 lakh	3.6	12.8	21.4	28.3
10 lakh to 1 crore	2.6	3.9	4.5	7.1
1 crore to 10 crore	1.2	3.1	4.1	5.7
10 crore to 25 crore	0.3	0.4	1.4	2.4
Above 25 crore		1.2	2.0	8.5
Total advances	100.0	100.0	100.0	100.0

Source: Reserve Bank of India (RBI), 'Basic Statistical Returns of Scheduled Commercial Banks in India', various issues.

It would be rare to find an Indian farmer taking a loan of size more than Rs 2 lakh for short-term cultivation purposes, which is what direct credit largely implies. In Table 7.7, we have used a broad size classification of the amount of direct credit; we have divided the amount of direct credit into those of size less than Rs 2 lakh and above Rs 2 lakh, as well as less than Rs 10 lakh and above Rs 10 lakh. If Rs 2 lakh is taken as a cut-off to indicate a typical agricultural loan, then the data in Table 7.7 show that only 48 per cent of the total agricultural credit reached the farmers in 2011. The corresponding share was 92.2 per cent for 1990, 78.5 per cent for 2000 and 66.7 per cent for 2005. A similar conclusion emerges from the classification of the amount of direct credit into sizes less than Rs 10 lakh and above Rs 10 lakh. In 1990, the amount constituted by loans of size above Rs 10 lakh was 3.3 per cent of the total amount; this share rose to 8.6 per cent in 2000, 12 per cent in 2005 and 23.8 per cent in 2011.

There is a probable reason why much of the direct credit to agriculture did not reach 'farmers' in the 2000s. A series of changes were introduced in the definition of direct credit from the late 1990s, and all of these either expanded the coverage of what constitutes direct credit or raised the upper limits for already existing direct credit. We list the definitional changes below.

Table 7.7 *Distribution of amount outstanding under direct agricultural advances by scheduled commercial banks, by broad size-classes of credit limit, 1985–2011* (per cent)

| Year | Share of amount of direct advances with credit limit (%) | | | | | |
	< Rs 2 lakh	> Rs 2 lakh	Total	< Rs 10 lakh	> Rs 10 lakh	Total
1985	na	na	100.0	96.7	3.3	100.0
1990	92.2	7.7	100.0	95.8	4.1	100.0
1995	89.1	10.9	100.0	93.6	6.4	100.0
2000	78.5	21.4	100.0	91.3	8.6	100.0
2003	72.6	27.4	100.0	87.5	12.5	100.0
2005	66.7	33.4	100.0	88.1	12.0	100.0
2006	60.8	39.2	100.0	86.3	13.7	100.0
2011	48.0	52.0	100.0	76.2	23.8	100.0

Source: Reserve Bank of India (RBI), 'Basic Statistical Returns of Scheduled Commercial Banks in India', various issues.

- From 1997 onwards, short-term loans to traditional plantations (such as tea, coffee, rubber and spices), *irrespective of the size of holdings*, were considered as direct credit to agriculture. Later, all loans (short-term, medium-term and long-term) to traditional and non-traditional plantations and horticulture, irrespective of the size of holdings, were considered as direct credit to agriculture.
- From 2002 onwards, the upper limit for loans given against the pledge or hypothecation of agricultural produce (including warehouse receipts) for a period not exceeding six months was raised from Rs 1 lakh to Rs 5 lakh for a period not exceeding twelve months. From 2007 onwards, the upper limit was raised from Rs 5 lakh to Rs 10 lakh. The upper limit was further raised to Rs 25 lakh in 2012 and Rs 50 lakh in 2013. Till 2007, these loans were given only to individual farmers who had sought crop loans from banks. From 2007, these loans were given to individual farmers irrespective of whether they had sought crop loans.
- From 2007 onwards, the entire amount of loans given to *corporates*, *partnership firms* and *institutions* for agricultural and allied activities (such as beekeeping, piggery, poultry, fishery and dairy) up to Rs 1 crore, and one-third of loans in excess of Rs 1 crore, in aggregate per borrower, were considered as direct credit to agriculture (the remaining two-thirds was considered as indirect credit). From 2013, loans extended to corporates, including

farmers' producer companies of individual farmers, partnership firms and cooperatives of farmers directly engaged in agriculture and allied activities (such as dairy, fishery, animal husbandry, poultry, beekeeping and sericulture – up to cocoon stage) of up to Rs 2 crore were fully included under direct credit. The rest was included under indirect credit.

Urbanization of Agricultural Credit

There was increased provision of agricultural credit by bank branches located in urban and metropolitan areas in the 2000s.[9] Agriculture is primarily a rural occupation, and most agricultural loans should typically be given by rural branches of banks. However, the share of agricultural credit outstanding from rural branches saw a fall in the 2000s (Table 7.8).

Let us here consider direct credit alone. Between 1995 and 2005, the share of direct credit to agriculture outstanding in rural branches fell

Table 7.8 *Share of agricultural credit outstanding, by population groups, by direct and indirect credit, India, 1995–2011* (per cent)

Year	Share of agricultural credit outstanding from branches				
	Rural	Semi-urban	Urban	Metropolitan	Total
Total agricultural credit					
1995	51.7	29.3	9.5	9.5	100.0
2005	43.0	26.4	11.7	19.0	100.0
2006	37.1	25.3	13.8	23.8	100.0
2011	37.9	29.0	18.4	14.7	100.0
Direct credit					
1995	56.5	31.2	8.2	4.0	100.0
2005	52.9	31.4	10.0	5.7	100.0
2006	48.0	32.0	12.6	7.5	100.0
2011	43.2	31.2	16.5	9.1	100.0
Indirect credit					
1995	23.9	18.5	16.8	40.8	100.0
2005	11.4	10.2	17.2	61.2	100.0
2006	9.1	7.8	17.0	66.0	100.0
2011	13.6	19.0	27.1	40.2	100.0

Note: On the periodization in this table, see notes in Table 7.1.
Source: Reserve Bank of India (RBI), 'Basic Statistical Returns of Scheduled Commercial Banks in India', various issues.

from 56.5 per cent to 52.9 per cent. Between 2006 and 2011, the corresponding shares fell from 48 per cent to 43.2 per cent. On the other hand, the share of direct credit outstanding in urban and metropolitan branches together rose from 12.2 per cent in 1995 to 15.7 per cent in 2005, and then from 20.1 per cent in 2006 to 25.6 per cent in 2011. Such a phenomenon implied a significant diversion of direct agricultural credit away from rural farmers, and towards urban-based dealers (as part of indirect credit) and urban-based corporates and joint-stock companies (as part of direct credit).

The urbanization of agricultural credit was clearly one of the most worrisome trends in the supply of agricultural credit in the 2000s. It corroborates the findings from the analysis of loans by size-classes of credit limit. It was argued that large loans typically indicate flow of agricultural credit away from farmers and crop cultivation *per se*, and indicate the rising importance of loans to large-scale, capital-intensive and export-oriented activities. It would appear that a large number of such loans were given out from urban and metropolitan branches of banks, where the headquarters of corporate entities involved in these activities are located.

The 'March' Phenomenon

The month-wise disbursement pattern of agricultural loans from commercial banks shows that most of the loans are disbursed in months with no agricultural activity. RBI does not publish data on month-wise disbursements, but a table in the 'Report of the Task Force on Credit Related Issues of Farmers', chaired by U. C. Sarangi, provides data for the year 2008–09 (see Table 7.9). According to the Report, about one-fourth (23.4 per cent) of the annual disbursement to agriculture by commercial banks was in the month of March; the Task Force noted this as 'a matter of serious concern' as March was 'not a critical month for agricultural production' (Ministry of Agriculture 2010: 34). Another 22.7 per cent of disbursement was in the months of January and February. Thus, together, about 46.2 per cent of all disbursements were in three months: January, February and March.

The Task Force suggested some reasons for this phenomenon. First, it noted that large disbursements might have been made to 'institutions' in these months. Secondly, there might have been significant disbursement of large loans through urban branches in metropolitan regions like Delhi and Chandigarh, but 'booked as agricultural lending'. Thirdly, there might have been 'window-dressing' by banks to meet government targets for credit, deposit and recovery. All these reasons listed by the Task Force corroborate the findings of this paper in earlier sections. The Task Force's findings were striking.

Table 7.9 *Share of agricultural credit disbursed, commercial banks, by month, India, 2008–09* (per cent)

Month	Share of agricultural credit disbursed
April	1.2
May	2.5
June	5.4
July	6.3
August	4.6
September	9.3
October	5.8
November	7.0
December	11.7
January	11.0
February	11.8
March	23.4
All months	100.0

Source: Ministry of Agriculture (2010).

The Task Force, while taking note of the doubling of agricultural credit, observed that *it did not reach large number of small and marginal farmers* who form the bulk of the farming community and are a critical contributor to the food security of the nation. Substantial loan disbursement by commercial banks takes place in March each year. It appears necessary to take a closer look at what is being termed 'agricultural' credit, especially by commercial banks. Given, too, that rather large 'agricultural' loans were being disbursed in urban centres, a closer look at who is being termed 'farmer' is also needed. (Ministry of Agriculture 2010: xviii)

Increasing Disconnect between Agricultural Credit and Agricultural Investment

Finally, changes in the nature of agricultural credit in the 2000s also led to a growing disconnect between credit and investment in agriculture. Two features of this disconnect are worth mentioning.

First, based on tenure, direct agricultural credit is classified into short-term and long-term credit. Short-term agricultural credit refers to credit given directly to cultivators for seasonal agricultural operations or

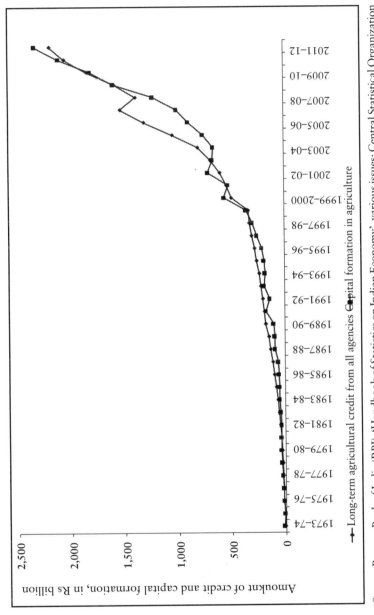

Figure 7.3 *Amount of long-term credit to agriculture and gross capital formation in agriculture, India, 1973–74 to 2011–12* (in Rs billion)

Source: Reserve Bank of India (RBI), 'Handbook of Statistics on Indian Economy', various issues; Central Statistical Organization (CSO), 'National Accounts Statistics', various issues.

Figure 7.4 *Share of short-term credit and long-term credit in direct agricultural credit, India, 1973–74 to 2013–14* (per cent)

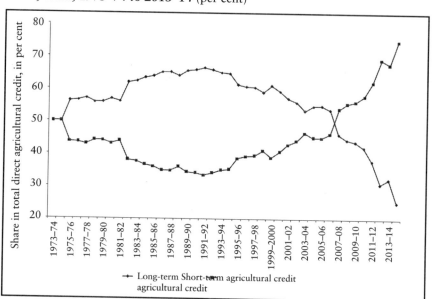

Source: Reserve Bank of India (RBI), 'Handbook of Statistics on Indian Economy', various issues.

Figure 7.5 *Trends in gross capital formation in agriculture and allied sectors and agricultural credit at current prices, 1973–74 to 2011–12, India* (Rs billion)

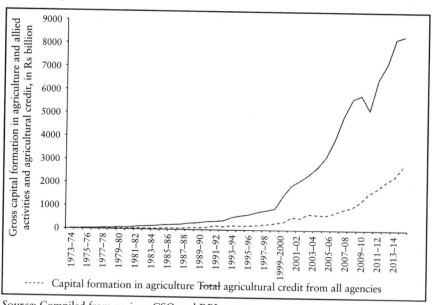

Source: Compiled from various CSO and RBI reports.

crop loans. Long-term agricultural credit indicates credit given directly to cultivators or producers in allied activities for minor irrigation, reclamation and land development, purchase of tractors and agricultural machinery, plantations, crop loans converted into term loans, and all loans given to allied activities like dairy, fishing, poultry and beekeeping.

Time-series data on long-term credit to agriculture and gross capital formation in agriculture shows an almost perfect positive association (Figure 7.3). Right from the 1970s itself, the plot of long-term credit has moved in perfect tandem with the plot of gross capital formation. Hence, any fall in long-term credit would have direct implications for investment in agriculture.

After 1991–92, right up to 2010–11, there was a sharp fall in the share of long-term credit (that aids investment) and a sharp rise in the share of short-term credit in the lending of commercial banks (Figure 7.4). In 1990–91, the share of long-term credit in total agricultural credit was about 66 per cent, which fell to 54.9 per cent in 2004–05 and 39.5 per cent in 2010–11. On the other hand, the share of short-term credit in total agricultural credit rose from 34.1 per cent in 1990–91 to 45.1 per cent in 2004–05 and 60.5 per cent in 2010–11. It is evident that the divergence between credit and investment in agriculture is a product of the changing composition of agricultural credit itself in the 1990s and 2000s (Chavan 2013).

Secondly, as a result, the difference between agricultural credit and gross capital formation in agriculture was insignificant till 2001–02 (Figure 7.5). Credit and capital formation were roughly at similar levels, and they also moved together every year. However, after 2001–02, trends in credit supply and gross capital formation began to diverge. From 2002–03 onwards, agricultural credit grew rapidly as compared to capital formation in agriculture, and the difference between the amounts of agricultural credit and agricultural capital formation grew. In other words, an increasingly smaller portion of credit supplied to agriculture was transformed into capital investment in agriculture in the 2000s.[10]

Concluding Points

An important feature of the trends in agricultural credit after 1991 is the revival of agricultural credit in the 2000s following a slowdown in the 1990s. After 2004, the government also announced a scheme to double the credit flow to agriculture over a period of three years. In this paper, our effort is to critically examine these changes using secondary data on commercial banks. In particular, our effort is to reconcile the results from two official sources: the first from the AIDIS, which showed a deterioration in the conditions of rural and cultivator households with respect to indebtedness; and the second from the RBI reports, which showed considerable expansion of rural bank branches and agricultural credit flow in the 2000s.

The paper points to a set of disquieting features in the supply of agricultural credit in the decade of the 2000s, which might help explain the paradoxical results from the AIDIS and the RBI. Here, we follow the suggestion offered by an official task force, chaired by the chairman of NABARD in 2010, that the doubling of agricultural credit 'did not reach large number of small and marginal farmers', and that 'a closer look at who is being termed "farmer" is . . . needed'.

First, even though the number of rural bank branches rose after 2005, it was unable to keep pace with the growth of the rural population. The rural population per bank branch in 2011 continued to be higher than it was in 1990 or 1995. The reduction of total population per branch was faster than the reduction of rural population per branch.

Secondly, the extent of revival would have been far less impressive in the absence of a sharp growth in indirect finance to agriculture. About one-fourth of the increase in agricultural credit between 2002 and 2010 was on account of an increase in indirect finance. Such growth did not originate from a growth in the traditional components of indirect finance, such as loans for the supply of inputs, power and credit to agriculture. On the contrary, the growth in indirect finance was the result of expansive changes in the definition of indirect finance since the late 1990s. These definitional changes broadly involved: (i) the addition of new forms of financing commercial, export-oriented and capital-intensive agriculture; (ii) raising the credit limit of many existing forms of indirect financing; and (iii) bringing loans given to corporates and partnership groups also into the ambit of agricultural credit. Indeed, meeting the task of doubling agricultural credit appears to have become much easier for banks as a result of these definitional changes.

Thirdly, a major driver of the revival of agricultural credit in the 2000s was the expansion of loans of large sizes. In fact, the share in total agricultural credit of loans of size less than Rs 25,000 fell from 58.7 per cent in 1990 to just 5.8 per cent in 2011. On the other hand, the corresponding share for loans of size above Rs 1 crore increased from 1.3 per cent in 1990 to 20.4 per cent in 2011. These large loans were advanced for financing the new activities – such as large agribusiness-oriented enterprises – added to the definition of direct and indirect advances since the late 1990s.

The increasing importance of large loans was apparent within direct credit to agriculture also. Taken together, the share in total direct credit of loans of size less than Rs 2 lakh fell from 92.2 per cent in 1990 to 78.5 per cent in 2000 and 48 per cent in 2011. In other words, the absolute amount constituted by loans of size above Rs 2 lakh exceeded the absolute amount constituted by loans of size below Rs 2 lakh. In 2011, the total supply of direct agricultural credit in India was Rs 3,77,991 crore. In the same year, only 41.4 per cent of the credit supply consisted of loans of size less than Rs 2 lakh. In other words, only less than Rs 1,90,862 crore is likely to have reached the farmers directly in 2011. The remaining Rs 2,70,158 crore is likely to have reached those not directly involved in agricultural production.

Fourthly, there was a major rise in the share of agricultural credit given out from urban and metropolitan branches of banks in the 2000s. In 2011, about 33 per cent of the total agricultural credit and about 26 per cent of direct agricultural credit were outstanding from commercial bank branches located in urban or metropolitan centres. At the same time, about 67 per cent of indirect finance was outstanding from branches located in urban or metropolitan centres. Following from the conclusions on the large sizes of loans, it becomes even more evident that there were major diversions of agricultural credit away from rural areas.

Fifthly, further corroborating the drifting of agricultural credit away from farmers, month-wise disbursement data showed that about 46 per cent of agricultural credit in 2008–09 was disbursed in the months January to March, which are not the normal periods of borrowal by farmers. About 23 per cent was disbursed in the month of March itself.

Sixthly, agricultural investment is closely associated with the disbursement of long-term loans to agriculture. However, after 1991, there was a sharp fall in the share of long-term agricultural loans, and a concomitant rise in the share of short-term agricultural loans, in total agricultural credit. Consequently, only an increasingly smaller portion of agricultural credit was transformed into capital investment in agriculture.

To conclude, the most important beneficiaries of the revival of agricultural credit in the 2000s were not farmers, who are direct producers in agriculture. The major beneficiaries were corporate groups, joint-stock companies and other organizations indirectly involved in agricultural production. Agricultural credit in the 2000s moved away from production *per se* and into post-production functions. In the 2000s, banks increasingly financed activities that aided the growth of specific sub-sectors within agriculture, which were large-scale, commercial, capital-intensive and export-oriented. In the 1990s and 2000s, these activities were also actively promoted by the government as part of a conscious shift in agricultural policy.

An earlier but slightly different version of this paper, co-authored with Pallavi Chavan, had appeared in the journal *Review of Agrarian Studies*, in 2013.

Notes

[1] The rise in the number of rural bank branches was an outcome of the policy of 'financial inclusion' adopted since 2005. The branch licensing policy was replaced by a 'branch authorization policy' in 2005. As part of the branch authorization policy, it was mandated that at least 25 per cent of new branches under the Annual Branch Expansion Plan (ABEP) of banks should be located in underbanked rural centres. Further, for each additional branch opened in tiers 2 to 6 (i.e. urban, semi-urban or rural centres), the banks were offered an incentive: they could open one branch in any metropolitan centre (tier 1 centres). Even here, the total number of branches opened in tier 1 centres was not to exceed the total number of branches proposed to be opened in tiers 2 to 6 centres.

[2] See also Ramakumar and Chavan (2007).

[3] According to Y.V. Reddy, the 'coverage of definition of priority sector lending has been broadened significantly in the recent years, thus overestimating credit flows to actual agricultural operations in recent years' (Reddy 2001: 5).

[4] To document the definitional changes, we have referred to the annual 'Master Circulars on Lending to Priority Sector' issued by the RBI in the month of July.

[5] However, in 2004, it was decided not to consider the investments made by banks after 1 April 2005 in the bonds of the Rural Electrification Corporation (REC) under indirect finance to agriculture.

[6] After 2007, the RBI has stopped reporting the figures for certain types of indirect credit, such as distribution of fertilizers and other inputs and loans to electricity boards. Hence, the comparison cannot be extended beyond 2007.

[7] It may be reiterated here that indirect finance to agriculture over and above 4.5 per cent of net bank credit is considered under total priority sector credit. This provision has provided an easy route for banks to meet the overall target set for priority sector credit.

[8] It is a different matter, however, that many of the changes in the definition of indirect finance to agriculture in 2004 were made on the basis of the report of the same Advisory Committee.

[9] On this point, see also Chakrabarty (2011).

[10] See also Ramakumar (2012).

References

Chakrabarty, K.C. (2011), 'Agricultural Productivity and Credit: Issues and Way Forward', speech delivered at the National Seminar on Productivity in Indian Agriculture, Pune, 2 September, available at http://www.rbi.org.in/scripts/BS_SpeechesView.aspx?Id=596, accessed on 15 December 2013.

Chavan, Pallavi (2002), 'Some Features of Rural Credit in India with Special Reference to Tamil Nadu: A Study of the Period after Bank Nationalization', MPhil thesis submitted to Indira Gandhi Institute of Development Research, Mumbai.

——— (2005), 'How "Inclusive" are Banks under Financial Liberalization?', *Economic and Political Weekly*, 40 (43), 22–28 October: 4647–49.

——— (2007), 'Access to Bank Credit: Implications for Rural Dalit Households', *Economic and Political Weekly*, 42 (31), 4–10 August: 3219–23.

——— (2009), 'How Rural is India's Agricultural Credit?', *The Hindu*, 13 August.

——— (2013), 'Credit and Capital Formation in Agriculture: A Growing Disconnect', *Social Scientist*, 41 (9–10), September–October: 59–67.

Indian Banks Association (IBA) (2008), 'Flow of Credit to Agriculture Sector: With Special Reference to Tenant Farmers, Oral Lessees and Agricultural Labourers', Report of the IBA Sub-Committee on Flow of Credit to Agriculture, Department of Social Banking, Mumbai.

Ministry of Agriculture (2007), 'Agricultural Credit', in *Annual Report: 2006–07*, New Delhi, available at http://agricoop.nic.in/AnnualReport06-07/AGRICULTURAL%20 CREDIT.pdf.

——— (2010), *Report of the Task Force on Credit-Related Issues of Farmers* (Chairman: U.C. Sarangi), submitted to the Ministry of Agriculture, Government of India, New Delhi.

——— (2007), 'Budget 2007–08: Speech of P. Chidambaram, Minister of Finance', New Delhi, 28 February, available at http://indiabudget.nic.in/ub2007-08/bs/speecha. htm.

National Bank for Agriculture and Rural Development (NABARD) (2013), *Annual Report 2012–13*, Mumbai.

Ramachandran, V.K. and Madhura Swaminathan, eds (2005), *Financial Liberalization and Rural Credit in India*, New Delhi: Tulika Books.

Ramakumar, R. (2012), 'Large-scale Investments in Agriculture in India', *IDS Bulletin*, 43 (1), Special Issue: *Standing on the Threshold: Food Justice in India*, July: 92–103.

Ramakumar, R. and Pallavi Chavan (2007), 'Revival of Agricultural Credit in the 2000s: An Explanation', *Economic and Political Weekly*, 42 (52), 29 December: 57–64.

——— (2011), 'Changes in the Number of Rural Bank Branches in India, 1991 to 2008', *Review of Agrarian Studies*, 1 (1), January–June: 141–48.

Reddy, Y.V. (2001), 'Indian Agriculture and Reform: Concerns, Issues and Agenda', *RBI Bulletin*, May, https://rbi.org.in/Scripts/BS_ViewBulletin.aspx?Id=2670.

Reserve Bank of India (RBI) (1991), *Report of the Committee on Financial Systems* (Chairman: M. Narasimham), Mumbai.

——— (2004), *Report of the Advisory Committee on Flow of Credit to Agriculture and Related Activities from the Banking System* (Chairman: V.S. Vyas), Mumbai.

Shetty, S.L. (2006), 'Policy Responses to the Failure of Formal Banking Institutions to Expand Credit Delivery for Agriculture and Non-farm Informal Sectors: The Ground Reality and Tasks Ahead', revised version of paper presented at seminar, Monthly Seminar Series on India's Financial Sector, 14 November, ICRIER, New Delhi.

8

Framing a Sustainable Development Policy for Indian Agriculture

U. Sankar

Introduction

In the context of the international community adopting sustainable development goals for the period 2015–30, there is growing awareness that 'the economy is embedded in a society and culture that are themselves embedded in an ecological life-support system' (Costanza *et al.* 2012). There is also recognition of the importance of conserving and sustaining natural capital because some components of natural capital are not substitutable by other forms of capital, and the greater dependence of the poor on natural resources for their livelihood. Two recent studies provide some evidence of the decline in India's natural capital. Arrow *et al.* (2012) find that in India between 1995 and 2000, reproducible capital grew at an annual rate of 7.3 per cent and human capital grew at a rate of 2.99 per cent, but natural capital grew at a rate of –0.16 per cent. Mani *et al.* (2012) note that in India, 'economic expansion is also often accompanied by rising demands on the already scarce and often degraded natural resources (soils, fossil fuels, water and forests) and the increasing pollution footprint will negatively impact human health and growth prospects', and that 'environmental sustainability could become the next major economic challenge as India surges along its growth trajectory'. They provide low and high estimates of environmental damage in billion rupees: degradation of croplands (4,80,910), of water supply, sanitation and hygiene (4,75,610), pastures (2,10,600), and forests (70,196).

The agricultural sector plays an important role in India not only in ensuring food security and in meeting industry demands for agricultural raw materials, but also in providing employment for 52.9 per cent of the total workforce.[1] The green revolution of the 1960s enabled India to achieve self-sufficiency in foodgrains. For the period 1950–51 to 2013–14, the compound annual growth rate of foodgrains production was 2.62 per cent while the compound annual growth rate of population was 1.95 per cent. India has become a net exporter of agricultural products. In 2012–13, the share of agricultural exports in agricultural gross domestic product (GDP) was 14.10 per cent while that of imports was 6.10 per cent (Government of India 2014a). However, the high water intensity and intensity of chemical fertilizers and pesticides have resulted in environmental damage to natural resources such as land, water, biodiversity and many ecosystem services.

M.S. Swaminathan forewarned in 1990:

> Intensive cultivation of land without conservation of soil fertility and soil structure would lead, ultimately, to the springing up of deserts. Irrigation without arrangements for drainage would result in soils getting alkaline and or saline. Indiscriminate use of pesticides, fungicides and herbicides could cause adverse changes in biological balance as well as lead to an increase in the incidence of cancer and other diseases, through toxic residues present in the grains or other edible parts. Unscientific tapping of groundwater will lead to the rapid exhaustion of this wonderful capital resource left to us through ages and natural farming. The rapid replacement of numerous locally adopted varieties with one or two high-yielding strains in large contiguous areas would result in the spread of diseases capable of wiping out the entire crops. (Swaminathan 2005)

Further, since most of the degraded and desertified lands belong to resource-poor farmers or are over-used and over-grazed commons, 'what nations with small farmers and resource-poor farmers need is the enhancement of productivity in perpetuity without associated ecological or social harm. The Green Revolution should become an *ever-green revolution* rooted in the principles of ecology, economics, and social gender equality' (ibid.).

The United Nations Conference on Sustainable Development (UNCSD) held at Rio de Janeiro in June 2012 urged the need for weighing and balancing the three pillars – economic, social and environmental – of sustainable development in policy formulation and implementation (UNCSD 2012). The need for considering locally appropriate institutional pillars was also recognized.

Design and implementation of policies for sustainable agriculture must recognize the multi-functionality of agriculture, the synergies and trade-offs among multiple goals, planetary boundaries and ecological constraints. The International Assessment of Agricultural Knowledge, Science and Technology for Development (IAAKSTD) (2009) uses multi-functionality of agriculture 'to express the inescapable interconnectedness of agriculture's different related functions and recognize agriculture as a multi-output activity producing not only commodities (food, feed, fibre, agrofuels, medicinal products and ornamentals) but also non-commodity outputs such as environmental services, landscape amenities and cultural services.'[2] These outputs/services are jointly produced and some of the non-commodity outputs/services exhibit the characteristics of externalities or public goods, and markets for these services function poorly or are non-existent. Agricultural ecosystems rely on ecosystem services provided by natural ecosystems including pollination, biological pest control, maintenance of soil structure and fertility, nutrient cycling and hydrological services, regulation of soil and water quality, and carbon sequestration.

When there are multiple goals and there are significant interactive effects among them, policy design becomes complex. Tinbergen (1952) suggested as many instruments as there are goals; however, he felt the need for supplementary or complementary tools to control side effects. With multiple goals, the problem of weighing and balancing benefits and costs of implementing policies assumes significance. This task will be easier if all the private, social and environmental costs and benefits can be expressed in a common monetary unit.[3] The difficulty arises both in valuation and implementation. Markets can be relied upon for valuation if the markets are perfect and the goods provided are 'private goods', but agricultural markets are not perfect because of government intervention in the supply of critical inputs and pricing; also, equity consideration is involved in the supply of inputs/outputs for the small farmers and the poor. Negative externalities arising from certain agricultural practices and positive externalities arising from certain ecosystem services are not captured in conventional cost and benefit estimates.[4]

In terms of the Millennium Ecosystems Assessment classification, markets do not exist for many regulating, supporting and cultural services. As most regulating and supporting services exhibit characteristics of 'public goods', public provision or a non-market mechanism is needed to ensure adequate supply. Another peculiar feature of agricultural policy is that it must be location-specific and hence there is a case for using local/indigenous knowledge in decision-making. Policies to deal with externalities such as eco-restoration, carbon sequestration, switch from modern farming to organic farming, and landscaping require a long time horizon (and hence low discount rate) to yield desirable results. As suggested by Costanza *et al.* (2012), we need a full-cost accounting system to internalize externalities, value non-market assets, reform the accounting system, and ensure that prices reflect actual social and environmental costs of production. This full-cost accounting system would enable a conscious and transparent assessment of trade-offs among the three pillars in devising public policies to promote sustainable development.

This paper reviews past agricultural policies relating to land, water, fertilizers and pesticides, organic farming, technology development and agriculture's linkages to ecosystem services, and their current status. It assesses the extent to which the full costs and benefits are captured in the accounting and the prices, and suggests what needs to be done to achieve sustainable development of Indian agriculture. The second section deals with availability of land – quantity and quality – and measures needed to augment this natural capital. The third section deals with the supply of irrigation water, and considers measures to conserve water and reduce water intensity of output. The fourth section reviews past policies relating to fertilizer and pesticide use, their impact on government budget and the environment. Issues relating to promotion of organic farming are addressed in the fifth section. The sixth section looks at the type of technology development in the past and considers reorientation to achieve agricultural sustainability. The seventh section deals with linkages between agricultural ecosystem and other ecosystems. The last section contains concluding remarks.

Land

The total geographical area of India is 328.2 million hectares. The net sown area increased 18 per cent between 1950–51 and 1970–71, and has remained almost constant at 140 million hectares from 1970–71 (see Table 8.1). Between 1950–51 and 2013–14, gross cropped area increased by 48 per cent, and cropping intensity increased from 1.11 in 1950–51 to 1.35 in 2013–14. The area under irrigation increased more than four times. The share of irrigated area in gross cropped area in 2013–14 was 46.88 per cent. Land is becoming increasingly scarce due to population growth and the demand for land for agricultural and non-agricultural uses. Groundwater is over-extracted. The potential for additional major irrigation is limited.

Land Degradation

Article 1 of the United Nations Convention to Combat Desertification (2012) defines land degradation as

> reduction or loss of the biological or economic productivity and complexity of rained cropland, irrigated cropland range, pastors, forests and woodlands resulting from land uses or from processes such as (i) soil erosion caused by wind and/or water (ii) deterioration of the physical, chemical and biological or economic properties of soils and (iii) long-term losses of natural vegetation.

Table 8.1 *Net sown area, gross cropped area and gross irrigated area, 1950–51 to 2013–14*

	Net sown area		Gross cropped area		Gross irrigated area	
	Mha*	Index 50–51 = 100	Mha	Index 50–51 = 100	Mha	Index 50–51 = 100
1950–51	118.75	100.00	131.89	100.00	22.56	100.00
1960–61	133.20	112.17	152.77	115.83	27.98	124.02
1970–71	140.86	118.62	165.79	125.70	38.20	169.33
1980–81	140.29	118.14	172.63	130.89	49.38	218.88
1990–91	143.00	120.42	185.75	140.84	63.20	280.14
2000–01	141.34	119.02	185.34	140.53	76.19	337.72
2010–11	141.56	119.21	197.32	149.61	89.63	397.30
2013–14	140.80	118.57	195.25	148.04	91.53	405.72
CAGR**	0.28%		0.64%		6.65%	

Notes: * Million hectares; ** Compound annual growth rate.
Source: Government of India (2014a).

The Indian Council of Agricultural Research (ICAR) and National Academy of Agricultural Sciences (NAAS) (2010) prepared harmonized statistics of degraded and wastelands in India. Table 8.2 gives information about types of degradation for arable land and open forest. Degraded and wastelands account for 37 per cent of the geographical area. Wind erosion and water erosion account for 79 per cent of the degradation, followed by chemical degradation (20 per cent) and physical degradation (1 per cent). Soil erosion lowers crop productivity and causes environmental damages. This report classifies degraded and wastelands under nineteen categories for each of twenty agri-ecological zones. This information is useful for planning reclamation, rehabilitation and eco-restoration in degraded and wastelands.

Three approaches are being used for estimating costs of degradation: productivity approach, preventive cost approach and replacement cost approach (Mythili and Goedecke 2016). The productivity approach compares the yield loss before and after degradation. It is a narrow measure. The replacement cost approach aims at estimating the cost of restoration to the original situation; in some situations this cost may be prohibitive. The authors use the total economic value approach to assess the costs and benefits, and find that in many cases the cost of action is cheaper than the cost of inaction. Once the full cost is known, the next question is, who is going to bear the cost? The rehabilitated/restored land may produce a

Table 8.2 *Harmonized area statistics of degraded and wastelands in India*

Type of degradation	Arable land (Mha)	Open forest (< 40% canopy) (Mha)	Total
1. Water erosion (> 10 tonnes/ha/yr)	73.27	9.30	82.57
Wind erosion (Aeolian)	12.40	–	12.40
Total (1)	85.67	9.30	94.97
2. Chemical degradation			
Exclusively salt- affected soils	5.44		5.44
Salt-affected and water eroded-soils	1.20	0.10	1.30
Exclusively acidic soils (pH< 5.5)	5.09		5.09
Acidic (pH<5.5) and water-eroded soils	5.72	7.13	12.85
Total (2)	17.45	7.23	24.68
3. Physical degradation			
Mining and industrial waste	0.19		0.19
Waterlogging (permanent surface inundation)	0.88		0.88
Total (3)	1.07		1.07
Total	**104.19**	**16.53**	**120.72**

Source: ICAR and NAAS (2010): 25.

private good, merit good or public good (local, regional or global). The land may be under private ownership, or under public ownership, or under common property with open or closed access. Institutional options for managing the restored land including public–private partnership and self-governing community-based organizations need exploration.

Bhattacharyya *et al.* (2015) analyse the causes of land degradation and recommend the following strategies to mitigate land degradation: soil erosion control, water harvesting, terracing and other engineering structures, intercropping, contour farming, watershed approach, integrated nutrition management, organic manuring, reclamation of acid salt-affected soils and drainage and conservation agriculture. The costs and benefits of these options and the trade-offs among the three pillars must be studied before an option is chosen.

Water

India has 18 per cent of the world's population but only 4 per cent of the world's renewable water. According to the Ministry of Water

Resources Strategic Plan (2011), utilizable water works out to only 1,123 billion cubic metres (BCM), out of which about 690 BCM is from surface water and about 433 BCM from groundwater. The per capita consumption fell from 5,177 cubic metres in 1951 to 1,820 cubic metres in 2001, and is likely to be 1,341 cubic metres in 2025. Irrigation accounts for 83 per cent of water use. The irrigation potential created is 108.2 million hectares (major and medium 45.26, minor surface water 15.84 and groundwater 47.11).

Water is being degraded because of discharge of untreated municipal and industrial effluents in water bodies, run-off from agricultural lands using chemical fertilizers and pesticides, and decline in groundwater quality due to over-extraction. The Central Pollution Control Board's (2013) monitoring of India's national aquatic resources shows that organic pollution continues to be the predominant form of pollution of aquatic resources. It finds that 63 per cent of the observations have biological oxygen demand (an indicator of oxygen-consuming substances) < 3 mg/ml, 19 per cent between 3 and 6 mg/ml and 18 per cent above 6 mg/ml. As for total coliform, 44–53 per cent have < 500 Most Probable Number (MPN)/100 ml; 28–39 per cent have between 500 and 5,000 MPN/100 ml; and 9–24 per cent have > 5,000 MPN/100 ml. As for faecal coliform, 48–70 per cent have < 500 MPN/100 ml; 20–35 per cent have between 500 and 5,000 MPN/100 ml; and 7–21 per cent have above 5,000 MPN/100 ml. Total coliform and faecal coliform are indicators of pathogenic bacteria.

It finds gradual deterioration in water quality from 1995 to 2011. As for groundwater, about 15 per cent of the assessment blocks are over-exploited, and about 14.5 per cent of the assessment blocks fall in the category of critical and semi-critical stages. NASA's Gravity Recovery and Climate Experiment (GRACE) study shows that groundwater is being depleted across northern India at the rate of 54 sq. km per year due to pumping for irrigation (World Bank 2010).

The Central Water Commission (2014) provides the following guidelines for improving water use efficiency in irrigation:

Conveyance
    – through linked canal for surface water   55–60.5 per cent
    – through lined canal for surface water   70–75 per cent
Flow irrigation   65.0 per cent
Furrow irrigation   80.0 per cent
Sprinkler irrigation   85.5 per cent
Drip irrigation   90.0 per cent

The National Water Policy Statement 1987 stated that water rates should be such as 'to convey the scarcity value of the resource to the user and to foster the motivation for economy in water use. They should be adequate to cover the annual maintenance and operation charges and a part of the fixed costs of irrigation works'. The Vaidyanathan Committee (Government of India 1992) observed that 'it is difficult to accept the case for subsidizing such user-oriented and capital-intensive infrastructure as irrigation'. It recommended a two-part tariff – a flat annual fee on a per hectare basis and a variable fee linked to the extent of the service (volume or area).The National Water Policy Statement 2002 said that the water charges for various uses should be fixed in such a way that they cover at least the maintenance and operation charges initially and a part of the capital costs subsequently. It suggested that the subsidy on water rates for the disadvantaged and poorer sections of the society should be well-targeted and transparent.

Despite various finance commissions' and official committees' recommendations on the need to ensure that the irrigation charges paid by farmers are adequate at least to cover the operational expenses and a part of capital cost, the situation has been far from satisfactory. The Central Water Commission (2010) reports that the present scenario is characterized by a subsidized price structure, infrequent and hesitant price revision, no provision in the water rates for automatic revision on account of inflation, and ineffectiveness of the governmental machinery in revenue collection. The time that has elapsed since the last revision of water rates in four states has exceeded twenty years, and ten years in most other states.[5] Many irrigation systems are operating at levels much below their capacity on account of poor maintenance and continued neglect.

There is ample scope for using water-saving technologies such as sprinkler irrigation and drip irrigation. These technologies are scale-neutral. The capital cost depends on type of soil, crop cultivated, spacing, proximity to water source and materials used. Narayanamoorthy (2009) reports advantages of drip irrigation over flow method of irrigation, such as water saving, higher yield, less weed problem and less soil erosion. The initial capital cost is high in drip irrigation, but he finds that drip irrigation is economically viable even without government subsidy. The main barrier to the adoption of drip irrigation is the lack of incentive for farmers to minimize costs because of subsidized water (zero marginal price of water in many areas). Lack of awareness about the social value of water and its scarcity is another factor responsible for the low adoption rate.

There is scope for augmenting water supply via rainwater harvesting, flood control, water recharge, and waste water treatment and re-use.

Remote sensing-based inputs have been useful in many areas of water resources development, planning and management.

As water is a scarce input, and as it is an essential commodity in consumption and production, conservation of water and reduction in water intensity/water footprint requires immediate policy action. Issues relating to water governance such as augmenting supply, demand management, pricing of water for different uses, adaptation to climate change and signalling scarcity value of water require immediate action. Water prices for different uses must reflect their social scarcity values. Subsidized water must be targeted only towards the poor.

Fertilizers and Pesticides

The green revolution of the mid-1960s increased the demand for chemical fertilizers for cultivation of high-yielding crop varieties. Fertilizer consumption increased by 11.24 times between 1970–71 and 2013–14. This increase was largely due to the subsidized prices of chemical fertilizers. As the subsidy for nitrogen fertilizer was higher than for potash and phosphate, there was over-use of urea. Compared with an ideal NPK (nitrogen–phosphorus–potassium) mix of 4:2:1, the actual mix was much higher than the ideal in Punjab. In 2013–14, the average mix for the country was 7.6:4.8:1.

Chemical fertilizers contributed to increases in yields of high-yielding varieties, thereby achieving the goal of food security. However, over-reliance on chemical fertilizers cause environmental problems like eutrophication of surface water, nitrate (NO3-) pollution of groundwater,

Table 8.3 *Fertilizer consumption in India*

Year	Nitrogen (thousand tonnes)	Phosphate (thousand tonnes)	Potash (thousand tonnes)	Total (thousand tonnes)
1950–51	58.7	6.9	–	65.6
1960–61	210.0	53.1	29.0	292.1
1970–71	1,487.0	462.0	228.0	2,177.0
1980–81	3,678.1	1,213.6	623.9	5,515.6
1990–91	7,997.2	3,221.0	1,328.0	12,546.2
2000–01	10,920.2	41,214.6	1,567.5	16,702.3
2010–11	16,558.2	8,049.7	3,514.3	28,122.2
2013–14	16,750.1	5,633.5	2,098.9	24,482.4

Source: Government of India (2014a).

heavy metal pollution of soil, atmospheric pollution due to emission of nitrate oxide and ammonia, acid rain, etc. Also, about 50 per cent of applied fertilizer nutrients are lost to the environment. In many places, nitrate pollution of groundwater exceeded the permissible limit of 45 mg/ml.

The government adopted the cost plus retention pricing scheme for fertilizer in the 1970s to protect farmers from the vagaries of crude oil prices and to ensure food security.[6] The price of urea was highly subsidized. Urea contains 46 per cent nitrogen; only about a third is used and the rest gets into groundwater or escapes into the atmosphere. As oil prices flared in 2008–09, fertilizer input prices – natural gas and naphtha used as feedstock – spiked. The subsidy bill increased to Rs 99,500 crore from Rs 43,000 crore in 2007–08. It was realized that this pricing policy was financially and environmentally unsustainable. In April 2010, the government decontrolled all fertilizers except urea; it scrapped the corruption-prone cost plus retention price scheme and replaced it with a nutrient-based subsidy system, and the list of nutrients eligible for subsidy was expanded to include sulphur, boron and zinc. In the budget of 2011, the Finance Minister announced that the subsidy will, in time, be given to farmers as a direct cash transfer.

Urea is highly subsidized: according to the *Economic Survey 2013–14*, farmers pay Rs 5,360 per tonne and government pays Rs 11,760 per tonne. Subsidies for other fertilizers have been capped since 2010 under the nutrient-based subsidy scheme. It says that the incremental output of the excess 4.2 units of nitrogen is zero or somewhat negative. It says that the fertilizer subsidy hurts everyone: farms, farmers, tax payers and consumers. Social sustainability can be taken care of by targeting subsidies towards marginal and small farmers directly using new technologies, i.e. biometric identification, mobile phones for targeting poor farmers and giving them cash transfers.

It is desirable to recognize the environmental costs of chemical fertilizers in tax policy by levying higher taxes on chemical fertilizers, and zero taxes and even provision of subsidies for biofertilizers. Biofertilizers nourish the beneficial micro-organisms in the soil and increase the soil's humus content. Unlike chemical fertilizers, biofertilizers are produced from renewable resources. Their disadvantage is that they contribute to increase in yield slowly. Biofertilizers can be combined with chemical fertilizers in the integrated plant nutrient system. To discourage overuse of chemical fertilizers some European countries tax chemical fertilizers and subsidize biofertilizers. Chelliah *et al.* (2007) recommended (i) reduction in subsidy for chemical fertilizers; (ii) capital subsidy for investment in R&D (research and development) to identify more suitable strains, and to develop better production technology and quality control methods for biofertilizers; and (iii) undertaking extension work in respect of use of biofertilizers.

India is the third largest user of chemical pesticides in the world. Spraying of chemical pesticides results in residues in drinking water, vegetables, fruits, milk, etc. Some pesticides are hazardous to human and animal health. Biopesticides are produced using renewable resources. The market for biopesticides is only about 1 per cent of the crop protection market. Chelliah *et al.* recommended the levy of an eco tax on chemical pesticides based on toxicity levels, and a reduction in the excise duty on biopesticides.

Organic Farming

According to the Food and Agriculture Organization (FAO) (2013), organic agriculture is a unique production management system that promotes and enhances agro-ecosystem health, including biodiversity, biological cycles and soil biological activity, and this is accomplished by using on-farm agronomic, biological and mechanical methods to the exclusion of all synthetic off-farm inputs. There is growing awareness that organic farming is sustainable. Its advantages are healthy food, improvement in soil quality, low incidence of pests, crop diversity, prevention of soil erosion and greater rural employment. This policy has the following thrust areas:

- Maintaining soil fertility by using natural resources
- Biological control of pests and diseases
- Biological and mechanical control of weeds
- Harnessing of technology and innovation
- Area approach
- Identification of crops: horticultural crops and export-oriented cereals like basmati rice, sorghum, pearl millets, pulses, soybean, groundnut, cotton, chillies, garlic, turmeric, coriander and ginger
- Employment generation
- Market development and domestic certification.

The National Project on Organic Farming, implemented from October 2004, envisages technical capacity building, information generation, technology development and dissemination, awareness creation, input production and quality control facilitation. The Organic Agricultural Produce Grading and Marking Rules were introduced in 2009. National standards for crop production, animal husbandry and beekeeping are available. Certification, a quality assurance initiative and accreditation standards exist. A Smallholder Group Certification scheme is also available.

The National Project on Management of Soil Health and Fertility

(NPMSH&F) aims to promote soil test-based balanced and judicious use of chemical fertilizers in conjunction with organic manures like farm yard manure (FYM), vermicompost and green manure to maintain soil health and fertility. The scheme was initiated in 2008–09. The major activities under the scheme are strengthening of soil testing services, promoting use of integrated nutrient management, strengthening of fertilizer testing services, and strengthening and modernization of pest management approach.

In India, as on March 2009, the total area under organic certification process was only 12 lakh acres. At present, India is exporting a few organic products such as basmati rice, coffee, tea and horticultural products. There is a need to scale up the efforts to increase the area under organic farming, improve productivity of organic crops and gain access to export markets. The FAO has attempted harmonization of national organic standards which are essential for global trade in organic products. The FAO and WHO (World Health Organization) has evolved Codex Alimentarius for organic products. Global sales of organic agricultural products were about $51 billion in 2008 as compared to $25 billion in 2003.

In India, farming techniques practised before the green revolution were basically eco-friendly, and they have not faded from the memories of the present elder generation of our farming community. In dry areas in most parts of the country, farmers still practise traditional farming methods. There are many hurdles to switch to organic farming. First, the yield rates for organic crops are generally lower than that for crops under modern farming. Secondly, due to lack of consumer awareness, the price premiums for organic products in domestic markets are low. Thirdly, the existing prices for non-organic products do not include external production costs and hence their prices are below their social costs. The low yield rate and small or no price premiums imply low short-run profitability for organic farmers. It is true that the long-run profitability of organic farming may be higher than modern farming, but the discount rates for farmers are high. Fourthly, most small farmers face market access problems because of poor post-harvesting facilities and high transaction costs of entry into organic markets. Fifthly, special programmes are needed to augment the supplies of organic inputs like biomass.

Development of Technology

The experiences of India as well as other developing countries in adopting high-yielding varieties (HYV) and modern biotechnology during the past four decades reveal that these changes did not benefit small and marginal farmers (IAAKSTD 2009). These technologies were confined to rice, wheat and maize, and to irrigated areas. They eliminated many traditional crop varieties and reduced biodiversity. IAAKSTD states that

> the institutional coupling between industry and university has encour-
> aged a steady narrowing of agricultural research agencies to funding on
> modern biotechnology. . . . The increasing influence of agrochemical
> and seed corporations over public sector agricultural research agencies
> risk weakening public institutions ability to fulfill their mandate to serve
> the public good.

It makes the following recommendations:

- Engage all stakeholders in open, informed, transparent and parti-
  cipatory debate about new and emerging biotechnologies.
- Introduce long-term environmental and health monitoring provisions, and conduct comparative technology assessment to better
  understand the respective risk, benefits and costs of different
  technologies and production systems.
- Use the precautionary approach in decision-making as per the
  Cartagena Protocol.
- Limit production of genetically modified organism (GMO) plants
  in regions that have wild relatives and show botanical characteristics that could contaminate the gene pool.
- Build institutions to support social equity and sustainability.

Linkages between Agriculture and Other Ecosystem Services

In policy formulation, it is important to recognize the ecosystem
services flowing to agriculture from other ecosystems, and ecosystem
services and disservices flowing from agriculture to other ecosystems,
understand the trade-offs, and develop environmentally sound agricultural
management practices to maximize the synergies and minimize the trade-
offs. Power (2010) explains the services flowing to agriculture from other
ecosystems under (i) biological pest control, (ii) pollination, (iii) water
quantity and quality, (iv) soil structure and fertility, and (v) landscape
influences on the delivery of ecosystem services to agriculture. Most of
these services are non-marketed; payment for ecosystem services like clean
water and pollination are being attempted in a few countries. Power men-
tions the following environmental disservices flowing from agriculture: (i)
loss of biodiversity, (ii) agricultural contamination and sedimentation of
water bodies, (iii) pesticide poisoning of non-target organisms, and (iv)
emissions of greenhouse gases and pollutants. It is possible to mitigate the
negative effects via agri-environmental policies incentivizing farmers and
public investment in ecosystem services.

Concluding Remarks

Our review of past agricultural policies shows that economic goals, particularly increasing food production to achieve self-sufficiency, have played a dominant role in policy-making. This is evident in policies such as development of HYVs, supply of irrigation water from major projects and electricity for pumpsets, and fertilizers at subsidized prices. Social considerations, i.e. equity, played a role in the establishment of a public distribution system (PDS) for foodgrains. This is because it is easier to frame policies with a single objective as it requires less information and is easier to monitor. Even in these cases, the means of implementation are questionable as they weakened the incentives for farmers to conserve scarce resources and avoid environmental damages from excessive use of the inputs, and PDS resulted in many leakages, wastages and inefficiencies.

Environment, the third pillar of sustainable development, has played no role in the formulation of agricultural policies. This neglect is partly due to lack of information on environmental costs and benefits in our national and regional accounting systems, and the difficulty in evaluating the trade-offs among the three pillars. Lately, India has developed the scientific capacity to gather information about the stocks and flows in natural capital via space-based and land-based statistics (e.g., the National Natural Resources Management System's harmonized statistics on land degradation), and initiated steps to develop green accounts (e.g., the Dasgupta report on green national accounts) and value ecosystems (The Economics of Ecosystems and Biodiversity). The National Environment Policy (2006) articulated India's environmental challenges, need for enhancing and conserving environmental resources, and policy reforms. The twelfth plan, chapter 4 on sustainable development notes that 'Economic growth and development have to be guided by the consideration of sustainability, because none of us has the luxury, any longer, of ignoring the economic as well as the environmental threat that a fast-deteriorating economic system poses to our fragile environment' (p. 112). The *Economic Survey 2013–14* contains a chapter titled 'Sustainable Development and Climate Policy'.

It is time to phase out subsidies for irrigation water, electricity for agricultural pumpsets, chemical fertilizers and pesticides, and the savings ploughed back as investment into ecosystem services. Attempts should also be made to implement payments for ecosystem services like clean water, pollination and carbon sequestration wherever feasible. Economists working together with scientists, policymakers and the affected people can provide valuable inputs in framing sustainable development policies, and weighing and balancing the three pillars.

Notes

[1] The share of agriculture in GDP fell from 41.8 per cent in 1951–52 to 11.8 per cent in 2012–13, but the share of employment is still high.

[2] The European Union uses agri-environment measures to protect and enhance the farm environment via payment to farmers for the following services: environment-friendly farm extension, management of low intensity pasture system, integrated farm management, organic farming, preservation of landscape and conservation of high value habitats. These measures also aim at shifting subsidies from amber box to green box.

[3] Intangibles cannot be assigned monetary values.

[4] Even the most comprehensive cost measure, C3, used by the Commission on Agricultural Costs and Prices (CACP) excludes the environmental costs of crop production.

[5] Competitive populism prevents price revisions. The worsening of state finances prompted the central government to add a new term of reference to the 14th Finance Commission: 'consider the need to insulating the pricing of public utility services like drinking water, irrigation, power and public transport from policy fluctuations through statutory measures'.

[6] This amounts to producer subsidy and weakens the incentive to minimize cost of production.

References

Arrow, K.J., P. Dasgupta, L.H. Goulder, K.J. Mumford and K. Oleson (2012), 'Sustainability and the Measurement of Wealth', *Environment and Development Economics*, 17 (3): 317–53.

Bhattacharyya, R., B.N. Ghosh, P.K. Mishra, B. Manda, C.S. Rao, D. Sarkar, K. Das, K.S. Anil, M. Lalitha, K.M. Hati and A.J. Fraanzlubbas (2015), 'Soil Degradation in India: Challenges and Potential Solutions', *Sustainability*, 7 (4): 3528–70, available at www.mdpi.com/journal/sustainability, accessed on 2 January 2016.

Central Pollution Control Board (2013), *Status of Water Quality in India*, Monitoring of Indian National Aquatic Resources Series: MINARS/35/2013–14, New Delhi: Central Pollution Control Board.

Chelliah, R.J., P. Appasamy, U. Sankar and R. Pandey (2007), *Ecotaxes on Polluting Inputs and Outputs*, New Delhi: Academic Foundation.

Central Water Commission (2013), *Pricing of Water in Public Distribution in India*, New Delhi: Ministry of Water Resources, Government of India.

——— (2014), *Guidelines for Improving Water Use Efficiency in Irrigation, Domestic and Industrial Sectors*, New Delhi: Ministry of Water Resources, Government of India.

Costanza, R., G. Alperovite, H.E. Daly, J. Farley, C. Frady, T. Jackson, I. Kubiszewski, J. Schor and P. Victor (2012), 'Building a Sustainable and Desirable Economy-in-Society-in-Nature', Report to the UN for the 2012 Rio+20 Conference.

Dasgupta, P. (2013), *Green National Accounts in India*, New Delhi: Ministry of Statistics and Programme Implementation, Government of India.

Food and Agriculture Organization (FAO), *Organic Agriculture*, available at www.fao.org/orgagriag/oa-hme/en, accessed on 30 December 2015.

Government of India (Ministry of Agriculture) (2014a), *Indian Agricultural Statistics at a Glance*, New Delhi: Oxford University Press.

Government of India (Ministry of Finance) (2014b), *Economic Survey 2013–14*, New Delhi.

Government of India (Planning Commission) (1992), *Report of the Committee on Pricing of Irrigation Water* (Chairman: A. Vaidyanathan), New Delhi.

——— (2012), *Twelfth Five Year Plan*, New Delhi.

Indian Council of Agricultural Research (ICAR) and National Academy of Agricultural

Sciences (NAAS) (2010), *Degradation and Wastelands of India: Status and Spatial Distribution*, New Delhi: ICAR.

International Assessment of Agricultural Knowledge, Science and Technology for Development (2009), *Synthesis Global and Regional Reports*, Washington, D.C.: Island Press, available at www.agassessment.org, accessed on 10 November 2015.

Millennium Ecosystems Assessment (2005), *Ecosystems and Human-Well-being Synthesis*, Washington, D.C.: Island Press.

Mani, M., A. Markandya, A. Sagar and E. Strukov (2012), 'An Analysis of Physical and Monetary Losses of Environmental Health and Natural Resources in India', Policy Research Working Paper 6219, *Ecology and Society*, 14 (2), Washington, D.C.: World Bank. Also in K.R. Shanmugam and K.S. Kavi Kumar, eds, *Environment and Development: Essays in Honour of U. Sankar* (2016), New Delhi: Sage Publications.

Mythili, G. and J. Goedecke (2016), 'Economics of Land Degradation in India', in E. Nkonya *et al.*, eds, *Economics of Land Degradation and Improvement: A Global Assessment for Sustainable Development*, Springer Open: New York.

Narayanamoorthy, A. (2009), *Water Saving Technologies with Demand Management Options: Potentials, Problems and Prospects*, available at www.iwmi.cgiar.org/Publications/Other/PDF/NRLP%20proceeding-3%20Paper%20-%205.pdf, accessed on 1 December 2015.

Power, A.G. (2010), 'Ecosystem Services and Agriculture, Tradeoffs and Synergies', *Philosophical Transactions of the Royal Society B*, 365: 2959–71, available at http://rstp.royalsocietypublishing.org/, accessed on 22 January 2016.

Swaminathan, M.S. (2005), 'Lessons from the Past and Policies for the Future: An Ever-Green Revolution', An International Dialogue on Agricultural and Rural Development in the 21st Century, available at www.fao.org/fileadmin/templates/esa/workshop_reports/Beijing/evergreen_revolution_swaminathan.pdf, accessed on 1 December 2015.

Tinbergen, J. (1952), *On the Theory of Economic Policy*, Amsterdam: North-Holland.

United Nations Conference on Sustainable Development (2012), 'The Future We Want', available at https://undocs.org/A/CONF.216/16, accessed on 1 March 2015.

United Nations Convention to Combat Desertification (UNCCD) (2012), 'Zero Net Land Degradation: A Sustainable Development Goal for Rio+20', UNCCD Secretariat Policy Brief, available at www.unccd.int/Lists/SiteDocumentLibrary/Rio+20/UNCCD_PolicyBrief_ZeroNetLandDegradation.pdf, accessed on 5 December 2015.

World Bank (2010), 'Deep wells and prudence: towards pragmatic action for addressing groundwater overexploitation in India', Tech rep, Washington, D.C.

9

Back from Hell, Marked Forever?

Trajectory of a Dalit Caste in South India

Staffan Lindberg

Introduction

This is an attempt at a sociological history of the Madharis, an
ex-untouchable caste in the Tirupur region of Tamil Nadu, over the past
half century or so. In this dry area, the Madharis, known by many as
Chakkiliyars, were leather workers who stitched the buckets for irrigation
and handled the irrigation works essential for agricultural production.
From a position as bonded village agricultural servants with customary
duties and rights (*urimai*) and survival insurance, their position changed
with the commercialization of agriculture under British rule to one in which
the majority were employed as permanent labourers on the larger farms.

With the advent of new technology, in this case mechanical pumps,
the need for Madhari labour reduced from the 1930s onwards. A severe
drought from 1947 to 1953 further spurred the introduction of this
technology, and many Madharis were retrenched from their positions as
permanent labourers. With no other work and income, this was a period
of great suffering for the Madhari community. Many of them converted
to Christianity in the hope of material relief, which was hard to come by.

The main part of this paper describes the situation of the Madharis
in fifteen villages near Palladam and Tirupur in 1967. The situation of this
Madhari community at that time illustrates the working of Indian caste
structures in the period following independence from colonial rule. This
was an extreme case of stability and reproduction, in which the structural
underdog position of the community within the local system did not change
despite transformation of the overall environment.

Of late, however, the economic situation of the Madharis has
changed for the better. With industrialization and urbanization, some
Madharis and most members of other caste groups in the villages have

left agricultural work. Scarcity of labour has benefited the Madharis, who continue to work as agricultural labourers and secure a much higher remuneration than was the case fifty years ago.

The paper builds on my own fieldwork from 1967, and on a number of books, articles and research reports by other scholars who have focused on the Madharis in this region over the last fifty years.

A Sociological Understanding of Indian Caste Structures

Social stratification and durable inequality mechanisms (Tilly 1999) are a central part of sociological theory and understanding of unequal societies. Tilly's basic concepts of *exploitation, opportunity hoarding, emulation* and *adaptation* are useful in analysing various social systems, and their reproduction and change over time. They form basic mechanisms in the class, cultural, religious and political power structure of a society. Exploitation, in his understanding, is based on asymmetrical categorical pairs such as men–women, landowners–landless, white–black, capitalists–workers, 'in which some well-connected group of actors controls a valuable, labour-demanding resource from which they can extract returns only by harnessing the efforts of others, whom they exclude from the full value added by that effort' (ibid.: 86–87).

Subordinate groups can *hoard opportunities* that open up via, for example, new technology, and the utilization of new resources, work migration, commerce and war. Relations of exploitation are often *emulated* in institutions and organizations in society, and *adapted* to the particular historical circumstances (local script) and need for legitimation.[1]

Exploitation is not unidimensional. Partha Mukherji discusses four asymmetrical domains that are directly involved: economic exploitation, political oppression, cultural discrimination and gender discrimination.[2] A fifth asymmetrical domain is eco-environmental exploitation, 'with differential consequences for the stratified and hierarchical population' (Mukherji 2012: 43). In Mukherji's understanding:

> The five conceptual cross-cutting domains of asymmetries are not mutually exclusive; they are analytically differentiated but interdependent, interpenetrating and interfaced. They, particularly the first four, constitute the abstraction of society or social system as a system of asymmetries in social interaction, given that the 'whole' is greater than the sum of its domains and their structures of asymmetries. (Ibid.: 44)

These two analytical frameworks provide very useful tools for understanding systems of exploitation and their dynamics.

They can be applied to Indian caste structures. Caste structures are similar to many other hierarchical structures of ethnic stratification in historical and contemporary societies.[3] In the 'traditional' society, dominant social groups in the form of castes have monopolies of wealth, land and political power, by means of which they can exploit other castes.[4]

There is at least one unique feature that makes castes stand out. This is the endogamy practised in all the social strata within the Indian structure, the *jati* (caste). The intermarriage pattern makes up the borderlines of caste, separating one group from another.[5] It gives a solid foundation to social stratification and sets limits to how social mobility can be achieved. This pattern facilitates the tracing of people from one generation to another. They are like 'ring-marked migratory birds' whose whereabouts are easy to track.

Another central feature is untouchability, in which around one-fifth of the Indian population is treated as outcastes and doubly exploited by all other members of the society.[6] The underlying social mechanism is that of the relation between the Established and the Outsiders (Elias and Scotson 1994). The mechanism provides for a bottom line of social conformity, below which the evil opposite is posited. A hierarchy, a turning point and a privileged interpretation by the 'Elite of the Established', keep up the rules and conformity to these. This is not to say that those thus outcasted subscribe to these interpretations (see below).

A Regional Phenomenon

Caste was always a regional phenomenon and still is to a great extent, as most researchers would agree. It is within historically emerging regions with the same political system, language, culture, ecology and production systems that we find concrete social structures operating under this common 'social logic'. However, since understandings of what constitute the central analytical dimensions vary, I will briefly define my view.

Within the caste system, a few castes typically have a monopoly of the main productive assets: land, capital and/or cattle.

The central analytical concepts are class and ideology.

Class: The landed and dominant caste, on the one hand, is grounded in the regional political and religious power structure (the kingdom), and on the other hand, makes up the elite in the local structure (the village). Most other castes are organized by the elite in a division of labour, in which caste is coupled with a particular occupation (priest, barber, *dhobi*, blacksmith, servants, tenants, agricultural labourers, etc.).[7] However, as we will see below, some castes may be organized on a regional basis through commerce and industry. In both cases 'class is embedded in caste', as expressed by Mukherji when analysing Srinivas' perspectives on 'traditional' caste structures (Mukherji 2012: 29; Srinivas 2003: 455).

Ideology: Each caste has a value on a scale from purity to impurity. The dominant caste and the Brahmin priests guarded a 'theory' of purity and the social order in which each caste was assigned to a particular vocation and task.

Thus, 'traditionally', there seemed to be a strong intersectionality and coherence between caste, class, culture and political power reproduced over time. Breaking out of caste structures was more or less impossible. Muslim or Christian conversions only resulted in new sub-castes with the old identity and status transferred to the new position. Conversions carried an element of opposition, but this was soon quelled by the treatment meted out to the converts by the dominant castes in the villages.

It must be stressed that caste structures were always changing over time. One decisive change came with the British census classifications from 1881 to 1931, when people were classified into castes and we also got the rather weird classification into *Forward Classes, Backward Classes, Scheduled Castes and Tribes*. 'Backward classes' included the local dominant and landowning castes in many regions! The whole census operation gave an impression of stability to the social order, which was presumably never the case (cf. Jodhka 2012). Today, with the transformation into an urban-industrial service society, caste structures have undergone several changes and transformations but they are still resilient (Jodhka 2015).

The interaction between class and caste became crucial with the advent of capitalism. The almost bewildering variety of forms of exploitation that one finds within contemporary Indian capitalism is created within a caste society and the kind of gender relations that this implies (cf. Harriss-White and Heyer 2015). One is tempted to speak of varieties of 'capitalism' or rather 'Indian capitalisms'.

These principles and mechanisms will now be illustrated by the story of the Madhari position in 1967[8] and its subsequent transformation.

The Madharis

The Madharis are called Chakkiliyars (leather workers) by the other castes in the villages, and belong to a larger caste of Arundathiyars, who used to be the tanners, scavengers and drumbeaters in many villages in Tamil Nadu.[9] They occupied an untouchable position[10] in traditional society, everywhere segregated from and discriminated against by the rest of the community.

My main concern during fieldwork in 1967 was with the changes experienced by the Madharis during the last century, foremost of which was the gradual transition from a mainly local-centred economy to an ever-growing market economy, with growing commercialization of agriculture and expanding industrial activities. During this period, many Madharis had converted to Christianity. Another change was the coming of Independence, which meant that a government committed to social and economic progress had come into power and initiated development programmes. Education, medical services, local democracy, etc., were some of the new institutions beginning to affect daily village life.

The Setting

The geographical setting of the then Coimbatore district (part of what was historically known as Kongu Nad) is characterized by its altitude of 1000 feet above sea level, rather poor soils (red and black sand), low rainfall, and a comparatively dry and mild climate. These factors have greatly influenced the development of the area. The feudal zamindar system was never common here.[11] Most of the landowners themselves work manually on the land. Lack of surface water has forced farmers to dig deep wells in order to get water for irrigation. The main crops in 1967 were ragi, *cholam* and *cumbu* – all millets – and groundnut. In the middle of the district there was an area with black soils, which was suitable for the cultivation of cotton.

Industrial growth in the district was impressive during the twentieth century. The textile industry dominated due to the dry climate and the availability of raw materials. What were originally subsidiary industries to the textile mills also developed into important industries along with smaller units of knitwear production. Other important industries included mechanical engineering producing pumps, electrical engines, etc. All of this led to rapid urbanization. Between 1901 and 1961, the urban population increased from 7 per cent to 29 per cent of the total population of Coimbatore district, which in 1961 was about 3.5 million.

The Gounder caste was the dominant caste in the district. Most of its members worked as farmers and they also owned most of the land. Next in importance was the Naidu caste, whose members were farmers but increasingly engaged in industrial production. Other important groups were the Chettiar and Mudaliar castes, most of whose members were weavers and merchants. There were three large Scheduled Castes – the Paraiyars,[12] the Pallans[13] and the Madharis. In 1967, most members of these castes worked as agricultural labourers. Many of them had recently converted to Christianity. In 1961, 94.6 per cent of the district population identified themselves as Hindus, 2.8 per cent as Muslims and 2.6 per cent as Christians. The absolute numbers identifying themselves as Christians were about 1,00,000.[14]

Coimbatore district offered a rich background for a study of the changing status of a Scheduled Caste community in 1967. How had it fared in different social-economic contexts? What were the implications of the economic, institutional and religious changes taking place? To ascertain this, I studied two different rural areas in Palladam taluk in the middle of the district.[15]

The first area selected for study, a pure *rural area*, consisted of ten typical mixed caste agrarian villages,[16] situated in a cluster 5 to 10 miles south of the small town of Palladam. It was in one of the driest areas of the whole district, and agriculture, although dominant, was complemented by handloom weaving in some villages. The main crops were ragi, *cholam* and groundnut cultivated on well-irrigated and dry land. The Gounders and the Madharis were the most numerous castes. The Madharis comprised 10–38 per cent of the population in the study villages. A small number of them owned small parcels of land and some had livestock. In four of these villages, most of the Madharis had converted to Christianity.

The second area consisted of five *urban fringe villages*, situated a few miles south of the rapidly expanding town of Tirupur, the population of which had increased from about 33,000 in 1951 to 1,00,000 in 1967. There were five big textile mills and some 350 small-scale banyan industries. The economy of the fringe villages was very different from that of the agrarian villages. First of all, agriculture was more diversified. Besides cereals, there was considerable cultivation of cotton and tobacco. There were also many non-agricultural activities including a fairly prosperous handloom-weaving industry, and various other small-scale industries. A large part of the population was employed in Tirupur.

In the fringe villages, the dominant castes were Gounders (farmers), Devanga Chettiars and Mudaliars (both handloom-weaving castes). Apart from the relative strength of the weaving communities, the caste composition was similar to that in the villages south of Palladam. Madharis constituted between 10 and 36 per cent of the population in each village. They had even less land and livestock compared to the first area. Quite a few of them had started work as day labourers in Tirupur town. In two of the five villages, the majority of the Madharis had become Christians.

Other castes in the two areas were represented in much smaller numbers. They included Brahmin (priests), Naidu (farmers), Pandaram (priests), Asari (carpenters), Udayar (potters), Boyár (house constructors), Navithan/Nasudar (barbers), Vannan (washermen), Nadar (petty shop owners), Koravan (basket makers), Pullavannan (agricultural workers), Valayar (agricultural workers), Kodangi (storytellers, beggars) and, finally, the Scheduled Caste Adi Dravida/Paraiyar (agricultural workers).

The caste ranking system in these villages was very similar to that found by Brenda Beck in her study of the culture and social structure of the Coimbatore area (Beck 1972 and 1979). As in most rural areas, the landowning castes and merchant castes had an intermediate *varna* position as Vaishya, but apart from this, two parallel status and prestige systems existed side by side (Beck 1972).[17]

The main core was a *land-based* caste system centred on Gounder landowners, their servant and artisan castes, and some of the Scheduled Caste agricultural labourers. In local terminology, these castes were called the *right-hand castes*. The other system consisted of *left-hand castes* which based their wealth on money and commerce, and included the merchants and the weavers, and those castes subservient to these as servants and artisans. Since they were not locally but regionally grounded, they were seen as outsiders or 'immigrants'. A lot of social interaction involved struggles between castes belonging to the two prestige systems at various levels.

Durable Inequality

The agriculturally based social system revolved around the two poles of Gounders as landowners and Madharis as workers, connected by interdependence and exploitation. The Gounder community was considered the lords of the land in Kongu Nad and carriers of an elaborate religious and kinship system tied to the soil.

From Tilly's analytical point of view, one can see here a stable structure of exploitation, 'in which some well-connected group of actors [the landowning Gounders] controls a valuable, labour-demanding resource from which they can extract returns only by harnessing the efforts of others [the landless Madharis], whom they exclude from the full value added by that effort' (Tilly 1999: 86–87). This 'internal' asymmetrical categorical pair (Tilly's term) is then reinforced by *emulation* (ibid.: 95), that is, by the 'use' of an 'external' asymmetrical categorical pair of pure and impure – touchable and untouchable, borrowed from the larger ideological framework of Brahmin theology.

A further aspect of the stability of this exploitation structure is the way it was *adapted* to local conditions and the way it was able to create vested interests in it among some of the Madhari labourers, through favourable conditions of annual employment in terms of remuneration, loans and gifts.

An additional crucial point in the structure was that the Madharis, though working as agricultural labourers for many generations, were still classified as a left-hand caste, that is, as outsiders. Thus, not only were they marked as 'untouchable', but they were also seen as outsiders,[18] as strangers not to be trusted like the 'sons of the soil' – a double underdog position and stigmatization! This made their relation to the Paraiyars very problematic. Though both castes were 'untouchable', the Paraiyars being classified as a right-hand caste always considered themselves far above the Madharis, since the latter were outsiders and moreover worked with the skins of dead animals. One consequence was that while Madharis were always made to live in separate colonies (*cheris*), the Paraiyar houses lay adjacent to the other caste residences in the villages.

Madharis as 'Immigrants'

According to a legend, the Madharis originally came to Coimbatore district from Telugu country, along with the intermediate Naidu caste. Telugu is still their mother tongue, although most of them have learnt Tamil. Their traditional occupation was to take care of dead animals, tan the hides and skins, and produce leather goods.

With the advent of extensive well irrigation in the Coimbatore region, the Madharis provided the leather buckets used in wells. They also operated the bullocks used for pulling water out of the wells for irrigation (a method called *kavalai*). Moreover, other than the buckets, they made several articles out of leather – shoes, sandals and drums for irrigation. In addition, they were assigned the task of cleaning and sweeping certain parts of village. Finally, they also served as drummers at religious ceremonies and were sent as messengers to inform relatives about deaths. There is evidence that the Madharis, due to their special skills, enjoyed a rather secure and decent subsistence position in Tamil Nadu at the turn of the former century (Sujatha 2002).

The Madharis were always more or less landless and few of them had livestock. They worked for the Gounders and other landowners. It is difficult to assess to what extent the so-called *jajmani* system, i.e. a regular exchange of goods and services between different castes in a village, was ever fully practised in the study villages, but remnants of it in the form of *urimai* existed as late as 1967. *Urimai* denotes a system of obligations and rights among the castes in a village. In exchange for work for the dominant community, the various service and artisan castes were entitled to a share in the village produce, typically distributed during harvest (Cederlöf 1997: 55–65). For the Madharis, the main right, besides a share of the village produce, was to receive dead cows and buffaloes whose hides could be tanned.

The nineteenth century brought increased cultivation of commercial crops, for which more irrigation was needed and thus the need for Madhari labour. At the same time, commercial estates in the hills as well as growing industries created labour markets with competition for the labour force. It was the farmers with enough irrigated land who employed labourers on an annual basis. The year-round cultivation associated with irrigation justified their employment on an annual basis.

The system under which the Madharis were permanently employed by the Gounders for one year at a time was called the *pannaiyal* system. *Pannaiyals* were paid on a monthly basis, the wage amounting to an average of 30 litres of millets and Rs 10 in cash per month in 1967. The *pannaiyal* was expected to work whenever the farmer needed him. His wife and children were also expected to work for the farmer whenever needed, with the children most often herding cattle. Advances and loans with a moderate rate of interest made sure the worker did not leave his employment. Often the loan would not have been paid at the end of the year, which meant that the *pannaiyal* had to continue with a new contract for another year (cf. Cederlöf 1997).

The fact that the Madharis had very low social status was a consequence of their weak economic position, their occupational activities and their status as 'immigrants'. They were regarded as unclean by other castes and treated as untouchables. They were residentially segregated from the rest of the community and had to live in special colonies, called *cheri*, outside the main village. Segregation extended to many other fields and still remained strong in 1967: the Madharis were not allowed to draw water from the common village well or to enter the houses or courtyards of other castes; they had to pay submissive respect to other villagers whenever they met them; and they were ordered to perform all lowly tasks. The exploitation, discrimination and oppression had seemingly no limits.

From 'Pannaiyal' to Day Coolies

During our interaction with the Madharis in 1967, we were shocked to learn about their miserable living conditions: lack of food, clothing, housing, drinking water, sanitation and all else necessary for a decent standard of living. They were a tragic sight – men, women, children and the old, thin-bodied and all clad in tatters.

After the 1930s, agriculture was increasingly mechanized. Electric pumpsets started to replace leather buckets and bullocks in drawing water for irrigation, and the tanning process had become industrialized too (cf. Cederlöf 1997). In the 1960s, the Madharis had become victims of a rationalization process, of which they were fully aware but about which they were unable to do anything. This theme was repeated in a number of interviews with the Madharis. In the words of a group of them:

This month we do not have enough to eat. There is no work for us. The

> harvest season is over. Can you give us some help? Now the Gounders are using the threshing machine and electric pumpsets. So we get less work and less income. They pay us only Rs 2 per day. Sometimes there is no work for all of us. Formerly it was better, but now there is surplus of labourers in this area.

And:

> For the last two years the threshing machine has been used by the Gounders, so there is no work for us at harvest. Now, there is electricity. Formerly, we used to prepare the leather buckets for drawing water from the wells. Now we go for daily coolie work for the Gounders. But not every day. Today, there is no work at all.

With no land of their own to cultivate, the Madharis had become casual agricultural labourers.[19] The casual work included ploughing, sowing, weeding, irrigation and harvesting. The daily wage was about Rs 2.50 for male workers and Rs 1.25 for female workers in 1967. Almost all wages were paid in cash. For this, they often had to work for more than ten hours a day.

In 1967, fewer Madharis than earlier were permanently employed as farm labourers, i.e. as *pannaiyals*, with a fixed monthly wage in cash and kind. In the rural area south of Palladam, about 25 per cent were *pannaiyals*, while in the urban fringe area there were fewer thus employed. In the latter area, however, one-third of the Madharis had annual employment as workers in the urban-industrial economy of Tirupur.

Interestingly, in 1981–82, the institution of *pannaiyal* was somewhat more resilient at 33 per cent, in villages northwest of Palladam studied by Heyer (2010). The difference may be explained by factors such as variations in the size of irrigated landholdings, cropping patterns and the distance from urban areas. The farther from the industrial conglomerate of Tirupur, the more common it appears, were permanently employed agricultural labourers at that time.

While in 1967 most of the Madharis in the vicinity of Palladam were formally free-wage labourers, they were in practice very often tied to the place where they lived. More than 80 per cent of them were heavily indebted either to friends or to moneylenders who were often their employers, with loans of Rs 100 or more. About half of all loans had an interest rate amounting to 12 per cent or more per month! The interest on employers' loans was often paid back through work without wages or at lower wages rates. The Madharis were seldom able to repay the original debt and so they got stuck in the place, bound for ever to insecure employment and income opportunities provided by the farmer-moneylenders.

In 1981–82, Heyer (2010) observed that the Madharis suffered from low wages. In theory, they could leave the employment and the village, 'absconding' as it was locally called, and leave the debt behind. But they seldom did, as they were hindered by the Madhari elders and the risk of even more insecure employment income opportunities elsewhere.

While the Madhari labourers and the Gounder farmers, male and female, mixed freely and worked side by side in the fields, the segregation of and discrimination against the Madharis persisted in all other respects. The Madharis used to say mockingly that it was strange to see how the Gounders refused to touch Madhari food or water, but at the same time could eat the food that they, the Madharis, had handled from seed to crop in the fields.

The Gounders treated the Madharis with contempt in 1967. Let me quote a Gounder in a village near Tirupur, where the Madharis had started to work as coolies in the town itself:

> The Madharis come irregularly for work and you cannot trust them. I am very much concerned about my village-fellows. Nowadays, they drink and gamble. Very few are honest and hard-working. It is especially so with the Madharis. They are dirty and unclean. If they were clean, I could think of eating with them. They do not come regularly for work. As soon as they have money, they spend it on liquor and so on. Then the women and the children have to suffer. Once I built a house for a Madhari and gave him permanent employment and good pay. Then he used to come regularly for work, but now he is not coming. The Madharis are ignorant and do not want to send their children to school. Instead, they let the children work for them in the fields.

Brenda Beck, doing fieldwork in the region in the late 1960s (see Beck1972), paints a very similar picture of the social and economic situation of the Madharis in those days. Her fieldwork also records the almost total submission of the Madharis to their Gounder masters. No organizations except religious ones had come near the Madharis and reduced the cause of their suffering. It was a situation of total servitude, it appears. Beck writes, comparing the Paraiyars and the Madharis: 'Both groups are ambivalent about their low status, of course, but in the case of the Matari, I have the impression that their low position is more fully internalized, and that members of this community are prone to a strong sense of self-inferiority' (ibid.: 134).

In my fieldwork, though, it appeared that the conversion to

Christianity had made some difference. Isolated from the rest of the community and without their traditional employment and income security, the Madharis had retained many of their old Dravidian customs, which were most readily seen in their religion. They worshipped the so-called village gods (*grama devatas*) – e.g., *Mariyamma*, the mother goddess. Facing material sufferings like illness they, like most people, took to religious worship. Yet their general notion of 'the other reality' seemed to be rather secular. 'There is no God but for man who created him.' Such expressions were fairly common. A yearly festival to the guardian goddess was celebrated in a manner similar to that practised by the higher castes, but it seldom took place due to the increased poverty of the Madharis.

Gender relations were different among the Madharis than among other and especially higher castes. As I saw it, Madhari women were often bold, and seemed to have greater influence in their caste group and in family affairs than women of other castes. The reason for this was probably that they often had to work as wage labourers in the fields and earn their own income. As a result, bride price was the persistent custom of the Madharis, which meant that the husband's family had to give a gift to the bride's family as compensation for the loss of a working hand. Also, in marriage they were freer than other Hindu women. If they were unhappy about the marriage, e.g., if the husband was drinking and not contributing to the expenses for food, etc., they would sometimes leave him, return to their parents' house and get remarried.

What we see here is a relative autonomy of gender relations among the Madharis in relation to the severe exploitation, oppression and discrimination that they all faced at the hand of the Gounders. In the fieldwork in 1967, we were all young men and interviewed mostly men, and were not very qualified to delve into women's situation. Thus, our observations carry limited weight in this regard. However, the relative 'freedom' of Madhari women that we observed seems to have persisted into contemporary time. Nitya Rao (2014) conducted focused life-story interviews with twenty Dalit couples, most of them Madharis, in a village in Tirupur district.[20] She found a limited but real space for women's agency to negotiate both choice of husband and everyday interaction in married life. Many marriages were self-arranged, that is, by active choice on the part of the women. Rao found that alcoholism and violence against women were common reasons for stress and oppression, but also for negotiations, including, in the end, divorce or at worst suicide. The space for women to act depended, among other things, on their social networks of peers and kin.

From Hindu to Christian

In the old society, there was a fixed role and status for the Madharis, even though low and detested. In their own understanding, in the 1960s they faced increased poverty and this led to a general disintegration of the networks of social relations in the local community. It was against this background that we can understand how the Madharis came to convert to Christianity. It was a kind of 'rebellion'.

The Church of Sweden Mission and, from 1919, the Tamil Evangelical Lutheran Church (TELC) had been working in this area since 1900.[21] The conversion of the Madharis began in the 1930s but it was during the severe drought from 1947 to 1953, from which the Madharis were the first to suffer, that conversion gained momentum. The Tamil Church was able to help with food and material gifts. In some cases, it even saved people from death from starvation. The centre of these activities was a mission station called Arulpuram,[22] on the road between Tirupur and Palladam.

> We were the first Madharis in this area to become Christians. We requested the Swedish missionary in Arulpuram and gave Rs 300 to the Church for our conversion. This was in 1951 or 1952. We were very happy to be converted to Christianity because at that time the Gounders were very hostile and sometimes used to beat us. To avoid this and to have somebody to come and help us we readily accepted the new faith. But nowadays, the Church is not taking care of us as it used to do. Formerly, it used to give wheat flour or beans or milk powder.

Conversion to Christianity also meant that the Madharis got some, though limited, protection against discrimination by the other castes. Group interview in 1967:

> *What is the difference between Hindus and Christians?*
> If we are Christians, there is one *durai* (pastor or missionary) and if the Gounders beat us, we are protected. When we are in need of foodgrains they will sometimes bring us one or two bags and supply to all of us. For some important festivals, like Christmas, *durai* will supply bengal gram and fried rice. The missionary who converted us talked our language and took photos. Those who are Christians, for them there is material help and protection.

The need for drinking water was another direct reason for conversion. The Tamil Church started a well-drilling programme during the severe drought of the 1950s. The programme was still in operation in 1967, another period of severe drought. The following exchange confirms this:

Are you happy as Christians?
Yes, we are.

Why did you become Christians?
We had water problems. To solve those problems, we became Christians and for nothing else.

Did you get water after becoming Christians?
Yes, they constructed a borewell and the water problem was solved, but after some time the pump was broken and for six months it was not taken care of, and then finally they [the Church] took it back. Now there is an open well dug for us by the government, but the water is salty.

The interviewer then came back to the difference between Hindus and Christians:

What is the difference between a Christian and a Hindu?
There is no difference.

Do you think that Hindus also are happy?
Yes, they are happy and we are also happy. There is no grievance for being Christian.

When did you become Christians and who converted you?
An old *natyar* (pastor). We do not know his name but he was a very good man. At the time of our conversion, many white people came here. We welcomed them all by beating the drums and presented garlands to them. Before we became Christians we asked the Gounders and they permitted us. They also came here when we were converted.

Are you going to church regularly?
Yes, we are. During Christmas celebrations, the *missiammal* used to bring sweets and even saris to some women like the widows here and also to the woman who kept the church clean. Dhankannu bible amma was here for more than eight years and she was a very nice bible amma.

Earlier, the Gounders had often objected to the conversions, fearing that they would lose control of the Madharis. There is one story in the studied villages about how the Madharis converted to Christianity in the late 1940s and how the Church built a school in the colony. The school was burnt down one night and the Madharis, fearing that it was the work of the Gounders, reconverted to Hinduism. Beck (1972: 138) notes this process based on missionary sources. Cederlöf suggests that the resistance from the Gounders abated when they no longer needed the permanent work of the Madharis, and they were perhaps happy to be 'free' of the responsibility for them (cf. Cederlöf 1997).

The Church also tried to help the Madharis to educate some of their children by sending them to boarding schools run by the Church. Generally Madharis were unable to send their children to the village school.

> *Do you send your children to the village school?*
> No, we don't. When a boy is able to follow some sheep, then we send him out to graze sheep. If we send him to school we do not even get that little amount of money.

> *But if the government would pay you Rs 50 per year for each child you sent to school, what would you think of that?*
> Rs 50 will not be enough. If we send a boy to the Gounder's field we will get Rs 100 as an advance. For this, the boy has to feed the Gounder's sheep for the whole year.

Many of the Madhari girls could not go to school either, because they had to take care of their younger sisters and brothers when the parents were away from the house working in the fields. Thus, poverty and the need for child labour accounted at least partly for the poor enrolment of Madhari children in the schools.

Another strong reason for not going to school was of course the persistent discrimination against the Madharis. They were not welcomed into the streets and houses of the main hamlet, where the school was most often situated. The Mission had little to offer against this. Only a very small number of Madhari children were enrolled at their boarding schools.

There is no doubt that the Madharis converted to Christianity for material rather than 'spiritual' reasons. I found in my interviews that the converts had very little knowledge about the Christian faith and they rather seldom participated in religious services (going through the congregation files). But this situation was not only because of their lack of interest. One important reason for their lack of engagement was the organization of the Church of which they had become members.

First of all, conversion was normally a collective act, in which the whole or majority of the members of the local caste group or lineage became Christians. Unable to maintain a network among scattered believers, the Church chose to implement mass conversions in the villages where they found an opportunity.

The Church was at the same time a typical Lutheran priest church with a heavy emphasis on baptism, confirmation and regular church-going. The inclusion of a large number of rural labourers spread out over large areas led to severe strains on the organization. The Church did not have enough pastors and other church workers to carry out the work. In charge of congregations in ten to fifteen hamlets, the pastor was normally able to visit each congregation on average only about three times a year. In the meantime, congregational care was the responsibility of evangelists and bible women. There were, however, also too few of these to be able to provide the necessary services. Many Madharis had to wait for long periods before being baptised. In 1967, the majority of them were not yet confirmed and those confirmed only attended communion services irregularly because of the infrequent visits of the pastor, who was the only one with clerical rights to provide such services.

But the Church was also, and that is perhaps more important, a caste- and class-based church, divided into two groups. One was the dominant minority of middle-class Christians in the towns, who were wealthy and who occupied all the important offices in the Church. The other group consisted of rural labourers, like the Madharis, who were unable to make their voice heard in the Church. They had been converted, often by means of resources from missionary societies abroad, resources that had short durability and could not suffice even in the short run, not to speak of the long run, to ameliorate their poor socio-economic situation.

This gulf between urban and rural areas and distinction between castes were also reinforced by reactions in the villages to the conversion of the Madharis by the Lutheran Church. In several of the villages, the Adi Dravidas had earlier been converted by the same Church.[23] Once the latter learned about the new converts from the Madhari caste, they quit the Lutheran Church and joined the Roman Catholic Church instead. The instability of the rural congregations was later seen when an American Free Church pastor started to travel around and enlist the Madharis for his new church, offering better 'terms of transfer and maintenance'.

An unrealistic approach had been adopted by the Church to overcome this situation. In 1960, a so-called village industry programme was started. Training and loans were given to individual Madhari Christians to enable them to practise their traditional vocation, viz., tanning, but also for the purchase of animals, instruments for mat weaving and material for house construction. Some Rs 6,000 was spent for these purposes in the study villages from the beginning of the 1960s up to 1967. The loans for tanning amounted to an average between Rs 200 and 500. There was also training in tanning, but the craft was not competitive with such a low investment, given the newly built tanning industries run by Muslim traders. It turned out to be an artificial revival of the old tanning activities. In 1967, the lasting result of the village industry programme seemed to be the houses that were built. Unfortunately, the poor status of the Madhari households made it very difficult for them to maintain their houses, so even these houses had deteriorated rapidly.

The missionaries interpreted the *pannaiyal* institution as very oppressive, based as it was on debt and bondage. They therefore sought to raise funds for the repaying of the debts, 'freeing', as they saw it, Christian Madharis. Since, however, there was no other way the Madharis could find stable employment and a livelihood, this would have resulted only in more misery. The intervention did not succeed. As many or slightly more Christian Madharis in the rural area were employed as *pannaiyals* in 1967 (29 per cent) as Hindu Madharis (23 per cent).

The change from Hinduism to Christianity thus had meant very little for the social and economic situation of the Madharis. Basically, they had remained in the same predicament as before. True, a few of their children had been educated in boarding schools, but that had only enhanced individual mobility and had not led to any improvement of the Madhari community as a whole. Educated Madharis seldom returned to their native places. Instead, they sought employment in the towns where they could find jobs suitable to their education, and where they could sometimes rid themselves of the marks of belonging to a debased caste. In this way, the Madharis left in the villages lost their most able members, who might otherwise have served as leaders for local emancipation.

State Development Programmes

Since Independence, the Indian government has made various efforts to promote social and economic development in rural areas. Two kinds of programmes were started early on. One was the Community Development programme, which aimed at the establishment of modern education and infrastructure in the villages. The other was the Harijan Welfare programme undertaken directly for the sake of the emancipation of the most depressed groups, the Harijans or the ex-untouchables.

Through the Community Development schemes, schools and medical dispensaries spread to a large number of villages. Local democracy was encouraged through the establishment of village panchayats. Loans for economic development, especially farming, were provided through cooperative societies. However, the Madharis did not benefit much from these.

Take the provision of education, for example. In thirteen out of the fifteen villages in our study, there were elementary schools, yet only 20 per cent of the Madhari school-age children went to school in 1967 and only 29 per cent of the Madhari households had any educated member at all. Those educated had normally attended school only for a few years, which meant that they either never learnt how to read and write, or had quickly forgotten how to do so after leaving school. One of the reasons for this ineffective process of learning was only too apparent: the Madharis possessed no books or magazines, they had no electric light in their houses, their work did not require or stimulate reading, and they were just too tired to read after a long day of hard work.

Most hamlets in the study had access to a medical dispensary within a distance of a few miles, but only one-third of the Madhari households had ever made a visit to these dispensaries. The Christians had made somewhat more visits, often brought there by church workers when taken ill. The same initiative was seldom taken by Community Development workers. When village workers of the Community Development programme approached the Madharis, it was rather to propagate family planning. The response of the Madharis to this was very negative. In a discussion some of them said:

> We do not like family planning. Perhaps in ten years' time we will adopt it. One agent has been here and has tried to convince us. Some of the old people are said to have gone for an operation.
>
> *But if you have three children is that not enough?*
> Yes, three children is enough. But what if they die? We have no money to go to the hospital and get our children treated. Only if we have money they will treat us well in the hospital. And family planning is not good for a man. Some Gounders from this village have been operated and now they are not able to work in the cold season. They cannot even come out of their houses when it is cold.

The family planning programmes one-sidedly stressed sterilization, for which most of the villagers – the Madharis were no exception – had little use. Most households had three children or less (55 per cent of all households), the mean number of children was three and the mean size of households was 4.7 persons. In 57 per cent of all households, one or more children had died.[24]

For a great many of the Madhari households, then, the problem was how to have more children and how to keep the children alive, rather than preventing more children from being born. In families in which there were more children, there was a more positive attitude to family planning. Yet almost everybody was scared of sterilization and even used rationalizations like that about illness caused by sterilization to strengthen their natural fears.

Finally, formal politics, both local and national, had so far left the

Madharis largely outside the sphere of influence. As regards local democratic institutions, their participation was low. Only 42 per cent of the male heads had participated in any local election to the local panchayat, which was still functioning in 1967.[25] This is not surprising. The most Madharis could hope for was to get one of their fellow caste members into a council of twelve members from various castes in the village.[26] The panchayat was completely dominated by the higher castes. The Madhari member had to sit on the floor while the others sat on chairs. He – and it was never a 'she' – was not expected to say anything unless directly asked.

More than 90 per cent of Madhari household heads had participated in the 1967 general elections. In those elections, the higher castes, who dominated the local party machinery, were interested in mobilizing as many votes as possible. Thus, patrons (landlords) laid claim on their clients (agricultural labourers) to vote for them or their party. Often encouraged by a small remuneration, the Madharis felt obliged to vote for a party about which they had little knowledge and a programme that took little interest in their problems. This lack of genuine political mobilization meant that the Madharis were uninterested in politics, or, as one of them expressed it:

> But what to do when you have promised to vote for two parties? Some of us voted for DMK (Dravida Munnetra Kazhagam) and a few voted for the Communists. Anyway, we don't know anything about politics and political parties. We are a depressed people, and who cares.

The direct aid to the Madharis through the Harijan Welfare Board had been of marginal importance with few exceptions: in one of the villages, the Madharis had built new houses by means of loans from the Board. However, in this village they had become very shy and afraid of outsiders because of their inability to repay the loans and, maybe also, fear of family-planning workers. A more general criticism of the programme is that it suffered from insufficient funding and therefore looked like random charity. Other direct programmes suffered from lack of applicability. For example, credit for implements and cultivation were to be given to Harijans who had land. But very few Madharis had land.

Industrialization
Standard development theories stress that industrialization is the means by which underemployed and unemployed rural people will be drawn into production and thereby share in the general increase in standards of living. In Tilly's analytical framework, growing industries open up the possibility for poor and landless rural workers to migrate to work in

urban areas. By drawing on successful first migrants, other members of the same family, kinship or caste group can then network with them, and get a job and a place to stay in the town. This is a primary example of what Tilly calls 'chain-migration', an opportunity hoarding mechanism for the non-elite (Tilly 1999: 149).

The pace of industrialization has generally been slow in India, but there are pockets, like for example Tirupur in 1967, where fairly rapid industrialization had taken place and theories of development could be put to a test. More specifically, we can ask: how had the Madharis fared in the industrialization process? By comparing the conditions of Madharis in the urban fringe villages with those of Madharis in the typical agrarian villages, we may get an answer to this question.

Industrialization had, first of all, meant some new employment opportunities for the Madharis in the fringe villages near Tirupur, mostly as day labourers in transport. A small number of them had become permanently employed factory workers, commuting every day to and from the town. Higher income and security enabled these few to raise their standard of living and they had become high-status members of their community. The vast majority of the urban entrants, however, were day labourers and continued to live in utter poverty. Fieldwork among urban Madharis in Tirupur revealed their meagre and precarious existence in sheds and mud huts along one of the major roads, with very insecure income. Only a few of their children went to school, most working as labourers like their parents.

The few successful Madharis could not provide *opportunity hoarding* for the vast majority of their fellow caste members. Another of the Scheduled Castes, the Adi Dravidas, had been more successful in this respect. Through early education in church schools and with networks forming among fellow caste members in the towns, they were able to secure stable and better-paid jobs.

The new employment opportunities had also led to a relative scarcity of agricultural labourers in peak periods, which in turn had led to a marginal rise in the wages for agricultural coolie work. The Madharis therefore had somewhat higher income in the urban fringe villages than in the typical agrarian villages. On the other hand, they were more indebted and owned less livestock in the fringe villages. So far, their overall economic conditions seemed not to have improved except in the few cases where they had become factory workers.

No improvement in the Madharis' educational standards could be found. Madhari children attended school in the fringe villages as little as elsewhere. A slight improvement was found in the use of medical institutions, but their general health status, measured for example by the child mortality rate, was very similar to that in the agrarian villages and shockingly poor.

What differed, and what perhaps contained some hope for the future, was the attitudes of some of the Madharis in the fringe villages towards their own situation. They were more discontent and grumbling about their situation, which was seen, for example, in their higher participation in both national and local elections.

As in the case of the Christian Madharis, the urban fringe Hindu Madharis were also more positive in their attitudes towards education, occupational mobility, inter-caste relations, etc., as compared to their rural fellow-caste members. But those attitudes were not very instrumental in their circumstances. The Madharis might be interested in the education of their children, but they could not afford to send their children to school even if they were invited to do so free of cost and even if midday meals were served in the schools. The children simply had to work for the survival of the family.

All in all, the situation of the Madharis in the urban fringe villages was much the same as that prevailing in the agrarian villages. Neither industrialization nor development programmes nor Christianity had been able to alter their condition.

Down and Out, and Then What?

More than fifty years have passed since I, along with five fellow students, conducted fieldwork among the Madharis in the Palladam area. It is where my interest in India's social development started.

This is now two generations ago and most things in rural India have changed since – changes that actually started in a broad way with the state-driven green revolution, and which intensified and raised incomes among the rural poor so that they could better feed and clothe themselves, build better houses, and so on. Along with this, there has been a formidable transformation into an urban industrial and service economy with agriculture today contributing less than 15 per cent to national income.

Most rural people now get their main income from non-farm employment. They still live in villages but work in small industries, services of various kinds, or commute to work in towns, just like some of the Madharis in the urban fringe villages. More recently, they have started to migrate and settle in urban areas in large numbers.

Today, most rural people send their children to school, enjoy simple but time-saving household machines and watch TV at night. As we know, it is not exactly a smooth and pleasant journey. On the contrary, most people are heavily exploited in the new capitalist economy and still lack good life opportunities and a green and healthy environment. Many still lack bare necessities (cf. Lindberg 2012).

What then of the Madharis – the poorest of all in 1967? How have they fared in this transformation?

A Historical Perspective

Gunnel Cederlöf from Uppsala has written a doctoral dissertation about the social and economic situation of the Madharis over a period of 70 years, from 1900 to 1970 (Cederlöf 1997). She used my undergraduate dissertation and other texts that I wrote at the beginning of the 1970s including my diaries and archive from the fieldwork.

The thesis is titled *Bonds Lost: Subordination, Conflict and Mobilization in Rural South India, c. 1900–1970*. It is a very telling title. Cederlöf's careful historical analysis largely confirms the fact that my study took place at what was most probably the worst ever situation of the Madharis as a community. From a subordinate but secure position as bonded labourers and leather workers with a guaranteed minimum of life necessities, they were more or less thrown on the garbage heap when modernization and mechanization came into agriculture. The coming of pumpsets, tractors, threshing and other machines from the 1960s onwards shattered their lives completely, like a storm over calm seas.

There is an old English proverb, 'The Devil takes the hindmost'. For the displaced Madharis there was no escape in sight. When I met them in 1967, the majority were either desperate about or resigned to their helplessness. Nobody could really help them, as I have shown above. Some of them had tried to convert to Christianity but that was of no avail to them. When the Christian missionaries, in their ignorance, sought to liberate tied farm servants from their debts by giving them new loans, they simply 'rescued' them into the insecurity of day-labourer work, growing scarcer by the day.

In 1967, industrial and town employment was still a distant dream for most Madharis. Their community was tight and locally bound with neither wider social networks nor the economic resources to go and find permanent and better-paid employment in towns. One can hardly imagine the kind of destitution and misery they must have lived through since then.

Back from Hell

'Wonder' is perhaps too strong a word for what has happened to the Madhari community since that time, but, thanks to meticulous contemporary research, we now know that they have fared much better than even the most optimistic of pessimists in the 1960s could have imagined (Heyer 2010, 2012, 2013 and 2014; Carswell 2012; Carswell and de Neve 2013 and 2014).

Who could imagine what Heyer (2012) tells us were two children, well-fed and well-clad and going to school? Who could imagine housewives in quite a few of the Madhari households who spend their time cooking, cleaning and looking after their children's education (Heyer 2014)? Who could imagine old women and men stopping work in their sixties and enjoying a small state pension? Who could imagine *pucca* houses, electric lights and TV (Heyer 2010, 2014)? The list of real improvements could go on.

I had a vague anticipation of this already in 1977 when I visited some of the villages from 1967. I sat among the Madharis who were working as labourers in Tirupur, transporting cotton and cloth on their hand-drawn carts. They had just been organized by the Centre of Indian Trade Unions (CITU), the trade union of the Communist Party of India (Marxist) (CPI[M]), and were proudly telling me about the sense of dignity it had given them.

Many Madharis, however, have stayed back in their villages and continued to work as agricultural labourers. The more important change has been the movement out of the village economy of workers from other castes, which has meant that Madharis got more employment and could bargain for higher wages in agriculture. Eventually, they formed gangs, called *kothus*, who labour-migrate in wider circles bargaining for the jobs they are being contracted for.

If we apply Tilly's concept of *opportunity hoarding*, we could perhaps say that the backward and isolated situation of the Madharis earlier, closely attached as they were to the Gounder farmers, meant that many of them could not get better-paid jobs in town, but they were now suddenly landed in a niche of better-paid work opportunities in agriculture, a kind of 'reversed opportunity hoarding'. One could also see the Madharis as being *socially immobile*, using Mukherji's analysis of social mobility (Mukherji 2012: 46), until a new and better opportunity emerged within the context of simultaneous agricultural development and exit of other working castes in their villages.

Thus, the almost phenomenal success of the so-called knitwear revolution in and around Tirupur city, with its ever-growing demand for wage labour, has tightened the labour markets also in agriculture. Agriculture, though beset with water scarcity, still thrives at a high level of mechanization, and increasing cultivation of high-value crops like turmeric, banana and sugarcane. Drip irrigation has been introduced.

Along with this, state social policy has made important inroads into village life, reaching also the poor. The public distribution system with outlets in villages, supplies a majority with subsidized rice and other basic amenities. The National Rural Employment Guarantee Scheme (NREGS) gives employment especially to landless women, also pushing up their wages in other work. Electricity is supplied to most households and house plots, and new houses are provided to many Dalit families. Schools enrol practically all children at the primary level with free midday meals, free textbooks and free travel for those going to middle and higher schools in other villages. The public health system has a better reach in the villages, especially when it comes to vaccination, and child and maternity care. There are legal provisions for old age and widowers' pensions and health care even if funds are lacking and the bureaucratic process of getting them is cumbersome (Heyer 2012).

The Tirupur region may be an extreme example of progressive social changes taking place under the joint impact of industrial, agricultural and social developments, but these findings are consistent with those of other studies of social transformation in rural Tamil Nadu in recent times (Athreya *et al.* 1990; Djurfeldt *et al.* 2008; Lindberg *et al.* 2014; and Harriss-White and Janakarajan, eds 2004).

Downsides

Social policy interventions finally reaching the villages is perhaps somewhat paradoxical in an era of increasing and highly exploitative Indian capitalism, with ever-old as well as new ways of exploiting, discriminating against and oppressing workers. But social policy interventions could be seen as a necessary way of ensuring the survival of the labouring classes and placating them.

The downsides of all this are not difficult to see. With mechanization, agriculture has become less labour-intensive and women get less workdays in agriculture than earlier. Uneducated Madhari women, constrained by patriarchy, are less equipped to get jobs in the non-farm sector than their menfolk. Home care and child care make it almost impossible to commute to any distance daily.[27] Increase in male wages, however, has made it an option for the women to stay home at least during pregnancy, childbirth and take care of small children. As many as one-third of all Madhari women in Heyer's 2008–09 survey stayed home as housewives, many of them also for prolonged periods, caring for their children going to school. Avoiding the drudgery of hard and ill-paid agricultural work, they considered themselves better placed and more autonomous than before (Heyer 2014).The downside of this was the strengthening of middle-class values and of patriarchy in their own homes (Rao 2014).

New forms of exploitation have emerged alongside free-wage labour in the urban economy. In some of the villages in the Tirupur area, a small-scale powerloom industry has come up. In these, most of the work-force is Dalit including Madharis. In order to control them and prevent them from seeking jobs in the garment industry, employers tie down the workers by giving them huge advances, amounting to more than a year's wages, thus making sure they are unable to repay their debts and leave their jobs (Carswell and De Neve 2013 and 2014). Thus, modelled on the old *pannaiyal* system, which is no longer there in the farms, a new form of 'bonded labour' has emerged. Emulation and adaptation of old and new forms of exploitation exist side by side.[28]

Environmentally speaking, the Tirupur region suffers from one of the worst polluted environments in India. Besides the chemicals and poisonous pesticides used in agriculture, as everywhere else, the textile industry more or less destroys the groundwater and soils in the area by not being forced effectively to purify the poisonous wastes produced.

Marked for Ever?

The workings of Indian capitalism and its intersection with the persisting caste-untouchability syndrome are such that even if real wages have improved and standards of living have taken a remarkable step upwards, the Madharis still occupy the lowest ladder in the hierarchy, and are well aware of their underdog position. Even the pride of the workers' union is now shattered with the disappearance of CPI(M) mobilization. The more recent promotion of the Untouchability Eradication Front by the CPI(M) cannot fully replace a workers' trade union in terms of caste eradication and social integration.

The feelings of relative deprivation are not particularly eased by viewing the rest of the society via colour television! Even though they are touched by the outside world, they are still 'untouchable' and unable to climb the social ladder. Their structural position in the system remains as before – at the bottom – and they know this. For example, no matter how their young would like to arrange their own marriages, these structures still force them into endogamy and they are stuck with their lot. Every attempt at cross-caste marriage on the part of the Madharis, especially between Gounder girls and Madhari boys, is repressed by the other castes, sometimes even with murders.

A glimmer of hope is attached to those educated young, often unmarried, Madharis who have shed work in agriculture and are now trying their luck in garment and other industries. Commuting for industrial jobs, some of those with more stable employment now convey a message of liberation from the remaining stigma and debasing treatment of Dalits in villages.[29] *'Stadtluft macht frei'* ('The city air makes you free'), as the German proverb goes. It remains to be seen if this holds true for Dalits in Indian cities in a generation or two.

I am grateful to Judith Heyer, Somerville College, Oxford University, and Gunnel Cederlöf, Royal Institute of Technology, Stockholm, for useful comments on an earlier version of this paper.

Notes

[1] According to Tilly, this is an analytical framework inspired both by Marx and Weber: 'It builds a bridge from Max Weber on social closure to Karl Marx on exploitation, and back' (Tilly 1999: 7). However, I think, as also concluded by Olin Wright (2015: 57–78), that the framework of *Durable Inequality* is as close to a Marxian position as you can get within a sociological analysis without explicitly recognizing it.

[2] One can discuss whether gender is a separate domain or subsumed under the first three domains (as in Tilly's analysis); cf. Mukherji (1999: 51 note 23).

[3] For a classical view, see Berreman (1963 and 1967).

[4] My understanding of caste structures concurs more or less with Surinder Jodhka's perspectives as presented in his recent authoritative work on caste (Jodhka 2012) and how caste structures change over time (Jodhka 2015).

[5] Caste-like systems based on social closure are found in many other societies, like the nobility in feudal societies, the craft trade communities in medieval Europe, especially the blacksmith communities there, and in West Asia and North Africa. A more recent example is racial stratification in the United States, with its predominant pattern of endogamy. But the traditional Indian structures are the most extreme since every nook and corner is organized along endogamous lines.

[6] Untouchability was a common phenomenon in feudal societies across the word. Visible remnants are outcaste groups in contemporary Japan and Romani people in southeastern Europe today.

[7] This is an idealized picture of the structure called the *jajmani* system. In border areas, there were villages in which several castes owned the land and commanded the local structure. There were also villages in which one 'caste' lived more or less in autonomy from the caste system, e.g., in tribal villages (Beck 1979: 64–110).

[8] This is based on my Bachelor degree thesis in Sociology in 1969 – 'The Madharis – An ex-untouchable caste in South India', mimeo., Department of Sociology, Lund – and networking around this study. Thanks are due to late Rev. Olle Johnsson, Coimbatore and Uppsala, for all assistance in this fieldwork. Thanks are also due to my fieldworker friends and student colleagues, Mr E. Jacob, Mr G. Kasturi, Mr T.B. Sankaran, Mr P. Solomon and Mr B. Oswald, and not least to Mr Khadiresan, our cook who fed us so well! Another important source is Cederlöf's historical study of the Madharis and their employment relations since about 1900 (Cederlöf 1997). In more recent time, in the 2010s, I have greatly benefited from interacting with Judith Heyer, Oxford University, going through my field material and discussing the changes over time studied by her up to the present.

[9] For a brief overview, see https://en.wikipedia.org/wiki/Arunthathiyar.

[10] Scheduled Caste (SC) is an official term used for the lowest group of castes in the Hindu caste classification. Scheduled Caste was used by the British with the

intent of affirmative action to ameliorate their status in society. Gandhi, in an effort to improve their status, introduced the term Harijan (children of God). Today, politically active Scheduled Caste groups call themselves Dalits (we the oppressed). In Tamil Nadu, however, the most commonly used term is Scheduled Caste.

[11] For information about the district, see Baliga (1966).

[12] The Paraiyar called themselves Adi Dravidas in 1967. They were considered above the Madharis in the traditional caste hierarchy; they sometimes owned land and had a somewhat better education than the Madharis.

[13] Devendra Kula Vellala is the gazetted name for Scheduled Caste Pallars in the Schedule, but most in the community use Pallar Moopan and Devendra Pallan (Devendra for short) interchangeably.

[14] Census of India (1961), *District Census Handbook, Coimbatore*, Volume IX: Madras, Part X–I, Volume–I.

[15] The fieldwork was carried out during April–June 1967. Altogether 415 male heads of Madhari households, 262 Hindus and 153 Christians were interviewed. The number of respondents represented 84.7 per cent of the total population in the selected villages eligible for interviews. The interviews were conducted with structured questionnaires. Other methods of investigation included group interviews and unstructured interviews with individuals on particular topics.

[16] The terms 'village' and 'hamlet' are used interchangeably in this study.

[17] This is according to Beck (1972), but it has to be added that this terminology was hardly used in everyday language in Tamil Nadu.

[18] With Telugu as their mother tongue, see below.

[19] Cederlöf (1997: 89–161) has traced this history in detail. While the new technologies arrived in the district in the 1930s, prompted by the state starting to instal electricity in the villages, it was only during the severe and prolonged drought of 1947–53 that the technologies became widespread and began to have a strong impact on farming practices. With boreholes and mechanical pumps water could be lifted from much deeper wells. Due to the lack of work during drought, most farmers simply cancelled *pannaiyal* contracts and started employing only day-coolies.

[20] The husbands and wives were interviewed separately 'by four researchers, two male and two female' (Rao 2014: 9).

[21] The Church was the result of German and Swedish missionary work starting in the late eighteenth century.

[22] Arulpuram later built a tannery and employed poor Christian Madharis in nearby villages. They stitched *chappals* (sandals) for sale abroad.

[23] The Adi Dravida converted in greater numbers than the Madharis according to Andreen (1955: 4–5). Cf. Beck (1972: 138) and Cederlöf (1997).

[24] A rough estimate is that about 300 per thousand of the children born live died before reaching the age of 5. In a further statistical analysis it would be possible to calculate the infant mortality rate, for which comparative figures are available. In Thaiyur village south of Chennai, where 90 per cent of the population belonged to a Scheduled Caste, the infant mortality rate in 1969–70 was 290 per thousand live births dead before the age of 1 (Djurfeldt and Lindberg 1975, 1980: 47).

[25] After the mid-1970s the panchayat system was more or less moribund in Tamil Nadu, only to be revived in 1996 with new laws and fresh elections.

[26] Being numerically in a minority position, the Madharis could at most elect one or two members from their own wards.

[27] Those women who now migrate to garment work in Tirupur are educated and unmarried.

[28] Debt-tied labour is common all over India today, for example, among migrant workers (see Breman 2003; Pattenden 2014; and Guérin *et al.* 2015).

[29] A similar experience is related by Jayaseelan (2014) while interviewing retrenched tea plantation workers who were forced to return to their original villages on the plains. There they found discrimination against Dalits still in full force, and far harsher as compared to the situation in the hills.

References

Andreen, Anders (1955), *Annual Report for the T.E.L.C. Pioneer Board, 1954–55*, Pollachi: Lutheran Church.

Athreya, Venkatesh B., Göran Djurfeldt and Staffan Lindberg (1990), *Barriers Broken: Production Relations and Agrarian Change in South India*, New Delhi: Sage Publications.

Baliga, B.S. (1966), *Madras District Gazetteers*, Coimbatore: Government of Madras Press.

Beck, Brenda (1972), *Peasant Society in Konku: A Study of Right and Left Subcastes of India*, Vancouver: University of British Columbia Press.

Beck, Brenda, ed. (1979), *Perspectives of a Regional Culture: Essays about the Coimbatore Area of South India*, New Delhi: Vikas Publishing House.

Berreman, Gerald D. (1963), 'Caste in India and the United States', in Raymond W. Mack, ed., *Race, Class and Power*, New York: New York American Book Company: 309–18.

——— (1967), 'Stratification, Pluralism and Interaction: A Comparative Analysis of Caste', in Anthony de Reuck and Julie Knight, eds, *Caste and Race: Comparative Approaches*, London: J.&A. Churchill Ltd.: 45–73.

Breman, Jan (2003), *The Labouring Poor in India: Patterns of Exploitation, Subordination, and Exclusion*, New Delhi: Oxford University Press.

Carswell, Grace (2012), 'Dalits and Local Labour Markets in Rural India: Experience from the Tiruppur Textile Region in Tamil Nadu', *Royal Geographical Society*, Transactions of the Institute of British Geographers.

Carswell, Grace and Geert De Neve (2013), 'From Field to Factory: Tracing Transformation in Bonded Labour in the Tiruppur Region, Tamil Nadu', *Economy and Society*, 42 (3): 430–54.

——— (2014), 'T-shirts and Tumblers: Caste, Dependency and Work under Neoliberalism in South India', *Contributions to Indian Sociology*, 48 (1): 103–31.

Cederlöf, Gunnel (1997), *Bonds Lost: Subordination, Conflict and Mobilization in Rural South India, c. 1900–1970*, New Delhi: Manohar Publishers.

Census of India (1961), *District Census Handbook: Coimbatore*, Volume IX: Madras, Part X– I, Volume I, Madras: Government Press.

Djurfeldt, Göran and Staffan Lindberg (1980), *Pills Against Poverty: The Introduction of Western Medicine in a Tamil Village*, New Delhi: Macmillan.

Djurfeldt, Göran, V. Athreya, N. Jayakumar, S. Lindberg, A. Rajagopal and R. Vidyasagar (2008), 'Agrarian Change and Social Mobility in Tamil Nadu', *Economic and Political Weekly*, 43 (45): 50–61.

Elias, Norbert and John L. Scotson (1994), *The Established and the Outsiders*, London: Sage.

Guérin, Isabelle, G. Venkatasubramaniam and Sebastian Michiels (2012), 'Labour in Contemporary South India', in Barbara Harriss-White and Judith Heyer, eds, *Indian Capitalism in Development*, Oxon: Routledge: 118–35.

Harriss-White, Barbara and Judith Heyer, eds (2015), *Indian Capitalism in Development*, Oxon: Routledge.

Harriss-White, Barbara and S. Janakarajan, eds (2004), *Rural India Facing the 21st Century: Essays on Long Term Village Change and Recent Development Policy*, London: Anthem Press.

Heyer, Judith (2010), 'The Marginalization of Dalits in a Modernizing Economy', in Barbara Harriss-White and Judith Heyer, eds, *The Comparative Political Economy of Development: Africa and South Asia*, London: Routledge: 252–74.

—— (2012), 'Labour Standards and Social Policy: A South Indian Case Study', *Global Labour Journal*, 3 (1): 91–117.

—— (2013), 'Integration into a Global Production Network: Impacts on Labour in Tiruppur's Rural Hinterlands', *Oxford Development Studies*, 41 (3): 307–21.

—— (2014), 'Dalit Women Becoming "Housewives": Lessons from the Tiruppur Region, 1981–82 to 2008–09', in Clarinda Still, ed., *Mobility or Marginalization: Dalits in Neo-Liberal India*, New Delhi: Routledge: 208–35.

Jayaseelan, Raj (2014), 'The Crisis and the Retirement: Alienation and the Struggle for Existence in a South Indian Tea Belt', paper presented at the workshop 'Inequality and Poverty in South Asia', London School of Economics, April.

Jodhka, Surinder S. (2012), *Caste*, New Delhi: Oxford University Press.

—— (2015), *Caste in Contemporary India*, New Delhi: Routledge.

Lindberg, Staffan (1969), 'The Madharis: An Ex-Untouchable Caste in South India', mimeo., Department of Sociology, Lund.

—— (2012), 'Rural India 1970–2005: An Arduous Transition to What?', *Indian Journal of Labour Economics*, 55 (1): 61–75.

Lindberg, S., V. Athreya, G. Djurfeldt, A. Rajagopal and R. Vidyasagar (2014), 'Progress over the Long Haul: Dynamics of Agrarian Change in the Kaveri Delta', in N. Gooptu and Johnny Parry, eds, *Persistence of Poverty in India*, New Delhi: Social Science Press: 344–69.

Mukherji, Partha N. (2012), 'Social Mobility and Social Structure: Towards a Conceptual-Methodological Reorientation', *Sociological Bulletin*, 61 (1): 26–52.

Olin Wright, Erik (2015), *Understanding Class*, London: Verso.

Pattenden, Jonathan (2014), 'Classes of Labour and Dynamics of Accumulation and Exploitation in Rural Karnataka', paper presented at the workshop 'Inequality and Poverty in South Asia', London School of Economics, April.

Rao, Nitya (2014), 'Marriage, Violence, and Choice: Understanding Dalit Women's Agency in Rural Tamil Nadu', *Gender and Society*, 29 (3): 410–33.

Srinivas, M.N. (2003), 'An Obituary on Caste as a System', *Economic and Political Weekly*, 38 (5): 455–59.

Sujatha, V. (2002), 'Tamil Nadu: Leather Processing: Role of Indigenous Technology', *Economic and Political Weekly*, 37 (47): 4672–75.

Tilly, Charles (1999), *Durable Inequality*, Berkeley: University of California Press.

10

Profit Inflation, Keynes and the Holocaust in Bengal, 1943–44

Utsa Patnaik

Keynesian demand management policies are usually associated with raising employment and incomes, but John Maynard Keynes also systematically discussed the exact opposite – measures for curtailing mass incomes, that he considered necessary to raise resources for financing wartime spending. In both *A Treatise on Money: The Applied Theory of Money* (1930, reprinted 1979) and *How to Pay for the War: A Radical Plan for the Chancellor of the Exchequer* (1940), specific measures for reducing mass consumption were explicitly discussed by Keynes.

During the Second World War, 6 million persons were put to death in Europe under fascist terror. But the death of 3 million civilians in undivided Bengal in India during a shorter sub-period of the war, from 1943 to 1944, has gone unnoticed in the international literature. This paper argues that these deaths were a direct result of the Keynesian policy of *profit inflation* deliberately followed at that time by the British and the colonial governments with a very specific purpose: to raise resources from the Indian population by curtailing mass consumption in order to finance the Allies' war in South Asia with Japan. Keynes himself was given the brief of advising the British government on Indian financial matters during the war. Because the policies followed were of demand management, which are always opaque to the general population, and remain opaque to this day even to the educated elite, the extreme compression of mass demand to raise forced savings that led to 3 million civilian deaths could be successfully camouflaged as simple famine, and attributed variously to natural phenomena like cyclone, or to food shortage, or to speculation and hoarding, or to not importing food in time, or to a combination of these factors.

Keynes had coined the term 'profit inflation' to describe a situation where in wartime, output prices are deliberately raised faster than wages in order to redistribute incomes away from wages and towards profits, and ensure substantial reduction of the consumption of wage earners. It can be applied equally to a situation where, in addition to wage earners, a large part of the working population comprises self-employed petty producers like artisans, fisherfolk, small peasants and so on, who have to buy food staples from the market since they produce either no food at all, or not enough to meet their needs. Without deliberate state policy of curtailing mass consumption, over £1,600 million of extra resources could not have been extracted from Indians during the war, with the bulk of this enormous burden falling on the population of Bengal, since Allied forces were located in and operated from that province. The state policy was to induce a very rapid *profit inflation* which redistributed incomes away from the working population towards capitalists and companies, which were then taxed. The colonial state directly spent in every war year after 1941, a *multiple* of its normal revenues by printing money – an extreme measure of 'profit inflation'.

Keynes was closely associated with Indian affairs from an early period of his life. He served in the India Office in London, leaving it when he was 25 years old, and used his experience gained there to write and publish *Indian Currency and Finance* (1913) five years later. He was a member of, or gave evidence to, successive Commissions set up to deliberate on Indian finance and currency (the Chamberlain, Babington–Smith and Hilton–Young Commissions, and for a while the Indian Fiscal Commission). He wrote articles on India and reviewed books on the Indian economy for the *Economic Journal* which he edited (such as T. Morison's *The Economic Transition in India* that discussed the drain of wealth). Keynes also gave lecture courses to students in Cambridge for many years on Indian monetary affairs.

In 1940, in view of the unusual financial situation arising from war, the British government appointed two economic advisors to the Chancellor of the Exchequer: an ex-banker, Lord Catto, and J.M. Keynes. *Indian financial and monetary matters were specifically entrusted to Keynes given his expertise in the area.* Keynes was the most influential figure at the Bretton Woods Conference in 1944, where the repayment of sterling owed by Britain to India was discussed by him with the Indian delegation.

Keynes's long India connection for four decades, his interest in the Indian monetary system and his part in policies followed in India during the Second World War have been neglected by his biographers (Minsky 1975; Moggridge 1995; Skidelsky 2001). His biographers appear to have had little interest in or understanding of the financial and monetary mechanisms underpinning the colonial rule that concerned Keynes, and they show no insight at all into India's role in sustaining the international gold standard even though literature on this was available (Saul 1960; de Cecco 1979). The severe impact on the colonies of the large forced loans Britain took from them is not mentioned, though Britain's refusal to honour its promise to repay debt immediately at the end of the war is discussed albeit cursorily.

That Keynes participated directly in formulating wartime policies in India cannot be in doubt as he was specifically given the brief of advising on Indian financial and monetary matters by the British government. Moreover, the war-financing policies implemented in India were uniquely Keynesian in nature, and were in most respects a textbook replication of policies he had advocated for raising resources in *A Treatise on Money* referring to the problem of financing the First War, and in *How to Pay for the War* referring to the Second War. We will first briefly discuss the specificity of the Indian fiscal and monetary system arising from the drain of wealth to Britain. Looking next at what Keynes had to say about war financing, his ideas will then be related to the main measures undertaken in India to finance war expenditure.

Economic Developments in India before the Second World War

The colonial government in India traditionally followed an *apparently* 'balanced budget' policy with expenditures strictly limited to revenues – the latter consisted mainly of land revenue supplemented by indirect taxes and revenues from government monopolies. 'Balanced budget' is a misnomer, however: the 'drain of wealth' imposed on India consisted in the fact that a large share (up to one-third of the budgetary revenues every year) was not spent in the normal manner of sovereign countries but was set aside under the head of 'expenditure abroad'. Effectively, the budget was kept in large surplus every year when domestic expenditure in relation to revenue is considered. The head of expenditure abroad always included the regular annual Home Charges incurred in sterling in Britain, additional variable items linked to military cost of wars abroad, and large 'gifts' from India to Britain.

The transformation of the rupees set aside in the budget in India under 'expenditure abroad' into sterling in the account of the Secretary of State for India in London took place (and could only take place) through the earning by India of gold and foreign exchange (forex) from its rising commodity export surplus to the world, entirely kept by Britain for its own use, while Indian earners of this export surplus were 'paid' out of their own taxes contributed to the budget. Not only were Indian producers deprived of international purchasing power they had earned, even the rupee equivalent of their export surplus earnings was not issued in the normal way since not even the colonial government was credited with any part of their net gold and forex earnings against which it could issue rupees. Rather, the Secretary of State for India in Council based in London kept all the gold and forex deposited with him as payment by foreign importers of Indian goods, and issued to them bills of exchange cashable only in rupees (termed Council Bills) to the value of these gold and forex deposits. The foreign importers sent the bills to the British-owned export houses and local export trading agents in India by post or by telegraphic transfer. These bills deposited with exchange banks were then paid out in rupees by the Treasury from the budgeted provision of 'expenditure abroad', and the exporting agents in turn paid to producers (peasants and artisans) from whom they sourced the goods, after keeping a hefty commission for themselves. Thus payment for India's commodity surplus earnings came not from equivalent issue of rupees but out of the producers' own tax contribution to the Indian budget, the part designated explicitly as expenditure abroad.

Y.S. Pandit (1937: 153) had pointed out that these rupee bills – termed Council Bills (CBs) – issued by the Secretary of State were a means of retaining the gold in London that would otherwise have flowed to India as foreigners' payment for its export surplus. Sunanda Sen (1992: 21–22) writes, 'the CBs provided a route for retaining in England the entire amount of India's export surplus. . . . Funds earmarked in the annual budget as "Expenditure Abroad" were used to honour the Council Bills.' The producers appeared to be paid, but in terms of real relations they were not actually paid since the 'payment' came out of their own taxes and not out of their foreign earnings. This is what made India's export surplus *unrequited* and constituted a tax-financed *transfer* to the metropolis, as had been correctly pointed out by those highly insightful authors, Dadabhai Naoroji and R.C. Dutt. This mechanism of transfer or 'drain' resulted in mass income deflation, monetary stringency and high interest rates in British India.

Data from the United Nations (1962) on the matrix of global trade show that for three decades up to 1928 (and very possibly earlier as well), India posted the second highest merchandise export surplus earnings in the world, second only to the United States. These rising global earnings were fully appropriated by Britain via the office of the Secretary of State as described, and accounting balance was maintained by administratively imposing the very same items of invisible liabilities on India's external account, now expressed in sterling, as were detailed in rupees in the budget under expenditure abroad. In fact the sum of the manipulated invisible demands put on India was deliberately pitched somewhat higher than actual commodity export surplus (no matter how fast the latter might rise), so that over a run of years the current account was always kept in deficit, and this deficit was shown as increase in India's debt to Britain. Large sums under 'gifts' were transferred whenever Britain required extra funds, with an accounting increase in Indian debt.

For example, in addition to the regular annual tax-financed transfer of about £25 million on account of Home Charges, an astonishing extra £100 million (that exceeded the entire annual budget of British India and amounted to over 3 per cent of Britain's national income) was transferred after the First World War as a 'gift' to Britain – a gift that no Indian knew about.[1] The important point to remember is that the actual producers and earners of the commodity export surplus, the local peasants and artisans, as mentioned, *were 'paid' in rupees out of the very taxes they themselves had contributed to the budget revenues.* Under this clever system, this part of the total taxes extracted from them merely changed its form from cash to goods embodied in export surplus. The budget was in perpetual surplus if these 'drain' items are excluded from the expenditure side, and the external current account was in matching surplus when the sterling value of the drain items were excluded.

Such surplus budgets entailing heavy tax-financed transfers every year (the 'drain') had a severely income-deflating effect: mass consumption was squeezed in order to release export goods. The greater the export surplus, the larger was the tax burden on the producers, and the more the decline in their consumption of basic staple foods (per capita annual foodgrains absorption in British India declined from 210 kg during the period 1904–09 to 157 kg during 1937–41, and reached its nadir of 137 kg by 1946).[2] While the masses suffered severe nutritional decline, the foreign export houses in India and the local export traders (*dalals*) benefited by taking a large cut from the price the producer received.

This mechanism, discussed elsewhere (U. Patnaik 1985, 2006, 2017; U. Patnaik and P. Patnaik 2016), was operated so successfully that even though India continuously posted the second largest merchandise export surplus earnings in the world for decades, the entire benefit of these huge earnings went to the metropolis. It used them not only to pay for its own deficits on current account with industrial Europe and North America, but also to export capital to these same regions, ensuring the diffusion of capitalism (Saul 1960; Bagchi 1972). By 1910, half of Britain's £120 million balance of payments deficit with USA, Canada and Continental Europe combined was being financed through Indian earnings according to Saul

(1960: Table XX, 58), while by 1911–13 two-fifths of Britain's balance of payments deficits with the entire world was being so financed, and our analysis of the United Nations (1962) data confirms this (U. Patnaik 2014). A discussion of the drain mechanism and a preliminary estimate of total drain from 1765 to 1938 are available in U. Patnaik (2017).

Keynes's deep interest in the Indian financial system is understandable because that system was unique in being so very different from any metropolitan one and, given the bimetallism prevalent at that time, it presented technical problems of maintaining monetary stability. Considerable finessing of the exchange rate between the silver rupee and gold-linked sterling was necessary in a volatile world economy, to achieve the rulers' multiple and connected aims of maximizing India's global commodity export surplus, while making sure that all such *financial gold* and forex earnings remained in London for Britain's use and did not leak back as payment to the actual producers in India (however, substantial *commodity gold* import was permitted). To this end, the rupee–sterling exchange rate was stabilized between 'gold points' carefully adjusted to a fraction of a farthing, to ensure that foreign importers of Indian goods would never find it more profitable to send financial gold directly to India but would follow the London Council Bill route. This enabled Britain to siphon off India's external earnings and rip off colonized producers by 'paying' them the rupee value of external earnings out of their own taxes – which meant not paying them at all.

The deflationary impact of annual surplus budgets in India was never explicitly discussed by Keynes to our knowledge, but it is not beyond the bounds of probability that the seeds of some of his later ideas were sown during his early engagement with the Indian fiscal and monetary system. The young Keynes was encouraged and patronized for many years by Edwin Montagu who, when serving as Secretary of State for India, put him on some of the commissions on currency and finance mentioned earlier. The India Office in London followed a traditional practice of obfuscating reality by fudging Indian accounts while maintaining technical correctness, and after his India Office stint Keynes did the same in *Indian Currency and Finance*. Keynes presented, in slightly modified form, the credits and debits of the Secretary of State's account; on the credit side, the actual receipts by the Secretary of State of gold and forex from global importers of Indian products were not mentioned, only their rupee equivalent that was shown as the Secretary of State's claim on the Indian budget; while the debit side comprised sterling expenditure by England out of these funds (Keynes 1913: 113). A studied silence was always maintained on how exactly rupees in the Indian budget ended up as gold and sterling with Britain.

The long bonanza for Britain based on its appropriation of India's booming export surplus earnings came to an end with the global agricultural depression followed by industrial depression, which saw a collapse of India's export surplus as indeed occurred for all primary product exporters. The United Nations (1962) data show that India's merchandise export surplus declined from its all-time high of $497 million in 1928 to only one-seventh at $73 million annual average by 1930–32 (see U. Patnaik 2014: 30). Bereft of the main prop of its balance of payments, Britain was unable to meet its global deficits and in 1931 was forced to devalue, finally abandoning the Gold Standard. Large distress financial gold outflow took place from India to Britain between 1931 and 1937 since Britain kept up its invisible demands on India despite the collapse of exchange earnings, but gold outflow was a once-for-all drain of assets and India's exchange earnings had no prospect of recovering to earlier heights in the changed world conjuncture. Since colonial transfers are not even recognized in standard economic literature, this important reason, among others, for the dethroning of Britain as world capitalist leader to this day finds no mention in the relevant literature on the Depression.

While the external 'drain' from India to Britain reduced to a trickle after 1938, the irruption of Allied forces into India during 1941–45 and suddenly increased military spending was met by using the budget to extract massive forced savings from the local population that had already suffered nutritional decline in the inter-war period. This was the background to the holocaust that claimed 3 million lives, whose economic cause is discussed below in Keynes's own words.

Demand Compression Advised by Keynes in *A Treatise on Money* and *How to Pay for the War*

Keynesian demand management policies are usually associated with state intervention to increase employment and incomes. But Keynes also repeatedly and systematically discussed measures for curtailing mass incomes and consumption that he considered a practical necessity to raise resources for financing wartime spending. In *A Treatise on Money: The Applied Theory of Money,* referring to the First World War, he said:

> The war inevitably involved in all countries an immense diversion of resources to forms of production which, since they did not add to the volume of liquid consumption goods purchasable and consumable by income earners, had just the same effect as an increase in investment in fixed capital would have in ordinary times. The investment thus required was – especially after the initial period – on such a scale that

it exceeded the maximum possible amount of voluntary saving which one could expect, even allowing for the cessation of most other kinds of investment including the replacement of wastage. *Thus forced transferences of purchasing power in some shape or form were a necessary condition of investment in the material of war on the desired scale.* The means of effecting this transference with the minimum of social friction and disturbance was the question for solution. (Keynes [1930] 1979: 152–53; emphasis added)

He then went on to discuss the three different methods through which such 'forced transferences of purchasing power' could be achieved: first, by reducing money wages while keeping prices steady; second, by letting prices rise more than money wages so as to reduce real wages; and third, by taxing earnings. Taking up the third course, he thought that 'the rich were too few' and therefore '. . . the taxation would have had to be aimed directly at the relatively poor, since it was above all their consumption, in view of its aggregate magnitude, which had somehow or other to be reduced' (ibid.: 153). But the additional taxation of wage earners would have to be substantial, it would meet trade union resistance and would be difficult for the government to implement.

'It was a choice, therefore, between the remaining alternatives – between lowering money wages and letting prices rise . . . it would be natural – and sensible – to prefer the latter.' (ibid.: 153–54). Keynes argued that it would be as difficult to enforce the required 25 per cent money wage cut, as to impose heavier taxes. *'I conclude therefore that to allow prices to rise by permitting a profit inflation, is in time of war, both inevitable and wise'* (ibid: 155, emphasis added).

Keynes was positing 'money-illusion' on the part of workers – they would oppose money wage cuts for given prices but they would not, to the same extent, oppose inflation without matching money wage rise, even though the second course lowered their real wages to exactly the same degree as the first. However, a profit inflation cutting real wages and raising profits would not by itself serve fully the aim of financing war spending, if all profits were retained by capitalists: taxation of profits was essential.

It is expedient to use entrepreneurs as collecting agents. But let them be agents and not principals. Having adopted for quite good reasons a policy which pours the booty into their laps, let us be sure that they hand it over as taxes and that they are not able to obtain a claim over the future income of the community by being allowed to 'lend' to the State what has thus accrued to them. *To let prices rise relatively to earnings and then tax entrepreneurs to the utmost is the right procedure* for '*virtuous*' *war finance*. For high taxation of profits and of incomes above the exemption limit is not a substitute for profit inflation but an adjunct of it. (Ibid.: 155; emphasis added)

Keynes's reasoning is clear – there had to be a substantial decline in the real consumption of the ordinary mass of the population and this could best be achieved without working class political opposition, not through additional taxation but by a *profit inflation*, by following policies which raised output prices without raising incomes at all, or to the same extent. This would redistribute incomes away from wages to profits, which should then be taxed.

Keynes's ideas on raising resources for war spending in Britain were further amplified in *How to Pay for the War: A Radical Plan for the Chancellor of the Exchequer* (1940), where he repeated the necessity of reducing mass consumption through an engineered inflation, and also discussed the methods of taxation and deferred payments. Keynes's ideas should interest us greatly for he was an influential advisor both to the British Chancellor of the Exchequer and to the Prime Minister; and in view of his expertise 'had special authority in discussion of Indian financial questions' (quoted in Chandavarkar 1990: 119). This fact throws light on how the balanced budget dogmas of the conservative bureaucrats in India were thrown to the winds when required for raising finance to serve the Allies' military spending.

War Financing through Extreme 'Profit Inflation' in India

India's export earnings recovered slowly from the mid-1930s as the developed world, especially USA, started following expansionary policies. India's total budget spending from 1938–39 to 1940–41 averaged Rs 88.8 crore, and annual deficit was only Rs 1.33 crore. (As the exchange rate averaged about Rs 13.50 to £1, the initial budget size was about £66 million). During 1939–40, Indian gold worth Rs 34.7 crore was transferred to London and the Reserve Bank of India (RBI) credited with equivalent blocked sterling, marking in effect a forced loan. After December 1941 the US entered the war against Japan, Allied forces poured into Bengal and war spending grew by leaps and bounds. The category 'recoverable war expenditure' had been created under the 1939 Indo-British financial agreement, specifying that the major costs of provisioning and operating Allied forces in India would be met through Indian resources until the end of the war. The RBI would be credited with the sterling equivalent of the rupees spent for the Allies: however, the account would be frozen, no sterling would be made available for actual spending and the account would be activated only at the end of the war, whenever that might be. Other heads of war spending were to be borne entirely by India. It was the 'recoverable war expenditures' that became a death warrant for 3 million persons in Bengal.

The movement of Allied troops and air forces into eastern India grew rapidly from early 1942; construction of airstrips, barracks and war-related industries was undertaken at a feverish pace. Private investment and output grew fast for munitions, chemicals, uniforms, bandages and the like as the government contracted with enterprises. The troops and supporting personnel had to be fed, clothed and transported at public expense. Table 10.1 details, from the RBI's 1945–46 Report, the unbelievably rapid growth of government expenditure, which is not matched in any other country – within a mere three years, by 1942–43, a sum amounting to 35 per cent of the pre-war national income of British India was being spent for war purposes, over two-thirds of this by printing money.

A war boom of unprecedented proportions resulted as total spending by the central government exploded to reach Rs 667 crore (£494 million) by fiscal 1942–43, *posting a 7.5-fold increase in a mere three years, over the Rs 88.8 crore (£66 million) annual average from 1937–38 to 1939–40.* Increased taxation had only doubled the revenues by 1942–43, so the government's own budget deficit ballooned from zero to reach Rs 112 crore, a sum substantially more than the entire normal budget. A much greater impact resulted, however, from the additional Rs 260 crore spent on average annually under 'recoverable expenditure' during 1941–42 and 1942–43, amounting to three times the normal budget. The total deficit by 1942–43 reached Rs 438 crore or £324 million (see Table 10.1), nearly five times the pre-war budget. Three-quarters of this arose from the 'recoverable war expenditures' undertaken for Allied forces, and one-quarter from the government's own excess spending.

This exploding deficit was entirely met by printing money, justified by treating Britain's sterling-denominated entries with the RBI in London, as reserves against which currency issue in India could be made up to two-and-a-half times (Joshi 1975: 405–06; Sen 1981: 75). That this was not only specious but disingenuous reasoning on the part of the monetary authorities, is clear enough. Assets or reserves, as the term itself indicates, are meant to be actually there to be drawn upon in case of need, while these sterling 'reserves' were a paper fiction, they did not actually exist since not a penny could be drawn. Nor was there any certainty of their being paid out in future as promised, after the war ended. The non-existent, so-called 'reserves' were an accounting device for extracting massive resources from the Indian people.

Table 10.1 *Central government total outlay, revenue and deficit, 1937–38 to 1945–46* (in Rs crore, 1 crore = 10 million)

	1	2	3	4	5	6	7	8
	Total govt outlay (4 + 6)	Per cent 3 to 1	Budget revenue	Budget expenditure	Budget deficit (3 − 4)	Recoverable expenditure (deficit)	Total deficit (5 + 6)	Merchandise surplus
1937–38	86.61	100.0	86.61	86.61	0.00	0.00	0.00	43.0
1938–39	85.15	99.3	84.52	85.16	−0.63	0.00	−0.63	78.0
1939–40	98.57	95.9	94.57	94.57	0.00	−4.00	−4.00	80.0
1940–41	167.18	64.4	107.65	114.18	−6.53	−53.00	−59.53	53.6
1941–42	341.26	39.4	134.57	147.26	−12.69	−194.00	−206.69	80.1
1942–43	667.04	26.5	176.88	289.05	−112.17	−325.48	−437.65	86.7
1943–44	857.17	29.4	252.00	441.85	−189.78	−377.87	−567.65	96.3
1944–45	970.38	34.6	335.57	496.71	−161.14	−410.84	−571.98	28.0
1945–46	894.20	40.3	360.67	484.57	−123.90	−374.54	−498.44	27.0
Total	4167.56	39.2	1633.04	2239.96	−606.84	−1739.73	−2346.60	572.7

Note: Up to 1941–42, Total government outlay is the sum of Budget expenditure plus the absolute value of Recoverable expenditure, as indicated. From 1942–43 onwards, Total government outlay is found to exceed this sum slightly owing to borrowing by government, not shown in the table. The exchange rate averaged about Rs 13.50 = £1.

In *The Cambridge Economic History of India* (*CEHI*), *Vol. 2*, edited by Dharma Kumar and Meghnad Desai (1984: Table 12.11, 943), some data were reproduced from the same Table 10 of the RBI Report 1945–46, but the figures in columns 1, 3 and 4 in the table above were not given. No idea of the actual increase in central government revenues and expenditure, or of total outlays and total deficit, can be obtained from the *CEHI*.

Source: Reserve Bank of India, *Report on Currency and Finance for the Year 1945–46*, Table 10.

Figure 10.1 *Central government total outlay, revenue and total deficit, 1938–39 to 1945–46* (in Rs crore)

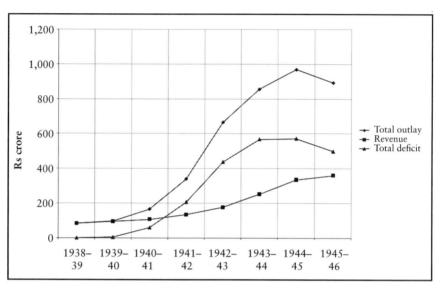

Source: Table 10.1; 1 crore = 10 million.

During the Depression years, administrators trained in classical theories of 'sound finance' and terrified of budget deficits had actually cut domestic spending, thus intensifying the adverse effects of depression. Such conservative officials in India did not decide on the opposite course of monetizing massive deficits every year to the tune of a multiple of the entire normal budget. Indian monetary policy was now being directed solely from London: all caution was thrown to the winds to serve metropolitan interests at the expense of the Indian people. The RBI, set up in 1935, served as a pliant tool and implemented the fiction that mere paper entries of sterling sums was the same as actual reserves. Corresponding to the suddenly expanding level of wartime activity, it expanded the money supply nearly seven-fold (Table 10.2). India lacked the technical means of printing paper currency at this frenetic rate, so the notes were printed in England. (Reportedly, highly efficient German-owned firms in England were given the task of printing notes, which if true would be ironic indeed: but this author has not been able to confirm this as a fact.)

The reckless deficit spending undertaken for the Allies grew fastest between 1940–41 and 1942–43. The 1940–41 outlay was already 69 per cent higher than the previous year; the next year it was more than doubled, and nearly doubled again the following year: over two years, government outlays expanded at 98 per cent per annum (Table 10.1). By

1942–43, total outlays reached a level equalling 35 per cent of the initial 1939–40 national income of British India, and reached 51 per cent of it as outlays peaked at Rs 970 crores during 1944–45.[3] Keynes cautioned against excessive spending, but solely in the interest of limiting Britain's post-war indebtedness: he showed no interest in the extent of adverse impact on the Indian population – after all, the objective was precisely to reduce their consumption.

The unprecedented explosion of public expenditure combined with the private investment boom generated, through multiplier effects that were strong for a poor population, a sudden and immensely increased demand for food, clothing and other necessities on the part of the rising numbers employed in war industries, in addition to the demands of the Allied personnel. While multiplier effects that raise demand call forth increased output, where most of the demand was for primary products and expanded with such abnormal rapidity in a matter of months, the adjustment was bound to be through price rise of these products, notably foodgrains, rather than output rise. Agricultural output could not possibly grow fast, and in Bengal, rice output had been in absolute decline for three decades owing to land and resource diversion to export crops. Nowhere in the world were such irresponsible monetary policies followed during the war as in India, and arguably nowhere else was inflation as rapid.

The personnel required for producing essential war goods and services were protected from price rise to a large extent through a system of food procurement and rationing which was rapidly put in place by the government (Sen 1981: 56). The urban population in one way or another had access to food, though it did have to take large cuts in real consumption. The burden of financing the mountainous extra public outlays was passed on to the unprotected mass of the rural population, which was severely affected, other than the small minority of landlords and moneylenders who benefited by foreclosing on the mortgaged assets of the majority struggling to survive.

Most of the government provisioning for the troops and supporting personnel, and for the new urban rationing system, was sourced from the surrounding hinterland of the towns in Bengal. Prices of all necessities started rising: the price of rice quadrupled over the eighteen months from the last quarter of 1941 to the middle of 1943 (RBI Report 1945–46; Sen 1981: 54). While wholesale prices trebled in India as a whole by 1943 (see Table 10.2), the inflation was much sharper and compressed within a shorter period in Bengal, where the bulk of the increased spending and sourcing of food from rural areas actually took place.

Not an iota of sterling owed to India as recoverable war expenditure was made available for food imports. India's own merchandise export surplus could have paid for food imports, but these earnings continued to be appropriated by Britain: from 1938–39 to 1943–44. India's export surplus totalled Rs 475 crore or about £352 million (see Table 10.1), taken in full by Britain for its own spending, and in the RBI accounts shown as repayment of India's sterling debt to Britain (Lokanathan 1946: 42). The 'debt' itself had been artificially created for invisible liabilities were imposed on India, always in excess of its total external earnings as earlier explained.

As rice prices doubled, quadrupled and rose six-fold, the rural labourers, artisans, fisherfolk and poor peasantry in Bengal did not know what had hit them. Rapid inflation is the most regressive possible method of raising resources because it adversely impacts to the greatest extent, the already poor rural labourers and net food purchasers. Food stocks physically disappeared as government bought up available supplies through contractors for urban distribution, and as traders held on to stocks anticipating further price rise. Many thousands of rural families, already at the margin of subsistence, sank first into dearth and then into hunger, then into famishment and finally into death. Many of those who migrated in search of food to the cities, in their weakened state, succumbed to disease. The final death toll during 1943–44 has been placed conservatively after reviewing the evidence at between 2.7 and 3.1 million by Amartya K. Sen (1981), while some authors cite up to 3.5 million taking into account secondary effects of enhanced morbidity.

The sample survey carried out by Mahalanobis, Mukherjea and Ghosh (1946), from the Indian Statistical Institute, on the after-effects of the famine found that among the survivors, half a million families had been reduced to utter destitution. British rule in India had started with the massive famine in Bengal in 1770 that decimated one-third of the population – the rapacity of the Company in trebling taxes over five years being a major reason for the high toll. British rule in India ended with a massive famine, yet again in Bengal, which was made to bear the brunt of resource extraction.

Amartya K. Sen, in *Poverty and Famines* (1981: 75), had correctly concluded, 'The 1943 famine can indeed be described as a "boom famine" related to powerful inflationary pressures initiated by public expenditure expansion', and had traced the 'failure of exchange entitlements' to such inflationary pressures. However, he did not give any data on the extent of the monetized deficit in relation to the normal budget, or link the policies followed to Keynes and his theory of profit inflation for raising wartime resources. This author a decade later (see U. Patnaik 1991) had identified the famine as arising from engineered profit inflation described by Keynes

Table 10.2 *Index of money supply, wholesale price index and total deficit, 1940–46*

	Index of money supply	Wholesale price index	Total deficit (Rs crore)
1940	100.0	100	4.00
1941	126.5	141	59.53
1942	215.1	187	206.69
1943	357.7	311	437.65
1944	486.5	302	567.65
1945	607.3	292	571.98
1946	686.8	328	498.44

Source: Reserve Bank of India, *Report on Currency and Finance 1946–47, 1947–48.*

in his *Treatise on Money* as 'virtuous war finance' but did not know then that Keynes was personally charged with advising on Indian monetary matters from 1940 – this information became available in A. Chandavarkar's *Keynes and India* (1989), it is not mentioned in any biography of Keynes. Digitization of the RBI records has made it easier to access the detailed data presented in Table 10.1,[4] while the publication of a definitive study of India's national income by S. Sivasubramonian (2000) has enabled us to relate deficit financing to national income.

Even though deficit financing through monetization continued at a high level and reached its peak in 1946, we see from Table 10.2 that prices ceased to rise after 1943. This was owing to the severe compression of mass demand throughout the country, and the 3 million excess deaths, that together outweighed the continued increase in demand from organized labour employed in war-related activities, whose wages were indexed however inadequately to inflation. In an advanced country with unionized labour and near-universal wage indexation, a wage–price spiral would have taken place, and the inflation might have acclererated. But in India, even at its height, the organized labour force was very small relative to the total labour force. Lacking bargaining power, the mass of unorganized labour along with petty producers simply suffered absolute immiserization.

Keynesian Profit Inflation was the policy followed in India albeit to a much more extreme extent than Keynes might have openly advocated, when the colonial government agreed to meet war spending for the Allies to an unlimited extent from the Indian budget, incurred deficits each war year to the tune of a mutiple of the entire pre-war budget, and monetized the deficits, printing money using the fiction that mere paper entries of sterling sums owed could be treated at par with actual reserves. The resulting sharply inflationary war boom did much more than 'pour the booty' into the laps of capitalists: the enormous excess of war expenditure over voluntary savings was brought to equality through the *forced savings* entailed in the inflation. The real consumption decline was so inequitably concentrated on the poorest segments of the population, and the decline was so large and rapid, that it physically eliminated 3 million persons who starved to death.

This author had earlier written: 'Such a savage and rapid compression of the real income and consumption of the most vulnerable sections of a population as a direct result of financing expenditures far in excess of voluntary savings, can find few parallels in the modern world' (U. Patnaik 1999: 336). Bengal's population was especially vulnerable because its per capita absorption of foodgrains had fallen to the largest extent by 38 per cent in the inter-war period compared to 29 per cent average for British India (Blyn 1966, Table 5.3: 102). During this period there was absolute decline in rice output in Bengal while exported commercial crops continued to grow.

While no previous author to our knowledge has linked Keynes directly to the holocaust in Bengal, after putting together all the facts we have cited, there is no doubt in this author's mind that Keynes himself, charged with advising on Indian monetary policy, was fully aware of and directly involved in Indian fiscal and monetary developments during the war. The profit inflation he had advocated in theory and watched unfolding

Table 10.3 *Increase in direct tax revenues, 1938–89 to 1944–45* (in Rs crore)

	Direct tax revenue			(Rs crore)	
	A Total tax	B Income tax	A / B Income tax / total tax %	Index total tax	Index income tax
1938–39	73.8	17.3	23.4	100	100
1939–40	81.9	19.4	23.7	111	112
1940–41	79.7	25.9	32.5	108	150
1941–42	103.3	44.1	42.7	140	255
1942–43	134.5	85.8	63.8	182	496
1943–44	199.2	138	69.3	270	798
1944–45	261.1	182.6	69.9	354	1055
(Budget) Total	933.5	513.1	55		

Source: Lokanathan (1946: 38); the last two columns have been calculated.

in practice resulted in forced consumption decline, hence forced savings of such a drastic magnitude that it killed 3 million people who starved to death. *This was no less a result of public policy than was the gassing of holocaust victims in Europe.* It amounted to genocide by economic means.

Inflation as a method of war financing, that had been termed as 'virtuous finance' by Keynes, turned out to be a most 'vicious' and uncivilized policy followed by Britain. Wholesale prices rose by 70 per cent in England comparing 1944 to 1935, while the rise was by over 200 per cent in India as a whole (Lokanathan 1946: 49) and even higher in Bengal. Keynes's advice that after 'pouring the booty' into the laps of capitalists they should be taxed, was also implemented faithfully. Table 10.3 shows that direct taxes in India including corporation tax rose more than tenfold, and their share in total tax revenues rose from below one-quarter to seven-tenths (ibid.: 38) . Increased taxes were woefully inadequate as a share of ballooning spending, as we have already seen from Table 10.1.

Contrasting Keynesian Wartime Policies in India and in Britain

In articles published in British newspapers in late 1939 and in *How to Pay for the War* (1940), Keynes repeated his earlier observations on the absolute necessity of reducing mass consumption in Britain, but his initial proposals of raising resources through inflation and compulsory savings, according to Skidelsky, met with a 'frosty reception' from the trade unions. Leaders like Aneurin Bevan certainly did not suffer from money illusion, and were fully aware of the highly adverse impact of inflation on the already needy within the working class, while the latter felt greatly offended by the presumption that workers would not voluntarily contribute resources for fighting fascism but had to be virtually tricked into doing so through inflation. Faced with strong opposition from labour leaders, Keynes was obliged to give up his initial proposals in favour of additional taxes graded by income levels. Strangely, Keynes opposed rationing of essentials even in wartime and his views on this coincided with those of Friedrich von Hayek, who commended Keynes's position. Wiser counsel from other members of government prevailed and rationing of all essential consumption items was introduced. (Skidelsky comments that Keynes did not believe in *dirigisme* as a general principle – it seems later authors attributed it to him incorrectly in view of his advocacy of state action to generate employment.) In order to ensure working class support, the socially divisive and highly regressive measure of inflation was given up as an explicit method of war financing by Keynes in favour of taxation, and he reformulated 'compulsory savings' as the better-sounding 'deferred incomes'. Additional taxation of £250 million was considered enough in the 1941 budget to cover the inflationary gap (Skidelsky 2001: 84–88).

Keynes worked out a preliminary estimate of national income for Britain and a detailed plan to distribute the proposed increased tax burden equitably over its population. He estimated Britain's net national income at market prices, at £6,229 million in 1940.[5] Those families earning below £5 per week were to be exempt, while graded taxation was to be imposed on higher income groups. Given a total population of 47.5 million, this meant a per capita annual income of £131.14, while in India in 1940 per capita income was Rs 64 (or £4.5).[6] The average income of the Briton was some thirty times that of the Indian; additional taxes in Britain's 1941 budget comprised £5.26 per capita, or 4 per cent of average income. The monetized deficit per capita in British India in 1942–43, however, was 28 per cent of the population's far lower average income.

Keynes's idea of *deferred income* was precisely what was entailed in the agreement signed by the British government with the colonial state, which put the onus of footing the war bill on India with a mere undertaking to repay after the end of war – except that the deferred income was to apply to an entire people, not particular classes which could afford to pay; the amount was astronomical relative to paying capacity; the method used was deliberate rapid inflation, highly regressive in hurting most the already poor among the peasantry and all rural net food purchasers; and there was no specific deadline by which repayment would take place, if at all. India was Britain's largest creditor: its sterling debt to Egypt was far smaller.

As far back as the 1860s, the administrator W.W. Hunter had identified the classes of persons in Bengal that were entirely dependent on purchasing food from the market and were therefore the most vulnerable in the event of food price inflation. These classes comprised labourers, artisans and fishermen. In his remarkable little book titled *A Famine Warning System for Bengal* (1867), Hunter had given the estimated numbers belonging to these classes for the different districts of Bengal Presidency, the prevailing price of rice, and the extent of rise in this price that should serve as a warning trigger for government to intervene to prevent famine (some of the data he compiled was reproduced in U. Patnaik 1991). Hunter's book is significant in showing that administrators did not think of famine as arising from decline in food availability alone, as in a drought, but clearly specified what A.K. Sen (1981) was later to term 'failure of exchange entitlements' of net food purchasers as a cause of famine, and advocated a warning system to prevent inflation beyond a point deemed to be safe.

Exactly the opposite policy followed during wartime, the measures to promote rapid inflation detailed so far, was not unwitting but quite deliberate: administrators were not so obtuse as to be unaware of the adverse impact of inflation on the population, a much higher fraction of which had become pauperized and landless after the Depression years and was more vulnerable than ever before. As the deaths mounted, the thrust of policy continued to be to suck foodgrains away from the famished rural population, and available food supplies with Britain donated by the US were directed not to India but to other countries in Europe (Mukherjee 2011). The rulers cared little for what they might have termed today 'collateral damage' of deaths from rapid inflation and its impact on production, since it was clear to them that the days of British rule and hence of tax collection in India were numbered.

Winston Churchill, with whom Keynes perforce worked closely during wartime, was an admirer of Mussolini and was unabashedly racist. According to Andrew Murray (2009: 20), 'The British Premier held that Hindus were "a foul race" who were "protected by their mere pullulation from the doom that is their due".' The term Hindus was often used by the rulers to refer to Indians in general. Murray draws a convincing parallel between the racism of imperialists and the racism of fascists. An urgent request by the then Secretary of State for India and Burma, Leopold Amery, that food exports be stopped in view of famine, was turned down by Churchill in the crudest terms, prompting even the conservative Amery to criticize his Premier for his 'Hitler-like' view of the colonized. Churchill had earlier 'flirted with eugenics' (ibid.: 20, 27), being much concerned with checking the growth of what he called the 'feeble-minded' in the British population.

Keynes too had a deep interest in eugenics and served during 1937 to 1944 as an important office bearer of the English Eugenics Society (ibid.: 27). Keynes had long held neo-Malthusian views on population, especially with regard to colonized people of the global South, as John Toye (2005) points out. In *Economic Consequences of the Peace* (1919) and later, Keynes worried about impending global food shortage, food price rise and decline in the terms of trade for 'civilized countries' threatening their standard of life, the responsibility for which he attributed to the present and future 'fecundity of the East' – the East presumably being where the 'non-civilized' countries were located (Toye 2005: 132–34).

Yet, the decennial censuses showed absolute population decline in India between 1911 and 1921, owing mainly to high mortality from the virulent 1918 influenza epidemic. India's population grew by 17 per cent between 1901 and 1931, lower than Britain's population growth by 22 per cent over the same period (despite a much higher rate of permanent out-migration from Britain). Keynes took no account of the fact that the growing poverty of the colonized offset their growth in numbers and their per capita food consumption had declined sharply. While the perceived threat of increasing food price allegedly posed by the 'fecundity of the East' had no rational basis, Keynes's remarks did reflect in a distorted way the very real fears of an economist hailing from the most import-dependent industrial country in the world.

On his views about population and the terms of trade, Keynes was roundly criticized by William Beveridge who pinpointed mistakes in his formal argument. (Toye 2005: 135–36). Economic developments later were to follow the opposite course, a secular decline in terms of trade for primary producers. It is interesting to note that the 2008 global food price spike was similarly fallaciously attributed by the then US President George W. Bush and economist Paul Krugman to rising demand from populous India and China, ignoring the fact that per capita grain consumption had fallen in both these countries and glossing over the huge diversion of grain to ethanol in the US.

Given his mephitic ideas, expressed in the crude language of an immature schoolboy, not surprisingly Churchill was quite unmoved by high famine mortality in Bengal created by British policy; indeed it is more than likely that he welcomed it as hastening the 'beastly' Indians towards the 'doom' that he considered as 'their due'. Keynes was not known ever to be abusive, but his liberal views did not survive the litmus test of a rational attitude towards a subject population. In a private letter to the editor of *The New Statesman* and *Nation* in 1943, as the famine raged, Keynes attributed the carnage in Bengal to the Indianization, hence a new-found alleged inefficiency, of the civil service (Chandavarkar 1989: 181).

It should be stressed that overt or covert racism on the part of important political leaders and public personalities was nothing but an expression of the latent, deep fear that the rulers who are in a minority always have of the numerically predominant ruled, and amounted to a form of self-exoneration, since policies of such inhumanity were imposed on subject populations as they well knew could have no moral justification. The rulers showed *bad faith* in the philosophical sense, in refusing to accept responsibility for their own actions. Their actions illustrated with text-book clarity the truism that exploitation not only degrades the exploited but ultimately dehumanizes the exploiters, however 'civilized' they may consider themselves to be. Those British officials on the ground in India who were not racist also became knowingly, or otherwise, complicit in these policies that followed from the very logic of a long history of colonial oppression. But with their direct contact with ordinary working people, a few developed a modicum of sympathy and understanding and did try sometimes to moderate the harshness of the policies they implemented.

Was there an alternative to the imposition of the enormous burden of war financing on India and the resultant extinguishing of 3 million lives? Indeed there was. The monetized budget deficit of Rs 606 crore (about £448 million) from 1940–41, and the consequent reduced real consumption by the population owing to this inflationary gap, would have entailed dearth but not death, and was absorbable as part of the war effort. It was the additional war expenditure arbitrarily imposed on India entailing forced savings three times higher at Rs 17.4 billion (£1.29 billion), which led to the extreme compression of rural consumption in Bengal and claimed 3 million lives. This was an impossible sum demanded of a people already overtaxed, drained for two centuries of exchange earnings and pushed into undernutrition; but it would not have been an impossible sum for the metropolitan population, amounting to only one-thirtieth of the burden actually placed on Indians. A sum of Rs 17.4 billion, or £1.29 billion, spent from 1940–41 to 1945–46 could have been raised by additional annual taxation in Britain of £4.5 per capita, while if the USA had chipped in, it would have been just over £1 per capita; or a combination of taxation to a lower extent, and crediting India with its own gold and dollar earnings that were entirely appropriated by Britain would have been the more humane solution.

At Bretton Woods in 1944 and later, Britain argued for cancelling part of its debt and for postponing repayment of the rest beyond the end of the war, citing lack of capacity to pay. Keynes took a strong position against that of the Indian delegation and scuttled its request for partial trilateral convertibility involving USA, which could have made some dollar funds available immediately to India for badly needed food imports, since only USA had goods to export. Keynes insisted that it was a bilateral matter between India and Britain (even though India had financed Allied forces, not Britain alone). The Indian delegation, including its British finance member, pressed Britain to honour its commitment of repaying sterling debt, citing the extreme suffering the population had gone through. The illogical response was that the suffering was in the past. It was even suggested by a member of the British delegation that writing off all sterling debt be made a condition for Indian independence, but fortunately this was opposed by Keynes (Skidelsky 2001: 413–14).

On the issue of sterling balances, the creditor nation, India, was in a weaker position than the debtor imperialist country that, using its political position, had unilaterally taken a forced loan of gargantuan proportions and when the time came for repayment, was implacable in trying to reduce its obligation drastically. With not a penny of sterling funds owed to India released, and with India's own wartime earnings from export surplus entirely taken over by Britain, very little food imports could take place: by 1946, per head grain availability had dropped further to 137 kg in India. And by April 1946, Keynes himself was prematurely dead from a long-standing heart problem.

Keynes was no doubt a liberal and even a humanist in the European context, where the working class had reason to be grateful for his employment-enhancing policies. But he was a member of the British ruling class and was every inch an imperialist in the colonial context. He never visited India, but formulated and influenced public policies there with apparently little interest in the extent of pauperization to which two centuries of drain of wealth had reduced the population, especially that of Bengal, longest under British rule. His Indian students in Cambridge later stated that he showed no interest in debates over the standard of living in India: all that interested him was the financial and monetary system (Chandavarkar 1989: 135–37, 182).

The policies followed in India to raise wartime resources were thus in sharp contrast to those followed in Britain. Keynes abandoned his initial proposal in the face of working class opposition in Britain and worked out an equitably distributed tax burden over classes at different levels of income, while part of extra taxes were to be repaid after the war ended. But no such considerations existed when it came to a subject population with one-thirtieth of the per head income of the Briton. Economic genocide through profit inflation – for that is what the Bengal famine was – was perfectly acceptable to the British administrators. The long British imperium in India was coming to a messy end; therefore no thought needed to be wasted any longer on preserving the lives, working capacity hence taxable capacity of the population. The scale and rate of this final act of resource extraction was arguably the most extreme, considering the entire period of British rule in India.

Justice delayed is justice denied. Sterling balances owed to India under interim agreements were divided into two accounts in 1947, the first containing only £65 million that could be immediately spent, while the second was frozen. In 1948, the balances in the two accounts were £80.58 million and £1,033.23 million; sterling devaluation against the dollar in 1949 greatly reduced purchasing capacity of the first while the second remained frozen until the 1950s, when the Korean War boom had reduced real values further. Whatever was paid up had been divided between India and Pakistan in proportion to their populations. India's share of the depleted sterling balances helped it to launch the ambitious Second Plan for development by providing a buffer against balance of payment worries for two to three years. The small fraction of sterling balances that Pakistan received is not likely to have been spent for the benefit of its eastern part which later became Bangladesh, from where the majority of the famine victims had hailed. Even in this very limited sense, no compensation was received for the enforced sacrifice of millions of lives.

Epilogue

History is the only laboratory that the scholar of the social sciences has. The holocaust in Bengal holds important lessons for analysing the current situation. It tells us that large-scale resource extraction entailing economic genocide is something that imperialist countries could get away with quite easily, attributing it to natural causes and abnormal external conditions. Owing to such misinformation, not a single demand was raised in India by patriotic political leaders or by any public intellectual, that the Allies should pay reparations for the lives wantonly lost owing to the extreme and inhumane measure of resource extraction from a population already greatly impoverished by preceding decades of tax-financed transfers and by the Depression. Barring individual exceptions, even the most intelligent persons in the country who actually lived through the famine period could be conceptually quite blind as regards its real cause. Or, if they did know the real cause, as perhaps some of Keynes's brightest Indian students did, they found it expedient to maintain silence.

It should not surprise us that there continues to be neo-imperialist resource extraction from the peasantry in India as indeed in other developing countries today, which is neither recognized nor analysed as such, imposing a prolonged toll on the lives of peasants and of petty producers generally. Demand management is a two-edged weapon: it can be 'virtuous finance' when used to expand public spending judiciously and reduce unemployment. Equally, when particular dominant Northern imperialist interests require a compression of mass consumption in developing countries to release primary resources for their own benefit, then these dominant interests can and do push for the implementing of 'vicious finance' by national governments, by peddling incorrect and self-serving theories.

Fiscal policies which reduce public spending in developing countries even though resources are unemployed, trade policies which remove protection to petty producers and urge removal of the meagre subsidies developing countries offer for food security, financial reform policies which withdraw credit on easy terms for small-scale producers and try instead to promote credit-financed consumption durables for the rich, all fall in the category of 'vicious finance'. They serve the same aim as taxation did under colonial systems, and as additional taxation plus profit inflation did during the war. These policies squeeze mass employment and incomes, leading to a fall in the aggregate demand for basic food staples and simple traditional manufactures. This releases the land and investment resources for increasing the output of a range of exportable crops including new perishable items, which can never be produced in industrially advanced, cold temperate countries, but which are essential for filling their supermarket shelves especially in winter when their land is frozen and nothing will grow. These policies shift income distribution in developing countries further in favour of the already well-to-do minority, a desired outcome for advanced country corporations which want market demand expanding for their high-end consumer durables.

The cost is high for the poor majority of developing country populations subjected to neoliberal policies. Given land constraint, more external demands without adequate investment leads to decline in domestic foodgrains output per head. Yet we see in India that stocks build up and massive food exports take place because income deflation through fiscal contraction and 'targeting', which denies access to affordable food from the public distribution system, reduces per capita demand even more than it reduces output. Such a severe decline of per capita foodgrain availability has taken India by now to a level below not only Sub-Saharan Africa, but also below the Least Developed countries. Exposure to global price volatility and removal of effective price support have resulted in debt-induced farmer suicides – the total number since 1997 by now exceeds 3,00,000. But the seriousness of these trends is not even recognized by either government or by public intellectuals – rather, fallacious arguments are advanced to rationalize and thus justify the adverse trends, including the idea that not economic but 'cultural factors' underlie farmer suicides.

It is important to remember that these overall policies which go by the name of neoliberal reforms, and have been systematically and successfully introduced by international financial organizations and transnational corporate interests, have but a single aim: to replicate imperialist control over developing countries including India, in new forms appropriate to the present era. Without an understanding of this overall context, even the best-intentioned micro-level analyses run the danger of supporting and serving the neo-imperialist agenda.

I thank Mihir Bhattacharya, Radhika Desai, Cristina Marcuzzo and Amit Bhaduri for their helpful comments on an earlier version of this paper.

This paper was published under the same title as a Special Article in *Economic and Political Weekly*, vol. 54, issue no. 42, 20 October 2018, pp. 33–43.

Notes

[1] See A.K. Bagchi (1997: 522). Share in British national income calculated by this author from G. Tily (2009, Table 5: 251). As India's wartime export earnings had not risen sufficiently to allow such a large transfer in full, the balance was shown as increase in Indian debt.

[2] U. Patnaik and P. Patnaik (2016, Table 7.2: 99), calculated from basic data in G. Blyn (1966).

[3] India's national income estimates from S. Sivasubramonian (2000), adjusted for British India by this author.

[4] I thank Arundhati Chowdhury for making available the digitized RBI Reports to me.

[5] See Tily (2009, Table 5: 251).

[6] For Indian national income, S. Sivasubramonian (2000) adjusted for British India by this author.

References

Bagchi, A.K. (1972), 'Some International Foundations of Capitalist Growth and Underdevelopment', *Economic and Political Weekly*, 8 (31–3), August: 1559–70.

——— (1997), *The Presidency Banks and the Indian Economy, 1876–1914,* The State Bank of India and Calcutta: Oxford University Press.

Blyn, G. (1966), *Agricultural Trends in India 1891–1949: Output, Area and Productivity,* Philadelphia: University of Pennsylvania Press.

Chandavarkar, A. (1989), *Keynes and India,* Basingstoke: Macmillan.

de Cecco, M. (1984), *The International Gold Standard: Money and Empire,* London: F. Pinter.

Dutt, R.C. ([1903–05] 1970), *Economic History of India,* Vol. 1: *Under Early British Rule 1757–1837* [1903], Vol. 2: *In the Victorian Age 1837–1900* [1905], Delhi: Government of India; second reprint, by arrangement with Routledge and Kegan Paul, 1970.

Hunter, W.W. (1867), *A Famine Warning System for Bengal,* London: Trubner.

Joshi, M.D. (1975), 'Currency', in V.B. Singh, ed., *Economic History of India 1857–1956,* Bombay: Allied.

Keynes, J.M. (1913), *Indian Currency and Finance,* London: Macmillan.

——— (1919), *The Economic Consequences of the Peace,* New York: Harcourt, Brace and Howe.

——— ([1930] 1971), *A Treatise on Money: The Applied Theory of Money,* in *The Collected Writings of John Maynard Keynes,* Vol. 4, London: Macmillan and Cambridge University Press, for the Royal Economic Society.

——— (1940), *How to Pay for the War: A Radical Plan for the Chancellor of the Exchequer,* Melbourne: Macmillan.

Kumar, D. and Meghnad Desai, eds (1984), *The Cambridge Economic History of India: 1757–1970,* Vol. 2, Delhi: Orient Longman.

Lokanathan, P.S. (1946), *India's Post War Reconstruction and Its International Aspect,* Delhi: Indian Council for World Affairs.

Mahalanobis, P.C., R. Mukherjea and A. Ghosh (1946), 'A Sample Survey of the After-effects of the Bengal Famine of 1943', *Sankhya: The Indian Journal of Statistics,* 7 (4), July: 337–400.

Minsky, H.P. (1975), *John Maynard Keynes,* New York: Columbia University Press.

Moggridge, D.E. (1995), *Maynard Keynes: An Economist's Biography,* London: Routledge.

Mukherjee, M. (2011), *Churchill's Secret War: The British Empire and the Ravaging of India during World War II,* New York: Basic Books.

Murray, A. (2009), *The Imperial Controversy: Challenging the Empire Apologists*, Croydon: Manifesto Press.

Naoroji, Dadabhai ([1901] 1962), *Poverty and Un-British Rule in India*, Delhi: Government of India.

Pandit, Y.S. (1937), *India's Balance of Indebtedness 1898–1913*, London: Allen and Unwin.

Patnaik, U. (1984), 'Tribute Transfer and the Balance of Payments in *The Cambridge Economic History of India, Vol. II*', *Social Scientist*, 12 (12): 43–55; reprinted in U. Patnaik (1999).

——— (1991), 'Food Availability and Famine: A Longer View', *Journal of Peasant Studies*, 19 (1), October: 1–25; reprinted in U. Patnaik (1999).

——— (1999), *The Long Transition: Essays on Political Economy*, Delhi: Tulika Books.

——— (2006), 'The Free Lunch: Transfers from the Tropical Colonies and Their Role in Capital Formation in Britain during the Industrial Revolution', in K.S. Jomo, ed., *Globalization under Hegemony*, Delhi: Oxford University Press.

——— (2014), 'India in the World Economy 1900 to 1935: The Interwar Depression and Britain's Demise as World Capitalist Leader', *Social Scientist*, 42 (1–2), January–February: 13–35.

——— (2017), 'Revisiting the "Drain" or Transfers from India to Britain in the Context of Global Diffusion of Capitalism', in Shubhra Chakrabarti and Utsa Patnaik, eds, *Agrarian and Other Histories: Essays for Binay Bhushan Chaudhuri*, Delhi: Tulika Books.

Patnaik, U. and P. Patnaik (2016), *A Theory of Imperialism,* Delhi: Tulika Books and New York: Columbia University Press.

Reserve Bank of India (RBI) (1946), *Report on Currency and Finance for the Year 1945–46*, Bombay: Times of India Press.

Saul, S.B. (1960), *Studies in British Overseas Trade*, Liverpool: Liverpool University Press.

Sen, A.K. (1981), *Poverty and Famine: An Essay on Entitlement and Deprivation*, Delhi: Oxford University Press.

Sen, S. (1992), *Colonies and the Empire: India 1870–1914*, Delhi: Orient Longman.

Sivasubramonian, S. (2000), *The National Income of India in the Twentieth Century*, Delhi: Oxford University Press.

Skidelsky, R. (2001), *John Maynard Keynes: Volume Three: Fighting for Freedom, 1937–1946*, London: Viking, Penguin.

Tily, G. (2009), 'John Maynard Keynes and the Development of National Accounts in Britain', *Review of Income and Wealth Series*, 55 (2), June: 331–57.

Toye, J. (2005), 'Significance of Keynes for Development Economics', in K.S. Jomo, ed., *The Pioneers of Development Economics*, Delhi: Tulika Books, London and New York: Zed Books.

United Nations (1962), *International Trade Statistics 1900–1960*, www.unstats.un.org/unsd/trade/imts/Historical1900-1960.pdf.

11

Land Acquisition and Income Disparities

Case Study of a Village in Jharia, Jharkhand

Vikas Rawal, Prachi Bansal and Vaishali Bansal

This paper presents a study of the impact of land acquisition and displacement on the livelihoods of people in Belgaria, a village in Dhanbad district in Jharkhand. The study village, Belgaria, is on the margins of the coal mines in Jharia. Agricultural land acquired from the village in 1982 was used to construct a township and rehabilitate about 1,200 families displaced by underground fires and land subsidence in Jharia. Using this village as a case study, the paper shows that in a location characterized by *ex-ante* unequal land relations, the impact of land acquisition on the livelihoods of people can vary across households belonging to different classes. Evidence from the new Belgaria township, where families displaced by underground fires were rehabilitated, shows that the resilience of displaced workers in coping with the disruption in access to livelihoods varied across male and female workers, and across the socio-economic status of displaced households. Livelihoods of workers who were engaged in casual labour in the coalfields, in particular women workers, were most adversely affected due to the displacement.

Jharia, in Dhanbad district, is one of the largest coalfields in India with estimated coal reserves of over 17 billion metric tonnes, and the only domestic source of high-quality coking coal that is needed for steel production. At present, there are two habitations in Belgaria – Belgaria village, where most of the land has been acquired from its inhabitants; and Belgaria township, where people displaced from Jharia have been resettled. This paper looks at income inequalities and livelihoods of people living in both these settlements. While Belgaria village is a former zamindari village with a long history of unequal agrarian relations, the township is a site where working class people living near the coal mines – and working as casual workers, coal scavengers or as providers of various kinds of services – have been resettled.

The paper is based on data from a survey conducted by the Society for Social and Economic Research and the Centre for Adivasi Research and Development in Belgaria in May 2015. The survey covered all households living in Belgaria village, and a randomly selected sample of 129 households living in Belgaria township.

The second section of the paper describes land acquisition in Belgaria village and its impact on livelihoods of households. The third section presents a brief account of resettlement in Belgaria township and the impact of displacement on the livelihoods of households there. The fourth section provides a comparative analysis of income inequality in Belgaria village and Belgaria township.

Belgaria Village

Belgaria village, located in Dhanbad district of Jharkhand, was once a zamindari village. It was inhabited some time in the late nineteenth century when three Rajput men from Ballia were awarded zamindari rights over the land in the village by Rani Hemkumari, the then zamindar of Jharia estate. Belgaria is a multi-caste village. All Rajput residents of the village trace their descent from the family of one of these three Rajput families. During the zamindari period, the land of Rajput landlords was cultivated by tenants belonging to the Mahato caste (now OBC or Other Backward Classes), and by landless Adivasi workers belonging to the Mahali tribe who worked as farm servants for the Rajput landlords apart from weaving baskets, which was their traditional craft.[1]

Abolition of zamindari led to transfer of ownership rights of some of the land to Mahato (OBC) households, though most of the land ownership remained concentrated in the hands of the Rajputs. Mahali Adivasis remained landless and continued to work as farm servants for Rajput landlords and large landowning peasants among Mahatos.

Land Acquisition in Belgaria Village

In 1982, Government of India acquired all land other than homesteads in Belgaria village and gave it to Bharat Coking Coal Limited (BCCL), a subsidiary of Coal India Limited (CIL). The resistance from the landlords and peasants to land acquisition was neutralized after Chief Minister Jagannath Mishra personally visited the village and assured the then *sarpanch*, who was also the biggest Rajput landlord in the village, that the landowners would be given a fair compensation and employment in BCCL for giving up their land. The terms of land acquisition in Belgaria were not only extremely discriminatory, but were specifically designed to gain the support of Rajput landlords in favour of land acquisition. Land owners were given a monetary compensation of Rs 9,000 per acre and, for every 2 acres of land acquired, a salaried job in BCCL. Since Rajput landlords owned most of the land, most Rajput families were entitled to multiple jobs in BCCL. Most households identified as many adult men as possible within the entitlement, and usually a woman was identified only if there was no adult male to take a job that was available. As we show in the second section, persons engaged in salaried employment in BCCL were well remunerated.

As against the Rajput households, the Mahato households had only small amounts of land. As a result, the Mahato households got fewer jobs; households that owned less than 2 acres of land were not given any job. In contrast, since the Mahali Adivasis were landless, they were not entitled to any compensation.

Although land was acquired for the purpose of building a coal depot, it remained unused by the BCCL for at least two decades. In 2006, the Jharia Rehabilitation and Development Authority (JRDA) started to construct a township on a part of this land to rehabilitate households affected by underground fires in the coalfield.

Impact of Land Acquisition on Livelihoods

Livelihoods of the inhabitants of Belgaria village were dramatically affected because of land acquisition. Land acquisition resulted in a drastic fall in the extent of cultivation in Belgaria village. Although all the agricultural lands were acquired by the government, landowners continued to have *de facto* possession of all their land from 1982 to 2006, and of the part other than land used for Belgaria township after 2006. However, given the imminent loss of land, landowners made no investment to improve the productivity of the land. Most of the land remained abandoned with shrubs growing on it, while a small part was used for rainfed cultivation in the kharif season. No investment had been made in irrigation over the last three decades to enable double cropping on this land. As a result, not only did the peasants leave agriculture as a source of livelihood, agricultural workers also had to seek wage employment elsewhere.

Implementation of land acquisition and compensation in Belgaria accentuated inequality in multiple ways. As is common in most projects where land is acquired, compensation was provided only to the landowners and that too according to the proportion of land they lost. But the compensation policy was doubly discriminatory against small landowners, tenants and landless agricultural workers. No jobs were provided to those who lost less than 2 acres of land. Neither did the tenants who cultivated land on informal contracts receive compensation, nor were the landless agricultural workers compensated for loss of agricultural employment. This further accentuated economic inequalities in Belgaria.

Salaried jobs in BCCL were highly remunerative. Table 11.1 shows that workers from 78 per cent of Rajput households and 86 per cent of Mahato households were engaged in salaried jobs. Most of these were jobs in BCCL that had been provided as compensation for land. On an average, these households received an income of over Rs 3 lakh from these salaried jobs. This accounted for 62 per cent of income for the Rajput households and 89 per cent of income for the Mahato households. In contrast, only 10 per cent of the Mahali households had incomes from salaried jobs. These jobs were also less remunerative and the average income of these households from salaried jobs was less than Rs 85,000.

With their accumulated wealth and surpluses from these remunerative salaried jobs, the Rajput households had made substantial investments in many other businesses. The construction of Belgaria township created demand for construction materials and many construction-related activities, as well as for services like shops and transport, supervisors and security guards. The Rajput households invested in these and entered into multiple businesses. They set up brick kilns on parts of the land that were still lying unused to provide bricks for construction. They started supplying other construction materials and started operating as labour contractors. In 2015, 28 per cent of the Rajput households had income from businesses. On average, these households received over Rs 4.5 lakh as income from these businesses, which accounted for about 30 per cent of their total income (Table 11.2).

Table 11.1 *Proportion of households with income from salaried employment, average annual income from salaried employment and share of salaries in household income, Belgaria village, 2014–15*

Social group	Proportion of households with income from salaried employment (%)	Average income from salaried employment (Rs)	Share of salaries in household income (%)
Mahali (Adivasi)	10	84,467	11
Mahato (OBC)	86	3,73,667	89
Rajput (Other)	78	3,32,744	62
All	44	3,17,376	61

Source: Survey data.

Table 11.2 *Proportion of households engaged in non-agricultural businesses, average annual income from businesses and the share of business income in total household income, Belgaria village, 2014–15*

Social group	Proportion of households in non-agricultural businesses (%)	Average income from businesses (Rs)	Share of businesses in household income (%)
Mahali (Adivasi)	3	1,00,420	5
Mahato (OBC)	5	84,000	1
Rajput (Other)	28	4,55,778	30
All	11	3,65,570	17

Source: Survey data.

It is noteworthy that although many Mahato families were also provided jobs, given the historical disparities between them and the Rajputs, they had not been able to invest in businesses like the Rajputs. While salaried employment became their main source of income, some of them continued to cultivate small parts of their land despite the acquisition.

At the time of the survey in 2015, there was a distinct difference in the socio-economic and political positions of the Rajputs and the Mahatos in the village. Rajput households had bigger, concrete houses, equipped with the most modern amenities and equipment. They wielded considerable social and political power in the village. While not as wealthy and politically powerful as the Rajputs, the economic status of Mahato households who had received salaried jobs in compensation for land had also improved considerably over the last three decades. And, with better economic status, they too had begun to assert themselves politically in the village.[2]

While provision of remunerative salaried jobs in compensation and opening up of opportunities for businesses resulted in considerable upward mobility among the Rajputs and the Mahatos, the Mahali Adivasi households were completely left out and had not benefited from any upward occupational mobility. Since these Adivasi households were landless, they received no monetary compensation or salaried jobs. Their main source of livelihood before the acquisition process was to work as farm servants for the Rajput landlords. Land acquisition took away this source of livelihood as well.

In 2015, the Mahalis were primarily dependent on basket weaving, their traditional occupation, and non-agricultural casual wage labour. Workers from about 83 per cent of the Mahali households were engaged in casual non-agricultural labour, as brick kiln workers, construction labour,

Table 11.3 *Proportion of households engaged in casual wage labour (farm, non-farm and MGNREGA), income from casual wage labour, and share of wage income in total household income, Belgaria village, 2014–15*

Social group	Proportion of households (%) engaged in casual wage labour	Average income from casual wage labour (Rs)	Share of wage in household income (%)
Mahali (Adivasi)	86	42,966	48
Mahato (OBC)	43	37,656	4
Rajput (Other)	19	71,678	3
All	59	44,881	11

Source: Survey data.

loading and unloading workers, and under the Mahatma Gandhi National Rural Employment Guarantee Act (MGNREGA). Non-agricultural labour accounted for about 48 per cent of their total income (Table 11.3). Almost all the Mahali households – 95 per cent to be precise – were engaged in basket weaving, a task in which all men and women, including the elderly and children, participated. Although bamboo basket weaving was seasonal activity, mainly from January to May, it accounted for about 31 per cent of their total income.

The discriminatory and unequal compensation for land acquisition also meant that any later demands for providing employment to the landless or for returning unused land did not get the support of households that had benefited from jobs in BCCL. There had been nascent attempts in the village to organize people around demands for returning large areas of land still lying unused, and for provision of employment to the landless and poor peasants. In the absence of support from the dominant classes in the village who had secured jobs in BCCL and did not want to jeopardize that prospect in any way, such efforts did not take off.

Belgaria Township

Over the almost century-long history of mining in the Jharia coalfields, underground fires and subsidence, marked by unsuccessful efforts at curbing them, have posed a huge problem. Subsidence of land continues to be a regular phenomenon in the coalfields, regularly resulting in loss of life and destruction of property. Expansion of open-cast mining since the mid-1970s has contributed to fanning underground fires. With fires raging in many underground veins of the mines, large parts of Jharia that are densely inhabited continue to face serious risk of subsidence (Gupta 2013).

Since 1983, several master plans have been made to deal with the problem. While these master plans have combined the need to control fires and subsidence with the need for rehabilitation of affected families, over the years, in view of the failure of efforts to control the fires, the emphasis has shifted to rehabilitation of affected families. In 1997, Haradhan Roy, CPI(M) Member of Parliament from Asansol, filed a public interest litigation (PIL) in the Supreme Court on the issue of displacement due to subsidence and fires in Jharia coalfield. The legal battle spearheaded by Haradhan Roy and the Jharia Coalfield Bachao Samiti forced the government to come up with a Jharia Action Plan in 2003 (Agarwal 2016). In 2004, the Jharia Rehabilitation and Development Authority (JRDA) was formed to spearhead the rehabilitation. In 2008, JRDA came up with an updated *Master Plan for Dealing with Fire, Subsidence and Rehabilitation in the Leasehold of BCCL.*[3] This updated master plan proposed construction of a total of 25,000 houses for BCCL employees and 54,159 houses for other affected families over a period of twelve years. However, by 2015, only a fraction of these houses had actually been constructed.

Resettlement in Belgaria Township

In 2006, JRDA started construction of Belgaria township to rehabilitate some families whose houses were in imminent danger of subsidence due to underground fires. Until 2015, this was the only location where affected families other than the families of BCCL employees had been rehabilitated. In the first phase, JRDA constructed 2,352 apartments in Belgaria township, each having a floor area of 203.36 square feet comprising two rooms, a kitchen and an attached toilet. The apartments were constructed in 196 three-storey blocks of twelve apartments each. However, since these apartments were very small and Belgaria was located far away from Jharia, the affected families had been unwilling to move to Belgaria. In view of this, JRDA provided two apartments to each family, thus managing to rehabilitate less than 1,200 families in Belgaria township (Phase I).

Historically, livelihood opportunities in the coalfields – either directly related to coal mining or to various other services needed to support this large coal economy – have attracted people from different caste and class backgrounds, and from different regions and linguistic backgrounds, to Jharia. Belgaria township was inhabited by families that were previously engaged in informal occupations – either as casual workers in coal-mining operations, or as coal scavengers, or as informal workers in provision of various services. These families belonged to different castes and traced their origins to many different places. As seen in Table 11.4, Dalits comprised

Table 11.4 *Proportion of population and households belonging to different social groups, Belgaria township, 2014–15*

Social group	Population (%)	Households (%)
Dalit	39	43
Adivasi	4	3
OBC	34	31
Other Caste Hindu	14	16
Muslim	8	8
All	100	100

Source: Survey data.

39 per cent of the population of Belgaria township, OBCs comprised 34 per cent of the population, Other Caste Hindus accounted for 14 per cent of the population, Muslims for 8 per cent of the population and Adivasis for 4 per cent of the population. Allotment of apartments in Belgaria township was caste-heterogeneous. However, the caste-heterogeneity of the habitation did not completely diminish the caste hierarchy. Caste barriers in social and economic relations within the township were pervasive and, in our survey, upper-caste families often complained about having to live in close proximity to Dalits, and talked about how they tried to avoid dealing with them.

Livelihoods of Households in Belgaria Township

Displacement on account of underground fires and subsidence of land caused a disruption in the livelihoods of households. Many forms of employment became either inaccessible or more difficult to be engaged in. These included various occupations related to coal mining including loading/unloading work, casual labour for private contractors and companies, and scavenging and transporting of coal. Shifting to Belgaria colony, which was far from most coal-related worksites, meant that many of these workers had to give up their work or had to reduce the amount of time they were able to work in the mines and other coal-related worksites. Similarly, many workers who worked in shops in Jharia were unable to continue doing so, since travelling from Belgaria early in the morning and returning there late in the evening was not possible. Livestock rearing was not possible for families that had been allotted apartments on first and second floors.

The problem of inaccessibility of worksites from Belgaria particularly affected the employment of women. In 2015, only 22 per cent of women in the age-group 15 to 59 years were employed, while the work participation rate of men in the same age-group was 82 per cent. Unemployment and marginalization of women workers were the most important economic effects of displacement and rehabilitation in Belgaria township.

While displacement caused severe disruption of access to wage employment initially, working class residents often got together to demand better housing conditions, improvement in transport, schooling and provision of other public services, and access to livelihoods. A few residents who were associated with the Communist Party of India (Marxist) took the lead in mobilizing the residents. Although very little was done to provide livelihood opportunities to the residents of Belgaria, collective protests did result in improvements in the availability of transport services, primary schooling and some other civic amenities.

As transport services became available, male workers started commuting to Jharia for work. Further, establishment of the township, where a large agglomeration of people lived, also opened up opportunities for provision of various services. In 2015, many workers of Belgaria township were self-employed, working as autorickshaw drivers, petty shopkeepers, barbers, cobblers, tutors, tailors, caterers, wedding decorators and owners of other small businesses. In all, as many as 40 per cent households had income from some form of self-employment, providing services not just in Belgaria township but also in various adjoining parts of Jharia. Average annual income from such businesses was Rs 80,140, which was about 34 per cent of the total household income of households in Belgaria township (Table 11.5).

Income from businesses, which was far more remunerative than casual manual employment, was the main source of economic inequality in Belgaria township. As shown in Table 11.5, participation in businesses was not unrelated to the caste status of households. The proportion of Dalit households that were self-employed, though substantial, was lower than the corresponding proportion for OBC, Other Caste Hindu and Muslim households. Despite the fact that Belgaria township was extremely heterogenous in respect of caste, religion, linguistic group and regional origin, there was a significant association of caste with the nature of business the households were engaged in. People belonging to the Nai caste worked as barbers, Lohras were engaged as blacksmiths, Ravidas were cobblers, OBC Halwais were street vendors selling sweets and other snacks, while other OBCs, Other Caste Hindus and Muslims were engaged in catering businesses and working as private tutors.

Although a relatively small proportion of Dalit households were self-employed, these households had substantial business incomes, earning

Table 11.5 *Proportion of households engaged in non-agricultural businesses, average annual income from businesses, and the share of business income in total household income, Belgaria township, 2014–15*

Social group	Proportion of households engaged in non-agricultural businesses (%)	Average income from businesses (Rs)	Share of businesses in household income (%)
Dalit	22	1,03,617	27
Adivasi	25	90,000	17
OBC	52	77,339	47
Other caste Hindu	50	79,960	34
Muslim	70	47,214	34
All	40	80,149	34

Source: Survey data.

Table 11.6 *Proportion of households engaged in casual wage labour, average income from casual labour and share of wage income in household income, Belgaria township, 2014–15*

Social group	Proportion of households engaged in casual wage labour (%)	Average income from casual labour (Rs)	Share in household income (%)
Dalit	87	56,114	57
Adivasi	50	23,700	9
OBC	55	47,234	30
Other	65	55,725	31
Muslim	70	57,636	41
All	71	53,347	41

Source: Survey data.

on an average over Rs 1 lakh per annum. Past savings and the monetary compensation provided to displaced families were used by these households for investment in businesses. Families which had been provided ground-floor apartments were at a significant advantage as they could open small shops in a part of their houses.

In contrast, many Dalit households were dependent on wage labour as their primary source of livelihood and had very low incomes (Table 11.6). Just as the proportion of households engaged in businesses

Table 11.7 *Proportion of men aged 15 to 59 years working in Jharia coalfield as manual wage labourers, Belgaria township, 2014–15*

Social group	Proportion of men (%)
Dalit	19
Adivasi	0
OBC	8
Other	6
Muslim	0
All	11

Source: Survey data.

was lowest for Dalit households among all social groups, the proportion of Dalit households engaged in manual wage labour was the highest (Table 11.6). Wage labourers in Belgaria worked in a variety of occupations, including loading and unloading in coal mines, as masons, tempo drivers and workers in construction sites. Of these, the most arduous and least remunerative was working in loading and unloading of coal. Table 11.7 shows that the proportion of workers who commuted from Belgaria to find manual wage employment in the coal fields was higher (19 per cent) for Dalit men than for male workers from other social groups. This disparity between those who managed to be self-employed and those who were forced to do manual labour was a source of substantial within-social-group inequality among Dalit households in Belgaria.

Income Inequality in Belgaria Village and Belgaria Township

Table 11.8 shows the proportion of households in different size classes of income in Belgaria village and Belgaria township. The table clearly shows that income distribution in both the township and the village was highly unequal. About 15 per cent households in Belgaria village and 26 per cent households in Belgaria township had annual household incomes that were less than Rs 36,000 (Rs 3,000 per month). Another 26 per cent households in Belgaria village and 35 per cent in the township had annual incomes ranging between Rs 36,000 and Rs 72,000. In contrast, 33 per cent households in Belgaria village and 7 per cent households in the township had incomes of more than Rs 2.5 lakh.

In terms of the Gini coefficient, income inequality in Belgaria village (0.57) was higher than the income inequality in Belgaria township (0.46) (Table 11.9).

Table 11.8 *Proportion of households belonging to different size-classes of annual household income, Belgaria village and Belgaria township, 2014–15*

Size-class of household income	Belgaria village (%)	Belgaria township (%)
0 to 36,000	15	26
36,000 to 72,000	26	35
72,000 to 1,08,000	11	16
1,08,000 to 1,44,000	9	9
1,44,000 to 1,80,000	1	3
1,80,000 to 2,16,000	3	4
2,16,000 to 2,52,000	2	1
Greater than 2,52,000	33	7

Source: Survey data.

Table 11.9 *Gini coefficient of annual household income, Belgaria village and Belgaria township, 2014–15*

	Gini coefficient
Belgaria village	0.57
Belgaria township	0.46

Source: Survey data.

Not only was inequality higher in Belgaria village, but historical patterns of caste disparities reflected clearly in the income disparities in Belgaria village. Table 11.10 shows some descriptive statistical measures of income disparities across the three castes. Of the three castes/tribes, Mahali Adivasi households were the poorest. Although they accounted for 52 per cent of the households, their share in total household income of Belgaria village was only 17 per cent. In contrast, Rajput caste accounted for 29 per cent of households and 53 per cent of the total village income. The median income of Mahali Adivasi households was only about Rs 58,000. In contrast, the median income of Mahato households was about Rs 3 lakh and that of Rajput households was about Rs 4 lakh. It is noteworthy that the highest income of an Adivasi household was Rs 3 lakh, while the highest among Mahato households was about Rs 12 lakh and among Rajput households, Rs 18 lakh. A similar pattern is evident from the boxplots shown in Figure 11.1(a).

In contrast, as seen in Table 11.11 and Figure 11.1(b), disparities across caste groups were much less striking in Belgaria township. Although

Table 11.10 *Measures of income disparity across social groups, Belgaria village, 2014–15*

Social group	Proportion of households (%)	Share in total income (%)	Median income (Rs)	Highest income (Rs)
Mahali (Adivasi)	52	17	58,115	3,21,710
Mahato (OBC)	19	30	3,16,500	12,39,267
Rajput (Other)	29	53	3,97,011	18,00,000

Source: Survey data.

Table 11.11 *Measures of income disparity across social groups, Belgaria township, 2014–15*

Social group	Proportion of households (%)	Share in total income (%)	Median income (Rs)	Highest income (Rs)
Dalit	43	39	58,600	7,35,640
Adivasi	3	4	98,000	2,88,000
OBC	31	29	64,750	4,58,096
Other	16	20	76,600	4,30,000
Muslim	8	8	1,10,100	1,55,000

Source: Survey data.

there were differences in median incomes of households belonging to different caste groups, it is clear that as a group, the income shares of different caste groups were not very different from their shares in the population.

We have formally tested for the extent of caste disparities using inequality decomposition techniques. Decomposition analysis of inequality is typically done using generalized entropy measures (equation 1), a class of inequality measures using which total inequality can be decomposed into inequality within groups (I_W) and inequality between groups (I_B) (Cowell 1977; Toyoda 1980).

$$\mathrm{GE}(\alpha) = \frac{1}{\alpha^2 - \alpha} \left[\frac{1}{n} 1 \sum_{i=1}^{n} \left(\frac{y_i}{y} \right)^{\alpha} - 1 \right] \qquad (1)$$

- where alpha represents the weights given to the distance between incomes at different parts of the income distribution
- n refers to the number of individuals in the sample
- y_i refers to income of individual i
- y refers to the mean of income.

Figure 11.1 *Boxplots of per capita income, by social group, Belgaria village and Belgaria township, 2014–15*

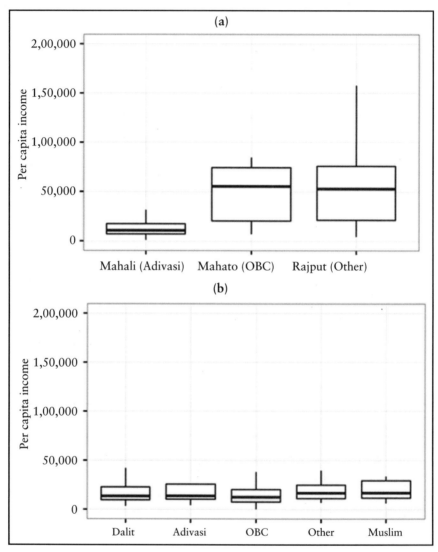

For decomposition of inequality, we use GE(2), a measure of inequality that corresponds to half the square of coefficient of variation. Inequality within the groups (I_w) is measured as the weighted sum of inequality of income within each sub-group, the weights being the relative population shares and income shares. Inequality between groups is calculated by assigning the mean income of each sub-group to all members of that sub-group and then estimating GE(2).

Table 11.12 shows the estimates of inequality decomposition across caste/tribe groups in Belgaria village and Belgaria township using GE(2). Results of the decomposition exercise further confirm that inequality in Belgaria village was primarily a result of caste disparities. In Belgaria village, about 30 per cent of total inequality was across different groups. In contrast, only 2 per cent of total inequality in Belgaria township was on account of caste disparities.

Elbers *et al.* (2008) have argued that given the relative size of different groups in a population, there is a maximum limit for inequality between groups, and that it is useful to look at observed between-group inequality in relation to the maximum between-group inequality. The observed between-group inequality was half of the maximum between-group inequality in Belgaria village, while observed between-group inequality was only 2 per cent of the maximum between-group inequality in Belgaria township.

In Belgaria village, within-group inequality was lowest among the Mahato households, followed by the Mahali Adivasis. Rajput households, which on average had the highest levels of income, also had the highest within-group inequality in Belgaria village.

In contrast, in Belgaria township, within-group inequality was

Table 11.12 *Decomposition of GE(2) inequality within and across social groups in Belgaria township and Belgaria village, 2014–15*

Social group	Belgaria township	Belgaria village
Dalit	85	–
Adivasi	29	38
OBC	50	29
Other	38	43
Muslim	10	–
Total within group inequality	56	57
Between group inequality	1	25
Total inequality	57	82
Maximum between group inequality [ELMO]	50	49
Between group inequality as a percentage of maximum between group inequality	2	50
Between group inequality as a percentage of total inequality	2	30

Source: Survey data.

highest among Dalits, the group that had the lowest average income. About 43 per cent households in Belgaria township belonged to different Dalit castes. While a majority of these households were engaged in manual labour, some had managed to invest in petty businesses and obtained substantial incomes from them.

Concluding Remarks

Acquisition of land for developmental projects has become a particularly contentious issue because state-led land acquisition is increasingly done for private sector-led projects and, in many such cases, is deemed to be detrimental to the livelihoods of people from whom land is acquired.

It has been argued by some scholars from within the Marxist tradition that, under the contemporary neoliberal order, appropriation of resources by capitalists with active aid of the state apparatus rather than appropriation of surplus value is the dominant form of accumulation. They have argued that appropriation of resources in the contemporary world can be usefully theorized as primitive accumulation (De Angelis 2000; Perelman 2000). David Harvey, one of the foremost proponents of this argument, coined the term 'accumulation by dispossession' to describe this phenomenon under neoliberalism (Harvey 2003, 2007). Within this body of literature, terms like 'land grab' are often used to talk about varied forms of land acquisition in the third world today.

Ben Fine points out that the concept of accumulation by dispossession has been used to 'homogenize what are diverse and complex moments in the economic restructuring of capital and the broader social restructuring of capitalism' (Fine 2006). Marx used the term 'primary' or 'primitive accumulation' to refer to a process through which the primary producers were separated from the means of production, and these means of production became the property of a class of people who would then constitute the capitalist class and would employ the now dispossessed class of erstwhile primary producers as wage labourers. Stated differently, primary or primitive accumulation is the process that leads to accumulation of capital prior to the establishment of the capitalist mode of production and the simultaneous dispossession of primary producers along with a fundamental change whereby the dispossessed primary producers are turned into wage labourers, primarily through the use of extra-economic coercion.

Would it be correct to characterize land acquisition in Belgaria village as primitive accummulation? There was considerable inequality in ownership of land between the Rajput landlords, the Mahato rich and middle peasants, and the Mahali landless Adivasi households when land was acquired in Belgaria. Landless Adivasi households laboured on the farms of the landlords and rich peasants, albeit under unfree conditions. Acquisition of land did not dispossess all households equally. Furthermore, it perpetuated caste–class disparities because of the extremely discriminatory terms on which land was acquired. While the landlords and the rich peasants were given monetary compensation as well as highly remunerative jobs, only a small monetary compensation was provided to poor peasants and no compensation was given to landless Adivasi households. Over time, taking advantage of opportunities that became available with the construction of Belgaria township, former landlord families established businesses that provided large returns. However, poor Adivasi households were left to seek casual employment in non-agricultural manual labour and continue with their traditional occupation of basket weaving.

The case of acquisition of land in Belgaria illustrates that applying the concept of primary/primitive accumulation to varied forms of appropriation of resources in the contemporary world is not only inaccurate, but also conceals wide variations and specifics that are crucial to understand the nature of accumulation and changes in class relations. The case study of Belgaria specifically shows that the impact of land acquisition in a village characterized by unequal class relations is differential across classes and social groups. Under conditions of unequal ownership rights and dominance of landlords and rich peasants, acquisition is negotiated differently with different classes and thus has differential outcomes.

Taking cognizance of this aspect is crucial for building resistance against discriminatory and forced land acquisition. Unless vulnerability of the working classes, poor peasants and other marginalized groups because of *ex-ante* disparities is identified as a core issue, the resistance against discriminatory and forced land acquisition runs the risk of being aligned to the interests of the dominant classes rather than with the poor and the working classes.

The trajectory of economic change was very different in Belgaria township. Relocation to Belgaria resulted in a short-term disruption of employment for male workers and a continued disruption of employment for women workers. With improvement in transport facilities, by 2015, most of the male workers had resumed work, although many had to find new occupations. Work participation rates among women, however, remained very low.

Belgaria thus turns out to be a site where a complex dynamics of change has unfolded in the wake of land acquisition and resettlement. The erstwhile landlords benefited the most from this process, while landless Adivasi households were the ones most adversely affected. There had been nascent attempts in the village to organize people around demands for returning large areas of land still lying unused, and for provision of employment for the landless and poor peasants. In the absence of support from the dominant classes in the village, who had secured jobs in BCCL and did not want to jeopardize that prospect in any way, such demands did not get adequate traction within the village. On the other hand, in Belgaria township, with a large concentration of working class households, demands for improvement of infrastructure, better connectivity with schools, hospitals and workplaces, and improvement in provision of basic services were made. Continuing problems such as lack of employment, particularly for women, and gaps in the provision of basic services like health care and schooling require that the residents are organized and their collective voice strengthened. This is the immediate future for Belgaria township to look forward to.

We are thankful to Ashok Agarwal, Venkatesh Athreya, Smita Gupta and Brinda Karat for their valuable inputs and support.

Notes
[1] In 2015, at the time of our survey, there were a total of 111 households in Belgaria village. Of these 111 households, 58 per cent were Mahali Adivasis, 21 per cent were Mahatos and 32 per cent were Rajputs.
[2] In 2015, the *sarpanch* of the local panchayat was a woman of the Mahato caste.
[3] See http://www.jrda.in/download/masterplan.pdf

References
Agarwal, Ashok (2016), 'The Case of Jharia', mimeo.
Cowell, F.A. (1977), *Measuring Inequality*, Oxford: Phillip Allan.
De Angelis, Massimo (2000), 'Marx's Theory of Primitive Accumulation: A Suggested Reinterpretation', Working Paper No. 29, Department of Economics, University of East London, available at http://homepages.uel.ac.uk/M.DeAngelis/PRIMACCA.pdf , accessed on 4 December 2018.
Elbers, Chris, Peter Lanjouw, Johan A. Mistiaen and Berk Özler (2008), 'Reinterpreting between-group inequality', *The Journal of Economic Inequality*, 6 (3): 231–45, available at https://core.ac.uk/download/pdf/81538676.pdf, accessed on 4 December 2018.
Fine, Ben (2006), 'Debating the "New" Imperialism', *Historical Materialism*, 14 (4): 133–56.
Gupta, Smita (2013), *Fanning a Fire in Jharia: Reap Windfall Profits and Loot the Coal*, Jharkhand: Communist Party of India (Marxist).
Harvey, David (2003), *The New Imperialism*, Oxford and New York: Oxford University Press.
——— (2007), *A Brief History of Neoliberalism*, Oxford and New York: Oxford University Press.
Perelman, Michael (2000), *The Invention of Capitalism: Classical Political Economy and the Secret History of Primitive Accumulation*, Durham and London: Duke University Press.
Toyoda, T. (1980), 'Decomposability of Inequality Measures', *Economic Studies Quarterly*, 31 (12): 207–46.

12

An Analysis of Cost and Income of Cotton Cultivation in India

A. Narayanamoorthy

Of late, pronounced discontent among cotton growers of the major cotton-growing states of the country has attracted considerable attention. Cotton farmers of Gujarat, Maharashtra, Rajasthan, Andhra Pradesh, Karnataka and Haryana, have been considering alternatives to the cotton crop. Surprisingly, the farmers of these states intend to shift from cotton, a high-value cash crop, to low-value crops such as *jowar*, *moong*, soyabean, corn, *tur*, *channa* and *guar*. In fact in Maharashtra, where cotton has traditionally been a principal cash crop, it is anticipated that if this trend continues, then the total area under cotton cultivation is very likely to be reduced. Undeniably, such a shift is likely to dampen cotton production across the country as well. What are the reasons that could be attributed to such a shift? Why is the cotton crop losing ground to coarse cereals? Could the failure of the government in announcing an appropriate minimum support price (MSP) for cotton be one of the reasons? Is poor returns from cotton cultivation another reason?

Apart from the above-mentioned, there must be other definite factors that are behind this disturbing trend. Officials at the Cotton Federations of the respective states cite aberrant weather conditions, the crop situation in other countries, prices in the international market and the fickle nature of the demand from the industry as being pivotal in prompting cotton farmers to move away from cotton cultivation. The distressed cotton farmers state that consecutive shrinking of cotton yield per acre and rising costs of cultivation are compelling them to abandon cotton cultivation and to go in for low-cost crops. Given the fact that the cotton crop is highly dependent on external inputs, is high cost of inputs escalating the money needs of the farmers and thereby the overall cost of cultivation? Is dwindling yield in any way related to rising cost of production of the cotton crop?

For quite a long time, India has been a closely watched frontier for cotton. In the world's cotton hierarchy, India has the largest share in area, occupying about 35 per cent of the area under cotton across the world, and the second largest share in production, accounting for about 24 per cent of the world's cotton production, while its yield is one of the lowest in the world (ICAC 2014). Low productivity (yield per hectare) has for long been a conspicuous feature of Indian cotton. It has been identified that this low productivity in cotton is partly due to the crop being largely grown under rainfed conditions, and partly due to multiple pest problems since cotton is highly susceptible to insects and diseases. The menace of pest attacks is so significant that they cause losses to the extent of about 50 per cent in cotton productivity. The losses, in fact, have increased from about 18 per cent in the early 1960s to about 50 per cent in 1990s (CICR 1998; Birthal *et al.* 2000).

It is estimated that cotton cultivation in India consumes about 44.5 per cent of the total pesticides used in the country. In fact, the per hectare pesticide consumption for cotton amounts to about 2.7 kg, which is much higher than the national average of 0.8 kg per hectare (Alagh 1988; WWF-India 2012). According to available estimates, the share of insecticide cost in the total cost of cultivation of the cotton crop in the cotton belt of Punjab has increased manifold, from about 2.1 per cent in 1974–75 to about 21.2 per cent in 1998–99 (Sen and Bhatia 2004). An escalation in the cost of cultivation and depressed yields due to pest attacks have not only rendered the cotton crop uneconomical, but also contributed to a large number of farmer suicides (Gandhi and Namboodiri 2006; Deshpande 2002).

The introduction of insect-resistant, GM (genetically modified) Bt cotton in India in March 2002 came as a relief to the country's cotton farmers, as it promised to reduce their dependence on pesticides and to increase cotton productivity by controlling pests in general and bollworm in particular (Narayanamoorthy and Kalamkar 2006). Bt cotton arrived in India amidst intense controversy with shrill invectives both for and against, and the respective sides vociferously proclaiming its success or failure on the farm. Nevertheless, the adoption rate of Bt cotton in the country was unprecedented and phenomenal, covering about 82 per cent of total cotton area in just eight years of commercialization since 2002–03 by occupying about 70 lakh hectares in the year 2008 (Gulati 2009).

While the majority of the 5 million adopters of Bt cotton in the country are smallholders, which no doubt points to the fact that farmers in general and resource-poor farmers in particular have accepted this new variety, there has been considerable debate regarding the performance of Bt cotton in India. Much of the debate has centered around whether Bt cotton consistently performs better than non-Bt cotton varieties, and whether the adoption of Bt varieties results in economic benefits to the farmers. Several studies have been undertaken to examine the efficacy of Bt cotton as compared to its conventional counterpart. It is the technological impact on the crop that fascinates them the most, rather than looking into the economic sustainability of the crop in the light of rising concerns among cotton farmers about the rising costs of cultivation since the 1970s (see ISAAA 2014).

Quite a few studies have attempted to analyse the profitability and productivity of the cotton crop in view of widespread agitations, resentment and suicides in the major cotton-growing states of the country, by using secondary and primary data. Critically, Bhatia (2006) pointed out that unlike paddy and wheat, where the MSP fixed by the government upon the recommendation of the Commission for Agricultural Costs and Prices (CACP) covers the economic cost (cost C2 in the major producing states), in the case of cotton, the MSP covered only 75–85 per cent of cost C2 in Maharashtra and 60–85 per cent in Punjab during the period 1996–97 to 2002–03. Besides, the paid-out cost of production of cotton in these two states was not covered by MSP in most of the study period. Chand and Raju (2009) stated that irrigation coverage played a vital role in bringing about variations in the area under cotton, which witnessed a decline during 1968–88 as compared to the pre-green revolution period, but increased thereafter between 1989–2007. In a very recent study in which about twenty-two crops were analysed, cotton was one among eight crops that was found to have reaped cent per cent or more gross profit (Vishandass and Lukka 2013). The study also found that the profitability of cotton between 2000–01 and 2010–11 increased between 45 per cent to 63 per cent. Gross returns per hectare as a percentage of paid-out cost plus family labour, i.e. A2 + FL cost, during 2008–09 to 2010–11 was found to be the second highest in cotton. Studying the economics of drip-irrigated cotton, Narayanamoorthy (2008) found out that drip irrigation reduces water consumption and cost of irrigation while increasing productivity of cotton significantly. The productivity of drip-irrigated cotton is about 114 per cent higher than the corresponding flood irrigation harvest. The profit of the cotton crop cultivated using drip method of irrigation is higher by about Rs 20,601 per acre than the corresponding profit realized through flood method of irrigation.

Focus of the Present Study

Much of the qualitative field-level information gathered from areas where farmers' suicides and indebtedness were reported concludes that the victims are mostly cotton farmers ravaged by escalating cost of cultivation and poor remuneration from crop cultivation. This necessitates analysis of the movements of costs and profitability in cotton cultivtion. A few researchers (Raghavan 2008; Dev and Rao 2010) have made serious efforts in analysing the issue of rising cost of farm inputs, albeit confining their profitability analysis only to wheat and rice. Bhatia (2006), on the other hand, studied the profitability aspect of cotton in selected states, but the study period consisted of only eight years. Narayanamoorthy (2013) analysed the profitability of some major crops with respect to cost C2 and cost C3, and concluded that the cotton crop in the selected state of Maharashtra was subject to huge losses owing to a steep rise in the cost of cultivation. However, this study looked at only the rainfed cotton-growing state of Maharashtra to analyse the profitability of cotton, leaving behind a trail of unanswered questions. Chief among them are: (i) What is the status in the other rainfed cotton-growing states of the country? (ii) Is irrigated cotton more profitable than rainfed cotton? (iii) Is the cost of cultivation of cotton very much influenced by the presence or absence of irrigation?

Keeping all this in view, the present study attempts to fill the gaps by analysing the movements of costs and profitability in cotton crop for a longer time period of forty-two years (from 1972–73 to 2010–11) in the major cotton-growing states. The study primarily uses the data generated under the cost of cultivation scheme (CCS) published by the CACP, Ministry of Agriculture and Farmers Welfare, Government of India, New Delhi.

Data and Methodology

The study uses secondary data for its entire analysis. Secondary data from two vital sources have been used to measure the profitability of cotton cultivation and the overall state of cotton cultivation in India. These include: (i) *Price Policy Reports* of the CACP, and (ii) *Agricultural Statistics at a Glance* and *Area and Production of Principal Crops*, published by the Ministry of Agriculture and Farmers Welfare, Government of India. For analysing trends in area, yield and production of cotton, the data period is divided into four phases: the pre-green revolution period (pre-GRP) (1950–51 to 1964–65), the green revolution period (GRP) (1965–66 to 1979–80), the post-green revolution period (post-GRP) (1980–81 to 1994–95), and the agrarian crisis period (ACP) (1995–96 to 2011–12). The years separating each phase were constructed so as to capture the marked changes

Table 12.1 *Area, irrigation coverage and yield of cotton in four selected states,*
TE 2011–12

States selected for study	Category of state selected	Area (mha)	Yield (kg/ha)	Under irrigation (%)
Punjab	HAHP	0.53	680	100
Gujarat	HAHP	2.68	637	57
Maharashtra	HALP	3.86	316	3
Andhra Pradesh	HALP	1.74	432	17
All India		11.18	464	35

Notes: HAHP = high area high productivity; HALP = high area low productivity; mha = million hectares.
Source: Computed using data from GoI (2014) and www.dacnet.nic.in

that have taken place in terms of area, yield and production of cotton. For studying the movements of costs and returns of cotton, although nine states have been recognized as the major cotton-producing states in the country, due to non-availability of continuous cost- and income-related data, a total of only four states have been taken up to study the profitability of cotton (Table 12.1). Since area and crop productivity does influence the profitability of the crop, data pertaining to the period TE 2011–12 have been used to categorize the selected states into high area and high productivity (HAHP), and high area and low productivity (HALP). As per this classification, Punjab and Gujarat are treated as HAHP states, while Maharashtra and Andhra Pradesh are considered as HALP states for the purpose of analysis.

Each of the selected cotton-growing states differs in its irrigation coverage. As per the data of TE 2011–12, the cotton-growing state of Punjab is fully irrigated, Gujarat and Maharashtra have irrigation coverage of about 57 per cent and 3 per cent respectively, and Andhra Pradesh has irrigation coverage of about 17 per cent. Very recent disaggregated analyses reveal that irrigated tracts give rise to higher levels of profitability (Vishandass and Lukka 2013); therefore, an attempt is made here to analyse whether irrigation coverage does impact the profitability of cotton cultivation. The CACP, which provides data on gross income and operation-wise cost of cultivation per hectare, makes use of nine different cost concepts (A1, A2, A2+FL, B1, B2, C1, C2, C2* and C3) for measuring the economics of cultivation of various crops. However, cost C2 is the preferred choice for our study as it includes all paid-out costs and fixed costs, including the imputed interest on owned fixed capital, imputed rental value of owned land and imputed value of family labour.

The significance of using cost C2 in our analysis is that if the cost C2 is covered, it would imply that farmers not only recover their paid-out costs, but also get rewarded for use of their own resources such as land, family labour and capital. Profit of cotton crop is computed by deducting cost C2 from the value of output. All the cost- and income-related data of the cotton crop have been converted into constant prices using Consumer Price Index for Agricultural Labourers (CPIAL) deflator at 1986–87 prices.

Trends in Cotton Cultivation

The main focus of this paper is to study the profitability of cotton cultivation. However, before that, let us try to understand the trends in the area, yield and production of cotton in India. As of 2012–13, cotton was grown in 11.98 mha (GoI 2014). About 6 million farmers were engaged in its cultivation as of 2011–12 (CICR 2011). India has the unique distinction of being the only country in the world to cultivate all four cultivable *Gossypium* species, viz., *Gossypium arboreum* and *G. herbaceum* (both Asian cotton), *G. barbadense* (Egyptian cotton) and *G. hirsutum* (American upland cotton), besides hybrid cotton. In India, while cotton cultivation is concentrated in the western half of the country, the cotton-growing regions can be broadly divided into three major ones based on climatic differences and regional heterogeneity in terms of availability of water and other natural resources. These are the northern region, comprising Punjab, Haryana and Rajasthan, which primarily produces short and medium staple cotton; the central region, comprising Maharashtra, Madhya Pradesh and Gujarat, which produces mostly medium and long staples; and the southern region, comprising Andhra Pradesh, Tamil Nadu and Karnataka, which produces long staples. Although cotton is grown in all these nine states, Gujarat, Maharashtra and Andhra Pradesh together contribute about 69 per cent of the total cotton production in the country, and accounted for about 75 per cent of the country's total area under cotton cultivation in 2012–13. About 65 per cent of India's cotton is cultivated under rainfed conditions and only about 35 per cent under irrigated conditions (WWF 2010).

At the all-India level, the average area under cotton, which was 7.71 mha during GRP (1965–66 to 1979–80), declined to 7.51 mha during post-GRP (1980–81 to 1994–95), but registered a huge rise to 9.23 mha during ACP (1995–96 to 2011–12) (Table 12.2). The rate of growth of area under cotton has thus slowed down considerably, especially after GRP. For instance, the area under cotton which registered a growth rate of 0.14 per cent per annum during GRP, slowed down at a rate of 0.04 per cent per annum during post-GRP, but marginally revived to 1.77 per cent per annum during ACP. Given the fact that a limit has been reached with regard to the

Table 12.2 *Trends in area, yield and production of cotton in India, 1950–51 to 2011–12*

Period	Area (mha)	Production (mt)	Yield (kg/ha)	Irrigation coverage (%)	Cotton area to GCA (%)
Pre-GR period (1950–51 to 1964–65)	7.51	4.57	102.00	11.58	5.08
GR period (1965–66 to 1979–80)	7.71	6.16	135.00	20.95	4.66
Post-GR period (1980–81 to 1994–95)	7.51	8.87	200.00	31.51	4.18
Agrarian crisis period (1995–96 to 2011–12)	9.23	17.74	314.00	34.68	4.85
Compound growth rate (per cent/annum)					
Pre-GR period	2.38	4.65	2.20	4.34	1.26
GR period	0.14	3.08	2.91	3.72	0.59
Post-GR period	0.04	3.59	3.56	1.51	0.57
Agrarian crisis period	1.77	6.10	4.25	0.15	0.24

Notes: GCA = gross cropped area; GR = green revolution; mha = million hectares; mt = million tonnes.
Source: Computed using data from GoI (2014) and www.dacenet.nic.in.

possibility of increasing net sown area on a substantial scale, the upward pace in the growth of area under cotton after the post-GRP can be attributed to cropping pattern changes and the spread of Bt technology. Commenting on the green revolution in rice and wheat cultivation during the late 1960s and early 1970s in a particular context, Gulati (2009) pointed out that if there is any other crop that has registered a phenomenal growth during the last six to seven years, it is cotton. This is exactly what happened after the post-GRP, when an upward pace in the area under cotton catapulted to a significant acceleration in the production and yield of cotton.

It is also useful to understand the trends in area and yield of cotton cultivation across the states of India, and the relative position of the states to the national-level scenario. Decadal trends in area under cotton in the major cotton-growing states depict that the area under cotton has increased in absolute terms in almost all the states except Punjab, Karnataka and Tamil Nadu. In Punjab, the area under cotton fell from 0.70 mha during 1990–91 to 0.56 mha during 2011–12, not ignoring the fact that the state's cotton area in fact witnessed a revival between 2000–01 and 2011–12 from 0.47 mha to 0.56 mha (Table 12.3). In Karnataka, the area under cotton declined from 0.60 mha in 1990–91 to 0.55 mha in 2000–01 and

Table 12.3 *Trends in area and yield of cotton in major growing states in India, 1990–91 to 2011–12*

States	Area (in mha)			Percentage change in area		Yield (kg/ha)			Percentage change in yield	
	1990–91	2000–01	2011–12	1990–91 to 2000–01	2000–01 to 2011–12	1990–91	2000–01	2011–12	1990–91 to 2000–01	2000–01 to 2011–12
Maharashtra	2.73 (36.69)	3.08 (36.11)	4.13 (33.91)	12.70	34.06	117	99	297	−15.11	198.57
Gujarat	0.92 (12.37)	1.62 (18.99)	2.96 (24.30)	75.39	83.37	244	122	689	−49.94	463.47
Andhra Pradesh	0.66 (8.87)	1.02 (11.96)	1.88 (15.44)	55.89	83.91	288	277	443	−3.92	60.24
Haryana	0.49 (6.59)	0.56 (6.57)	0.64 (5.25)	13.27	15.50	401	424	703	5.72	65.90
Punjab	0.70 (9.41)	0.47 (5.51)	0.56 (4.60)	−32.38	18.14	463	430	698	−7.11	62.37
Madhya Pradesh	0.61 (8.20)	0.50 (5.86)	0.71 (5.83)	−18.14	41.85	111	84	482	−24.48	475.24
Rajasthan	0.45 (6.05)	0.51 (5.98)	0.47 (3.86)	12.18	−7.86	343	268	483	−21.83	79.90
Karnataka	0.60 (8.06)	0.55 (6.45)	0.55 (4.52)	−7.40	0.40	197	263	368	33.89	39.76
Tamil Nadu	0.24 (3.23)	0.17 (1.99)	0.13 (1.07)	−29.00	−21.72	290	317	575	9.11	81.57
All-India	7.44 (100.00)	8.53 (100.00)	12.18 (100.00)	14.65	42.79	225	190	491	−15.68	159.12

Note: Figures within parentheses are percentages of all-India.
Source: Computed using data from GoI (2014) and www.dacenet.nic.in

continued to remain the same in 2011–12 as well. In the state of Tamil Nadu, the area under cotton shrank from 0.24 mha in 1990–91 to 0.13 mha in 2011–12.

Besides actual area, some significant changes have taken place in the share of cotton area occupied by different states since the late 1990s. Except Gujarat and Andhra Pradesh, the other cotton-growing states, including the traditional cotton-growing states of Punjab and Haryana, have lost a considerable share of cotton area since the late 1990s. For instance, the share of cotton area occupied by Punjab declined from 9.41 per cent during 1990–91 to 4.60 per cent during 2011–12; in the case of Haryana, it declined from 6.59 per cent to 5.25 per cent. The state of Tamil Nadu, which has the least area under the cotton crop, has seen a drastic decline in its share in the all-India total. The share of cotton area occupied by Tamil Nadu witnessed a decline from 3.23 per cent during 1990–91 to 1.07 per cent during 2011–12.

On the yield front, a very impressive picture seems to emerge. Cotton yield across all the states increased dramatically between 1990–91 and 2011–12. Similar to national-level trends, the pace of increase in the area and yield under cotton accelerated in the major cotton-growing states between 2000–01 and 2011–12, as compared to the periods 1990–91 and 2000–01. It was in the states of Rajasthan and Tamil Nadu that the area under cotton underwent a decline during the aforementioned period. The increase in cotton yield was found to be marked in almost all the states. However, in Gujarat, Madhya Pradesh, Haryana and Punjab, cotton yield witnessed a phenomenal increase between 2001–01 and 2011–12 as compared to the period 1990–91 and 2000–01. What could have triggered the increase in cotton yield in these states?

As per the available data, the area and yield of cotton in the major growing states stepped up significantly between 2000–01 and 2011–12 as compared to the period of 1990–91 and 2000–01. If this is so, why are the voices of discontent emerging from the cotton fields of these states? In spite of a noticeable rapid growth in cotton yield in these states, why do the farmers lament that cotton cultivation is no longer remunerative? Why have these farmers taken the grave decision of committing suicide? Are the cotton farmers denied a decent profit from cotton cultivation? Let us try to answer these questions in the following section using cost of cultivation survey data.

Profitability in Cotton Cultivation

The four states selected for analysis here are not homogeneous in agricultural characteristics; therefore, the analysis of profitability of cotton is carried out separately for each of these states. Table 12.4 presents the results on cost C2, cost A2, VOP (value of output) and profit (at 1986–87 prices) for cotton cultivation for HAHP states from 1970–71 to 2011–12. To begin with, the state of Punjab accounts for about 4 per cent of the total area under cotton with cent per cent irrigation facilities in 2012–13. The results of Punjab show that cotton farmers were able to make profits over cost C2 in eight out of ten time periods. In the remaining time periods, the farmers were unable to cover the cost of cultivation. Even the profits realized by the farmers in the eight time periods did not exhibit a definite trend; profits either remained almost stagnant in certain time periods or fluctuated every alternate year. In fact, during the mid-1990s, the profit margins remained almost constant. Significant changes in cost C2 and VOP trends are observed before and after the 1990s as well. During the pre-1990s, cost C2 increased by about 21 per cent, whereas the VOP from cotton cultivation did so by 35 per cent. But in the post-1990s, these figures are 49 per cent and 45 per cent respectively. It is clearly evident that in spite of cultivating cotton under fully irrigated conditions, profits reaped by the farmers are not explicit. In relation to cost A2, the cotton farmers of the state reaped profit throughout the time period – amidst fluctuations, however. With cent per cent irrigation coverage, farmers from Punjab incurred losses in two time periods, which clearly brings out the fact that irrigation is not the only determinant of farm profitability. Can a similar picture be expected from the state of Gujarat, where the cotton crop has irrigation coverage of about 56 per cent?

Gujarat is another state which is selected as HAHP for analysis. It accounted for about 21 per cent of India's total cotton area and for about 26 per cent of total production in 2012–13 (GoI 2014). The per hectare cotton yield during 2012–13 in Gujarat was as high as 603 kg/ha, and it was ranked fourth next to Haryana, Tamil Nadu and Madhya Pradesh. Does higher cotton yield translate into higher profits? Does higher yield imply that the cost of cultivation of cotton in the state is fairly stable? Are cotton farmers reaping the benefits of higher yield in the form of a steady flow of income? The analysis shows that the cotton farmers of Gujarat reaped profits in seven out of nine time periods considered for the analysis. Similar to Punjab farmers, the cotton farmers of Gujarat too have incurred losses from cotton cultivation in two time periods, viz., 1985–86 and 2000–01 (Table 12.4). It is also evident that the profitability trend lacked a definite path amidst a sharp escalation in cost C2. Considering cost C2, it is observed that in over three decades, the cost of cultivation of cotton in the state has risen by about 300 per cent, from Rs 2,248/ha to Rs 9,499/ha. The VOP from cotton cultivation, on the other hand, rose

Table 12.4 *Profitability in cotton cultivation in high area and high productivity (HAHP) states, 1970–71 to 2011–12 (Rs/ha at 1986–87 prices)*

Year	Punjab							Gujarat						
	Cost A2	Cost C2	VOP	VOP/ A2	VOP/ C2	VOP- A2	VOP- C2	Cost A2	Cost C2	VOP	VOP/ A2	VOP/ C2	VOP- A2	VOP- C2
1970–71	1875	4049	4890	2.61	1.21	3015	841	NA	NA	NA	NA	NA	NA	NA
1975–76	1976	3624	3103	1.57	0.86	1127	-521	1533	2248	2562	1.67	1.14	1029	314
1980–81	2369	4483	4822	2.04	1.08	2453	339	3482	5107	5600	1.61	1.10	2118	493
1985–86	2556	4917	6638	2.60	1.35	4082	1721	2559	3750	3211	1.25	0.86	652	-539
1990–91	3468	6239	6500	1.87	1.04	3032	261	2983	4727	5671	1.90	1.20	2688	944
1995–96	3709	7296	7721	2.08	1.06	4012	425	3009	5202	6670	2.22	1.28	3661	1468
2000–01	4262	7540	7349	1.72	0.97	3087	-191	2283	3505	2851	1.25	0.81	568	-654
2005–06	4815	9589	10942	2.27	1.14	6127	1353	5240	8906	11268	2.15	1.27	6028	2362
2010–11	4760	10511	14550	3.06	1.38	9790	4039	4838	9526	18133	3.75	1.90	13295	8607
2011–12	5906	10916	11199	1.90	1.03	5293	283	5415	9499	12760	2.36	1.34	7345	3261

Note: NA = data not available; due to non-availability of data for some years, data from the nearest point were used in the analysis.
Source: Computed using data from CACP (various years).

relatively faster as compared to cost C2, by about 400 per cent during the same period, triggering the profit to shoot from Rs 314/ha to Rs 3,261/ha. However, as noted earlier, although the profit from cotton rose by Rs 2,947/ha in over three decades, the increase in profit was marred by fluctuations, the most conspicuous being the downward fluctuations ranging between Rs 1,468/ha and Rs 654/ha during 1985–86 to 2000–01. Such precipitous fluctuations in profit have taken place against the backdrop of plummeting VOP of the cotton crop, from Rs 6,670/ha to Rs 2,851/ha, with cost C2 oscillating between Rs 5,202/ha and Rs 3,505/ha. Even during 2010–11 and 2011–12, the profits over cost C2 declined by Rs 5,346/ha, which is indeed very worrying.

Elsewhere, in a different context, Gulati *et al.* (2009) reported that the main source of Gujarat's agricultural growth post-2000 has been the massive boom in cotton production. Has higher agriculture growth translated into higher farm earnings for the cotton farmers of Gujarat? Evidently, during 2005–06 to 2010–11, profit increased by over four times, benefiting the state's cotton farmers immensely. However, during 2010–11 and 2011–12, the profit from cotton suffered a setback with the profit margin varying between 90 and 34 per cent. Supposedly, a decline in VOP by about 29 per cent was the primary reason. It was expected that the state government's imposition of a price ceiling on locally produced Bt cotton seed, the spread of micro-irrigation and a high MSP for cotton, all would gather momentum during the post-1990s, and this would have a cumulative positive impact on the cost of cultivation of cotton and on its profitability as well. However, cost C2 is found to have risen relatively faster during the post-1990s than during the pre-1990s, thereby disabling the state's cotton farmers from earning appreciable and stable profits during the post-1990s (except during 2005–06 to 2010–11).

Although the cotton farmers of the state have not incurred any loss from cotton crop cultivation, profits fluctuated every alternate year. In certain time periods, for instance, during 1980–81 and 1985–86 and during 1995–96 and 2000–01, profit over cost A2 fluctuated very sharply. Profit during 1980–81 and 1985–86 fluctuated between Rs 2,118/ha and Rs 652/ha, while during 1995–96 and 2000–01 the fluctuation was between Rs 3,661/ha and Rs 568/ha. Plummeting VOP over cost A2 during these time periods is the basic reason behind such sharp fluctuation in profit. The profit margin over cost A2 obtained by the cotton farmers of the state during the entire period of analysis is not very impressive, although it is found to be relatively better during the post-1990s than in the pre-1990s. Profit margin over cost A2 declined during the pre-1990s, varying in the range of 67 to 25 per cent, while it improved marginally during the post-1990s. Similar to the irrigated-cotton farmers of Punjab, the irrigated-cotton farmers of Gujarat also failed to obtain definite profits from cotton crop cultivation.

Maharashtra is considered for analysis as the state with the largest cotton acreage but lower crop yield (HALP category). It accounted for 34.62 per cent of the total area under cotton in 2012–13 (GoI 2014), and is indisputably the largest cotton-growing state of the country. The state is often caught in the midst of water-related problems, and on the irrigation front it earns the dubious distinction of possessing the lowest irrigation coverage in the country. As of 2011–12, the irrigation coverage of cotton in the state was merely 2.70 per cent, clearly indicating that the cotton crop is subject to vagaries of the monsoon. This implies that the cotton crop is overwhelmingly rainfed in this central part of the country. Fluctuations in crop output and farm profitability under rainfed farming are well known. Under such circumstances, are the rainfed cotton farmers of Maharashtra entangled in the midst of fluctuating profits?

The results presented in Table 12.5 reveal that the cotton farmers of the state are able to reap profits over cost C2 in only four out of eight time periods, with the profit hovering somewhere in the range of Rs 344/ha to Rs 1,791/ha. The profit is not substantial, owing to the fact that the VOP from cotton cultivation, although it outstripped cost C2, moved in close tandem with cost C2, resulting in profit that was only enough to cover the escalating cost. In the remaining four time periods, the state's farmers were in the grip of considerable losses, as cost C2 surpassed the VOP from cotton crop. Much of this loss occurred during the post-2000 period, when cost C2 rose by about 117 per cent. It is ironical that it is during this period that Bt cotton cultivation gathered momentum in India, which promised to bring down costs of insecticides and labour.

In the absence of a steady flow of income from the crop cultivation, what is the incentive for the cotton farmers of the state to cultivate the crop? Given the fact that cotton is a cash crop that is supposed to bring cash to farmers cultivating it, if it erodes whatever cash is left with them instead, it is no more than a *killer crop*. Moreover, when the income from cotton cultivation fluctuates every now and then, and when the rising cost of cultivation sees no respite for a long period, obviously, the farmers will be prompted to opt for some other alternative where the element of uncertainty would be negligible. This is exactly what is happening in the cotton fields of Maharashtra where distressed voices hint at the abandoning of cotton cultivation. The profitability analysis of Maharashtra state brings out a vivid picture that the state's cotton farmers are cultivating cotton in the hope that a single good harvest would yield sufficient income to mark

Table 12.5 Profitability in cotton cultivation in high area with low productivity (HALP) states, 1971–72 to 2011–12 (Rs/ha at 1986–87 prices)

Year	Maharashtra							Andhra Pradesh						
	Cost A2	Cost C2	VOP	VOP/A2	VOP/C2	VOP–A2	VOP–C2	Cost A2	Cost C2	VOP	VOP/A2	VOP/C2	VOP–A2	VOP–C2
1970–71	NA	NA	NA	NA	NA	NA	NA	NA	NA	NA	NA	NA	NA	NA
1975–76	1066	1762	2106	1.98	1.20	1040	344	7639	10847	9239	1.21	0.85	1600	–1608
1980–81	1810	2762	2894	1.60	1.05	1084	132	6093	10090	12138	1.99	1.20	6045	2048
1985–86	1647	2360	1970	1.20	0.83	323	–390	2201	3938	4463	2.03	1.13	2262	525
1990–91	NA	NA	NA	NA	NA	NA	NA	NA	NA	NA	NA	NA	NA	NA
1995–96	2870	4434	5281	1.84	1.19	2411	847	5232	9288	8634	1.65	0.93	3402	–654
2000–01	3031	4667	3983	1.31	0.85	952	–684	4068	6962	8186	2.01	1.18	4118	1224
2005–06	4078	5891	5023	1.23	0.85	945	–868	4330	7826	6887	1.59	0.88	2557	–939
2010–11	5613	9323	11114	1.98	1.19	5501	1791	4266	8759	11002	2.58	1.26	6736	2243
2011–12	6178	10132	10025	1.62	0.99	3847	–107	5483	10087	10821	1.97	1.07	5338	734

Note: NA = data not available; due to non-availability of data for some years, data from the nearest point were used in the analysis.
Source: Computed using data from CACP (various years).

adequate profit in the current year as well as compensate losses in the past under abysmal conditions.

The cotton crop in the HALP state of Andhra Pradesh was grown under minimal irrigation coverage of about 18 per cent in area that accounted for about 20 per cent of the total area under cotton in India during 2012–13 (GoI 2014). With yield that is far behind the other major cotton-growing states of Haryana, Punjab, Gujarat and Tamil Nadu, but better as compared to Maharashtra, cotton crop in this southern part of the country is often controversially associated with crop failure, farmer suicides and acute farm indebtedness. Is cotton in Andhra Pradesh, which is the third largest producer of cotton in the country, not remunerative for the farmers? Are the cotton growers of the state able to cover the costs of cultivation?

It can be seen from Table 12.5 that out of nine time periods, the cotton farmers of Andhra Pradesh obtained profit over cost C2 in almost five time periods, with the profit hovering somewhere in the range of Rs 2,048/ha to Rs 734/ha. However, the profits were not at all substantial, nor were they steady. The state's farmers were in the grip of considerable losses in three time periods, ranging between Rs 1,608 and Rs 939/ha, as cost C2 surpassed the VOP from the cotton crop. Both substantial losses and fluctuating profits have occurred during the pre-1990s itself, which reflects the fact that melancholy and despair among the state's cotton farmers is not entirely a new phenomenon; rather it was very much present even before the entry of Bt cotton into India. The despondency of the state's cotton farmers continued in the post-1990s as well in the form of fluctuating profits, which can very well destabilize farmers' earnings by eroding their past savings. Thus, the return from cotton has been unpredictable in Maharashtra, Gujarat and Punjab, and continues to be so in Andhra Pradesh state as well. Compared to the irrigated cotton farmers of Punjab and Gujarat, the plight of the less irrigated and unirrigated cotton farmers of Maharashtra and Andhra Pradesh is equally ravaged by relentless oscillations in cost C2.

Number of Years of Profit Realized by the Farmers

As mentioned earlier in the profitability analysis, profit margins in almost all the selected states have remained unsteady and dismal too. Under such circumstances, it has to be investigated as to in how many years the cotton crop has benefited the farmers of the selected states. Of the total thirty-seven years for which data are available, the irrigated cotton farmers of Punjab have harvested profits over cost C2 for twenty-eight years (see Table 12.6). The crop turned out to be a loss in nine of the thirty-seven years

Table 12.6 *Number of years profit reaped or loss incurred by cotton farmers in relation to cost C2, 1970–71 to 2011–12*

States	Category of states	Green revolution period (1970–71 to 1995–96)			Agrarian crisis period (1995–96 to 2011–12)			Entire period of analysis (1970–71 to 2011–12)		
		>1.30	>1.00 to <1.30	<1.00	>1.30	>1.00 to <1.30	<1.00	>1.30	>1.00 to <1.30	<1.00
Punjab	HAHP	8/20 (40.00)	10/20 (50.00)	2/20 (10.00)	2/17 (11.76)	8/17 (47.06)	7/17 (41.18)	10/37 (27.03)	18/37 (48.65)	9/37 (24.32)
Gujarat	HAHP	2/14 (14.29)	10/14 (71.43)	2/14 (14.28)	9/16 (56.25)	5/16 (31.25)	2/16 (12.50)	11/30 (36.67)	15/30 (50.00)	4/30 (13.33)
Maharashtra	HALP	3/10 (30.00)	5/10 (50.00)	2/10 (20.00)	0/15 (0.00)	8/15 (53.33)	7/15 (46.67)	3/25 (12.00)	13/25 (52.00)	9/25 (36.00)
Andhra Pradesh	HALP	1/7 (14.29)	4/7 (57.14)	2/7 (28.57)	2/15 (13.33)	11/15 (73.34)	2/15 (13.33)	3/22 (13.64)	15/22 (68.18)	4/22 (18.18)

Note: Figures within parentheses are percentages of total number of years.
Source: Computed using data from CACP (various years).

(24.32 per cent), most of which has occurred during ACP. Farmers from the HAHP state of Gujarat have reaped profits in twenty-six out of thirty years (86.67 per cent), incurring losses in only four years (13.33 per cent). It is indeed commendable that with only about 50 per cent of irrigation coverage, the farmers were able to make a profit in most of the years.

The cotton farmers of Maharashtra have harvested profits in sixteen years (64 per cent) out of the total twenty-five years for which data are available. This means that these farmers were subjected to losses in nine years (36 per cent); much of these losses have taken place during ACP. This period has a significant relevance to the state of Maharashtra, as it marks the period of widespread adoption of Bt cotton. In this context, some scholars argue that Bt cotton has resulted in crop loss and is responsible for the unprecedented number of suicides of cotton farmers, which shook the entire world. Did the cotton farmers of the state incur losses only during the Bt cotton era? In the profitability analysis that was conducted in the previous section of this paper, it was stated that the cotton farmers of Maharashtra were struggling for a decent profit margin and consistent profit right from 1975–76 onwards. The state's farmers in the mid-1970s and mid-1980s were in the grip of fluctuating profits, which are as damaging as incurring losses. Neither were any cases of mass suicides reported nor did any massive relief package come to the rescue of the farmers who were languishing for lack of a decent and steady flow of income from cultivating cotton during the mid-1970s and 1980s.

We noted, to our surprise, that the cotton crop has turned out to be profitable in eighteen out of twenty-two years (81.82 percent) in Andhra Pradesh, which is a HALP state. Cotton cultivation proved to be a loss-making venture in only four years (18.18 per cent). If the cotton crop has proved to be beneficial to farmers, then why is the state ravaged by mass farmer suicides? Here too, Bt cotton was held responsible for the spate of suicides and crop losses among farmers. If Bt cotton is the villain responsible for crop losses and the subsequent damages, then what explanation can be rendered for the crop losses that farmers incurred during the pre-1990s? Why were no such distress issues reported in that period when the VOP to C2 cost ratios were less than 1 (<1)? It is astonishing that the less irrigated/unirrigated state of Andhra Pradesh is far ahead of Punjab and almost at par with the irrigated state of Gujarat in terms of earning profits in a larger number of years. Does this mean that irrigation alone is not the most important factor in determining the profitability of cotton?

Furthermore, as per the analysis, all the cotton-growing states except Gujarat and Andhra Pradesh have reaped profits in relatively less number of years during ACP as compared to GRP (see Table 12.7). The

Table 12.7 *Number of years profit reaped or loss incurred by cotton farmers in relation to cost A2, 1970–71 to 2011–12*

States	Category of states	Green revolution period (1970–71 to 1995–96)			Agrarian crisis period (1995–96 to 2011–12)			Entire period of analysis (1970–71 to 2011–12)		
		>1.30	>1.00 to <1.30	<1.00	>1.30	>1.00 to <1.30	<1.00	>1.30	>1.00 to <1.30	<1.00
Punjab	HAHP	20/20 (100.00)	0/20 (0.00)	0/20 (0.00)	14/17 (82.35)	3/17 (17.65)	0/17 (0.00)	34/37 (91.81)	3/37 (8.11)	0/37 (0.00)
Gujarat	HAHP	12/14 (85.71)	2/14 (14.29)	0/14 (0.00)	15/16 (93.75)	1/16 (6.25)	0/16 (0.00)	27/30 (90.00)	3/30 (10.00)	0/30 (0.00)
Maharashtra	HALP	8/10 (80.00)	2/10 (20.00)	0/10 (0.00)	11/15 (73.33)	4/15 (26.67)	0/15 (0.00)	19/25 (76.00)	6/25 (24.00)	0/25 (0.00)
Andhra Pradesh	HALP	6/7 (85.71)	1/7 (14.29)	0/7 (0.00)	15/15 (100.00)	0/15 (0.00)	0/15 (0.00)	21/22 (95.45)	1/22 (4.55)	0/22 (0.00)

Note: Figures within parentheses are percentage of total number of years.
Source: Computed using data from CACP (various years).

cotton farmers of Punjab and Maharashtra were able to reap profits of 80 to 90 per cent of the time periods considered for analysis during GRP, but only about 50 per cent of the time periods during ACP. Besides, the farmers in the largest cotton-growing state of Maharashtra and the fully irrigated state of Punjab incurred losses in most number of years during ACP. Therefore, it can be concluded that the profits from cotton not only fluctuated but also differed significantly between GRP and ACP among the states considered for analysis. The highlight of the wide variations in the margins of profit during the two crucial periods is that the cotton farmers of almost all the selected states were severely hit by uncertain and meagre farm earnings during ACP. Such adverse situations may have compelled some of them to take the extreme step of committing suicide.

Conclusion

Poor returns from cotton cultivation due to a perpetual increase in the cost of cultivation have been reported by the farmers in the recent years. In this study, an in-depth analysis was undertaken to cross-check with data from the cost of cultivation survey published by CACP as to whether the discontent in the cotton belts of the country is justifiable or not. The analysis reveals that although the profit from cotton cultivation increased across all the selected states at constant prices, the farmers were struggling to garner a consistent margin of profits throughout the period of analysis. The VOP from cotton cultivation outstripped cost C2 in almost all the states; however, it moved in close tandem with C2, resulting in profit that was merely enough to cover the escalating cost C2.

The profit margin over cost C2 in the highly irrigated state of Punjab was not impressive in the pre- and post-1990s, with losses occurring in both the periods. When the cotton farmers of the irrigated states of Punjab and Gujarat were struggling to make profits during the post-1990s, their counterparts in the less irrigated/unirrigated state of Maharashtra had to face the brunt of losses. In Andhra Pradesh, the crop losses that occurred during the mid-1970s reflect the fact that melancholy and despair among the state's cotton farmers is not entirely a new phenomenon. It is also found that dwindling profit over cost C2 is not confined to less irrigated/unirrigated farms; it is equally seen in the highly irrigated states. In an examination of how many times (years) cotton farmers were able to reap profit over cost C2 during the period of analysis, it was found that cotton farmers in all the states except Gujarat and Andhra Pradesh reaped profits a fewer number of times during ACP.

The analysis also brings out an important hidden truth, that profits from the cotton crop have been in oscillation right from the pre-1990s onwards, and assumed mammoth proportions in the post-1990s. This particular finding assumes significant relevance in the context of the decade-long raging debate that extensive crop losses and the spate of suicides among cotton farmers are primarily due to Bt cotton. It has to be underlined here that as per the analysis, cotton farmers of the major cotton-growing regions selected for analysis have incurred losses right from the 1970s onwards, a period when Bt technology had not set foot in India. The profit margins during those periods were also low but cases of farm suicide never came to the fore. Under these circumstances, how can it be claimed that farmers were ruined during the Bt cotton era? The bottom line is that the crop losses that prevailed during the pre-1990s gathered momentum in the post-1990s. Why has the crop loss not seen any respite in the post-1990s? More than any other factor, it is the persistent rise in the cost of cultivation of cotton that is playing havoc with the crop earnings of the farmers.

Amidst such disturbing trends from the country's cotton fields, what can be done to improve the returns from cotton cultivation? One-time relief packages or loan waiver schemes will not solve the problem that is being faced by the cotton growers. The real issue is the rising cost of farm inputs which, in recent years, has led to widespread discontent among all crop growers including cotton farmers. While raising the minimum support price in tune with the rising cost of cultivation is essentially required to safeguard the interests of the farmers, it is not a permanent solution for the issue of rising cost of cultivation. It can at the most be a temporary solution to compensate the rising cost of cultivation in the absence of yield-increasing incentives. Therefore, besides announcing remunerative MSP, there is a need to strengthen farmer-friendly market infrastructure with other non-price incentives such as adequate credit and improved surface irrigation facility.

One way of solving the problem is to popularize the drip method of irrigation in cotton cultivation as it has proved to increase profitability by reducing the cost of cultivation and water resources (Narayanamoorthy 2008). Drip irrigation will also be highly beneficial for cotton farmers in all the four selected states (Punjab, Gujarat, Maharashtra and Andhra Pradesh) as they are unable to cultivate cotton due to the fast-depleting groundwater table. All such initiatives can provide increased farm productivity and profitability; an assured income that can take care of the farmers' family needs and leave them with a little surplus to sow the next crop. If there is a delay in implementing these measures, the country's cotton farmers will continue to cultivate the crop under abysmal conditions, and hope and despair will continue to visit the cotton fields of the country every alternate year.

This paper was completed when the author was working as Professor and Head, Department of Economics and Rural Development, Alagappa University, Karaikudi, Tamil Nadu. The author wishes to thank Dr P. Alli and Dr R. Suresh for their research assistance in completeing the paper. The views expressed in the paper are personal.

References
Alagh, Y.K. (1988), 'Pesticides in Indian Agriculture', *Economic and Political Weekly*, 23 (38): 159–64.

Bhatia, M.S. (2006), 'Sustainability and Trends in Profitability of Indian Agriculture', *Agricultural Economics Research Review*, 19 (Conference No.): 89–100.

Birthal, P.S., O.P. Sharma, S. Kumar and A. Dhandapani (2000), 'Pesticide Use in Rainfed Cotton: Frequency, Intensity and Determinants', *Agricultural Economics Research Review*, 13 (2): 107–22.

Commission for Agricultural Costs and Prices (CACP) (various years), *Cost of Cultivation of Principal Crops in India*, New Delhi: Commission for Agricultural Costs and Prices (CACP), Ministry of Agriculture, Government of India.

Chand, R. and S.S. Raju (2009), 'Instability in Indian Agriculture during Different Phases of Technology and Policy', *Indian Journal of Agricultural Economics*, 64 (2), 283–88.

Central Institute of Cotton Research (CICR) (1998), *Annual Report*, Nagpur: Central Institute of Cotton Research.

——— (2011), *Vision 2030*, Nagpur: Central Institute of Cotton Research.

Deshpande, R.S. (2002), 'Suicides by Farmers in Karnataka: Agrarian Distress and Possible Alleviatory Steps', *Economic and Political Weekly*, 37 (25), 2601–10.

Dev, S.M. and N.C. Rao (2010), 'Agricultural Price Policy, Farm Profitability and Food Security', *Economic and Political Weekly*, 45 (26–27), 174–82.

Dhawan, B.D. (1988), 'Impact of Irrigation on Farm Economy in High Rainfall Areas: The Kal Project', *Economic and Political Weekly*, 23 (52–53), A173–A180.

Gandhi, V. P. and N.V. Namboodiri (2006), 'The Adoption and Economics of Bt Cotton in India: Preliminary Results from a Study', Working Paper No. 20060904, Ahmedabad: Indian Institute of Management.

Government of India (GoI) (2014), *Agricultural Statistics at a Glance: 2014*, New Delhi: Directorate of Economics and Statistics, Ministry of Agriculture, Government of India.

Gulati, A. (2009), 'Emerging Trends in Indian Agriculture: What Can We Learn From These?', paper presented at 2nd Prof. Dayanatha Jha Memorial Lecture, 2 May, New Delhi: National Centre for Agricultural Economics and Policy Research (NCAP).

International Cotton Advisory Committee (ICAC) (2014), *Cotton Statistics*, Washington, D.C.: International Cotton Advisory Committee.

International Service for the Acquisition of Agri-Biotech Applications (ISAAA) (2014), *Global Status of Commercial Biotech/GM Crops: 2014*, Ithaca, New York: International Service for the Acquisition of Agri-Biotech Applications.

Narayanamoorthy, A. (2008), 'Drip Irrigation and Rainfed Crop Cultivation Nexus: The Case of Cotton Crop', *Indian Journal of Agricultural Economics*, 63 (3), 487–501.

——— (2013), 'Profitability in Crops Cultivation in India: Some Evidence from Cost of Cultivation Survey Data', *Indian Journal of Agricultural Economics*, 68 (1): 104–21

Narayanamoorthy, A. and S.S. Kalamkar (2006), 'Is Bt Cotton Cultivation Economically Viable for Indian Farmers?: An Empirical Analysis', *Economic and Political Weekly*, 41 (26): 2716–24.

Raghavan, M. (2008), 'Changing Pattern of Input Use and Cost of Cultivation', *Economic and Political Weekly*, 43 (26–27): 123–29.

Sen, A. and M.S. Bhatia (2004), *State of the Indian Farmer: Cost of Cultivation and Farm Income*, 14, New Delhi: Academic Foundation.

Vishandass, A. and B. Lukka (2013), 'Pricing, Costs, Returns and Productivity in Indian Crop Sector during 2000s', Discussion Paper No. 7, New Delhi: Commission for Agricultural Costs and Prices, Department of Agriculture and Cooperation, Ministry of Agriculture, Government of India.

World Wide Fund for Nature (WWF) (2010), *Better Management Practices for Cotton Cultivation: A Guide on Sustainable Cotton Production for Field and Agricultural Extension Workers*, New Delhi: World Wide Fund for Nature.

——— (2012), *Cotton Market and Sustainability in India*, New Delhi: World Wide Fund for Nature.

Venkatesh B. Athreya: A Profile

Venkatesh Balasundaram Athreya was born on 30 December 1947 in the village of Pattamadai in Tirunelveli district as the youngest of ten surviving children at the time of his birth. His father, T.A. Balasundaram, was the headmaster of the high school in the village. He passed away in November 1949 at the age of forty-eight years, when Athreya was barely twenty-two months old. His mother, Narayani Ammal, did not have formal schooling; a self-taught woman of great resilience, she brought up her children under difficult circumstances. The family had no inherited or other landed property or other real assets of any significance. The loss of the sole earning family member was therefore a serious blow, especially with a large number of children to take care of. Vital and sustained help came from the eldest daughter, Lakshmi (twenty years older than Athreya), and her husband, V.K. Ganapathi. Some other close relatives also chipped in. The fact that Balasundaram was very fondly and highly regarded by many of his students from Madras (where he had taught for sixteen years before moving to Pattamadai), who were relatively well placed and influential, helped the two eldest brothers of Athreya (elder to him by a decade and a half) find employment in Kolkata. Their remittances, modest as they were, and the earnings of other elder siblings in due course helped ease the crisis over time. By the time Athreya entered college, the family was better off (though still modestly placed) and no longer struggling for survival. He considers the remarkable resilience and mental strength of Narayani Ammal and her household budget management skills as the key to this gradual emergence, and also values highly the contributions of all his siblings to minimizing the deprivations he experienced in his childhood and adolescent years.

Athreya had his primary schooling in Saraswathi Elementary

School in Pattamadai, an experience he recalls fondly. When the family moved to Chennai in 1957, he was admitted in P.S. High School in Mylapore, where his late father had taught from 1926 to 1942. After spending six happy years in this school finishing his high school studies and completing a year of pre-university education at Vivekananda College in Chennai, Athreya successfully cleared the entrance examination to the B.Tech programme in Indian Institute of Technology (IIT) and joined IIT Madras for a B. Tech in Chemical Engineering, supported by a merit-cum-means scholarship.

During his undergraduate years in IIT Madras, Athreya was taught the one compulsory course in economics by a professor named Anantharaman who was a very good teacher. The experience of this course and an emerging humanist concern with issues of poverty and deprivation massively present in his social milieu, propelled Athreya to a study of economics. Following his graduation from IIT Madras, he proceeded to the United States of America to study for a doctorate in economics from University of Wisconsin–Madison which had offered him admission and financial support. Athreya emphasizes that none of this would have been possible but for the support and guidance of his siblings as well as their spouses, and the tremendous, profound support of his mother, suppressing her own grief and suffering, and dedicating herself entirely to the task of ensuring the progress of her children.

The decision to pursue higher studies in economics was, in his own words, probably a turning point in his life. The late 1960s and the early 1970s were times of great ferment in several US campuses. The civil rights movement of the early 1960s was succeeded by a growing movement against the war being pursued by the US government in Vietnam, Laos and Kampuchea. Athreya walked into this ferment in 1969, and was greatly influenced by the legitimate questions that students on campus at Wisconsin–Madison were asking, such as, 'Why was the US government bombing Vietnam when Vietnam did no such thing to the US?'

Athreya completed the course work of his doctoral programme quickly, securing, with distinction, the highest 'A' grade in all but one of the courses he took and a distinction in his preliminary exams. While this meant that he had learnt rigorously and reasonably thoroughly the then dominant paradigm of neoclassical economics, Athreya's exposure to the anti-Vietnam war movement and the critical literature on international political economy that traced the US government's pursuit of the Indo-China war to its imperial ambitions and the pursuit of profit by large US business corporations across the world had led him to a very dim view of mainstream economics, which had no credible explanation for what was happening across the world at that time. It was at this time that he came to Marx via such critical thinkers as Joan Robinson, a well-known and outstanding economist who was then at Cambridge, UK. He embarked on a study of Marx's political economy by closely and repeatedly reading *Das Kapital*, Marx's magnum opus. Athreya says that reading *Das Kapital* changed his entire world outlook and the course of his life.

The period of Athreya's stay in the US – from late 1969 to mid-1975 – was also a period that saw the rise of the movement for gender equality and the powerful movement of the black people in the US against racism. Anti-colonialism and anti-imperialism, anti-racism and the fight against the structures and values of patriarchy became three major pillars of Athreya's world view, with Marx's approach to political economy providing the vital analytical fourth pillar. Athreya continued to pursue his studies of both mainstream economics and Marxist political economy while at Wisconsin as well as subsequently.

While in the US, Athreya taught at University of Wisconsin–Madison in 1973–74 and at Bucknell University in 1974–75. He returned to India in late 1975 and joined the Centre for Development Studies at Thiruvananthapuram as a visiting fellow. In early 1977, he joined as Reader-in-charge of the Department of Economics at the Autonomous Post-Graduate Centre of the University of Madras in Tiruchirappalli. That year proved to be a turning point in his personal life as he met Chandra, who worked as a teacher of economics in Holy Cross College for Women, and the two became good friends very quickly. They got married in July 1977. This proved to be a great match of shared interests and social concerns. Chandra and Athreya have one daughter, Poornima, who is now a senior HR professional.

The Autonomous Post-Graduate Centre that Athreya joined in 1977 as a reader was upgraded into Bharathidasan University in 1982. Athreya was promoted as Professor of Economics at Bharathidasan University in 1984 and as Head of the Department of Economics in 1990. He retired from the university in 2008. While at the Centre for Development Studies, Athreya had carried out a study of the Indian fertilizer industry. While this was linked to some extent to his training as a chemical engineer, it led naturally to an interest in studying the agrarian economy. Given Athreya's approach to issues of economic development from a Marxian perspective, it was but natural that his research interests turned towards India's rural and agrarian transformation as part of the overall political economy of the development and growth of the Indian economy. His research on agrarian change in collaboration with two sociologists then at the University of Lund, Staffan Lindberg and Göran Djurfeldt, began in 1978. The three scholars continued their research collaboration for more than three decades. The first round of this collaboration led to the publication of the book *Barriers Broken* by Sage Publications in 1990. It was a study of production relations and agrarian change in Tamil Nadu, based on a large sample farm and household-economy survey in six revenue villages of the then Tiruchirapalli district of Tamil Nadu. The second round of the research collaboration that began in 2004–05 was based on a resurvey of the same households, thus enabling an investigation of the transformation that had occurred over a twenty-five-year period which had seen dramatic developments in economic policies, including, in particular, the accelerated implementation of neoliberal policies from 1991 onwards with serious implications for the agrarian economy. Over the last four decades, a consistent concern of Athreya's has been the development of capitalism in India and its complex relationship with the exploitative structures of class, caste and gender as they have been and as they have changed on the ground.

He has not, however, been exclusively an academic economist. He became an activist of the People's Science Movement (PSM) and its Tamil Nadu contingent, the Tamil Nadu Science Forum (TNSF). He was active in the mass literacy campaigns of India in the 1990s, and coordinated the campaigns in the state of Tamil Nadu, taking leave from the university for two years to pursue these responsibilities. Some of this work has been documented in the book *Literacy and Empowerment*, co-authored by Athreya with Sheela Rani Chunkath of the Indian Administrative Service, who was the head of the administration in the district of Pudukkottai in Tamil Nadu at that time. The book, published by Sage Publications in 1996, provides an analytical account of the mass literacy campaigns enriched by a large number of narratives highlighting the role of the grassroots activists of these campaigns.

Athreya has also worked in the fields of education and health policies, both as an activist of the PSM (serving from 1996 to 1998 as the president of the All India Peoples Science Network) and as an academic seeking to play a role in shaping pro-people policies. His work, in collaboration with Sheela Rani Chunkath, on gender, focusing on infant and maternal mortality, declining female to male ratios among children six years and younger, and the horrific practices of female infanticide and foeticide has been published in *Economic and Political Weekly* and elsewhere. It has also contributed to community-based campaigns and interventions which have had some impact in reducing the incidence of these practices.

Athreya has been associated for more than four decades with

Left and progressive movements and has been a resource person to many organizations in these fields.

A prolific writer, Athreya continues to write on various issues in both English and Tamil, increasingly in the latter. His public speeches present a critical perspective and understanding on many contemporary issues. Through his different interactions, he continues to learn from the people. He is a passionate teacher and has always held the view that the practice of teaching entails constant learning. He has guided twelve PhD students and a far larger number of MA and MPhil students during his academic tenure. He remains an intellectual force inspiring young people to contribute to this great country of ours from a modern, scientific standpoint. Now in his early seventies, Athreya continues to be involved in teaching, research and social activism.

Contributors

Prachi Bansal is a research scholar at the Centre for Informal Sector and Labour Studies, Jawaharlal Nehru University, New Delhi and a research associate at the Society for Social and Economic Research, New Delhi. Her research spans agrarian issues as well as issues related to industrial development. She has been a part of several studies on agrarian relations in India, food security, employment and land acquisition, and has carried out fieldwork in Jharkhand, Andhra Pradesh and Haryana. She is writing her doctoral dissertation on labour absorption in Indian agriculture.

Vaishali Bansal is a research scholar at the Centre for Economic Studies and Planning, Jawaharlal Nehru University, New Delhi and a research associate at the Society for Social and Economic Research, New Delhi. She is writing her doctoral dissertation on food insecurity in India. She has been a part of many field-based and secondary data-based studies on issues related to agrarian relations, land, labour and nutrition. Her areas of interest include agriculture, industry and public policy.

R.V. Bhavani is Director, Agriculture Nutrition Health Programme at the M.S. Swaminathan Research Foundation (MSSRF), Chennai. Rural development, food and nutrition security, and leveraging agriculture for nutrition are the focus areas of her work. Between 2004 and 2006, she was on deputation to the National Commission on Farmers, Government of India, as officer on special duty to the chairman. Bhavani has coordinated several research projects at MSSRF on food and nutrition security, engaged in policy advocacy, organized national and international conferences, and authored reports and research papers. From 2012 to 2018, she was project manager of a multi-country, multi-institutional research programme consortium, Leveraging Agriculture for Nutrition in South Asia (LANSA), led by MSSRF. Before joining MSSRF in 2000, Bhavani worked as an officer in State Bank of India for a decade and was a Chevening scholar in 1997 on a programme for Young Indian Bankers at the London School of Economics and Political Science.

She has an MPhil degree in Planning and Development from Indian Institute of Technology Bombay, and a PhD in economics from Madras University.

Göran Djurfeldt is Senior Professor of Sociology, Department of Human Geography, Lund University, Sweden. He specializes in research on the sociology of agriculture and on development studies with long research experience in India. Together with colleagues, he conducted three major phases of fieldwork in rural Tamil Nadu, and has made numerous research and consultancy trips all over India. Since 2000, he has also been working on agrarian transformation in sub-Saharan Africa. His publications include books and articles on rural development in this subcontinent as well as Western Europe. His co-authored books on India include *Behind Poverty* and *Pills against Poverty* (both 1975, co-authored with Staffan Lindberg), *Barriers Broken* (1990, co-authored with Venkatesh Athreya and Staffan Lindberg), and *Structural Transformation and Agrarian Change in India* (2017, co-authored with Srilata Sircar).

Barbara Harriss-White is Professor Emeritus of Development Studies and Emeritus Fellow at Wolfson College, University of Oxford and a Visiting Professor in the Centre for the Informal Sector and Labour Studies at Jawaharlal Nehru University, New Delhi. Since driving from Cambridge to New Delhi in 1969, she has studied and taught about India's political economy. Her approach, published widely, requires fieldwork and has two strands: (i) rural transformations and informal capitalism; (ii) aspects of deprivation and their relation to market economy. She connects with Venkatesh Athreya through shared interests of agrarian change in Tamil Nadu and in the success of capitalism at hiding its failures. In retirement, she has fused a working lifetime's interest in the political economy of food systems with that in the economy as a waste-producing system.

Judith Heyer was a member of the Economics Department at the University of Oxford from 1975 to 2005, before which she held posts in Nairobi University's Institute for Development Studies and Department of Economics. She is now an Emeritus Fellow of Somerville College, Oxford. Much of her earlier work focused on rural development in Kenya. Her more recent work has drawn on fieldwork in western Tamil Nadu conducted over more than three decades. It focuses on the oppression of Dalits in the agrarian economy, the limited opportunities for Dalits in the industrial economy, the role of social policy in the rise in material standards of living of Dalits in recent decades, and gender issues in Dalit and non-Dalit communities. She has written and edited a number of books, including *The Comparative Political Economy of Development: Africa and South Asia* (2010, edited with Barbara Harriss-White) and *Indian Capitalism in Development* (2015).

Staffan Lindberg was Professor Emeritus, Department of Sociology, University of Lund, Sweden at the time of his passing away in January 2019. He was the founder-director of the Swedish South Asian Studies Network (SASNET) and had done extensive work, over five decades, on rural social transformation in India, focusing on rural Tamil Nadu in particular. He authored and co-authored several books, including *Barriers Broken* (1990, co-authored with Venkatesh Athreya and Goran Djurfeldt).

Mohan Mani is a graduate engineer from Indian Institute of Technology, Madras and has a Master's degree in management from Indian Institute of Management, Calcutta. He worked for twelve years in areas of finance and business planning with various private and public sector enterprises before changing sides to work with trade unions, helping them with research on enterprise and labour issues. He is a part of the Centre for Workers' Management, a small trade union resource centre set up in the early 1990s by independent trade unions. He is also a Visiting Fellow at the National Law School of India University, Bengaluru.

Gautam Mody is the general secretary of the New Trade Union Initiative (NTUI), which represents both regular and irregular workers across sectors throughout the country.

A. Narayanamoorthy is Member (Official), Commission for Agricultural Costs and Prices (CACP), Ministry of Agriculture and Farmers Welfare, Government of India, New Delhi. He is on deputation from Alagappa University, Tamil Nadu, where he was working as Senior Professor and Head, Department of Economics and Rural Development. A recipient of the Professor Ramesh Chandra Agrawal Award of excellence, awarded for outstanding contribution in the field of agricultural economics by the Indian Society of Agricultural Economics, Mumbai, he specializes in the area of irrigation including micro-irrigation, watershed management, farm profitability and cost–benefit analysis in agriculture. Narayanamoorthy has published ten books and over two hundred research papers in well-known journals. He has completed over thirty research projects sponsored by national and international agencies. The National Bank for Agriculture and Rural Development (NABARD), Mumbai, has awarded Narayanamoorthy the coveted NABARD Chair Professor position. He has, in addition, worked as a member of policy committees constituted by the Government of India, New Delhi.

Prabhat Patnaik is Professor Emeritus at the Centre for Economic Studies and Planning of Jawaharlal Nehru University (JNU), New Delhi, where he held the Sukhamoy Chakravarty Chair until his retirement in 2010. Before joining JNU, he had been a member of the Faculty of Economics and Politics at the University of Cambridge, United Kingdom, and a Fellow of Clare College, Cambridge, between 1969 and 1974. His research interests are in the areas of macroeconomics, political economy and development economics, where he has written a number of books and articles. His books include *Time, Inflation and Growth; Economics and Egalitarianism* (1988), *Whatever Happened to Imperialism and Other Essays* (1995), *Accumulation and Stability Under Capitalism* (1997), *The Retreat to Unfreedom* (2003), *The Value of Money* (2009), *Re-envisioning Socialism* (2012) and *A Theory of Imperialism* (2017, co-authored with Utsa Patnaik). He was the vice-chairman of the Kerala State Planning Board from June 2006 to May 2011, and is the editor of the journal *Social Scientist*.

Utsa Patnaik is Professor Emeritus at Jawaharlal Nehru University, New Delhi, where she taught economics from 1973 until retiring in 2010. She has researched extensively on problems of peasant transition from traditional to modern economy, both in history and at present. Her recent work relates to critiquing poverty estimates, and estimating the contribution of colonial transfers to Northern industrialization. These themes have been explored in over one hundred essays published in books and journals. Her books include *Peasant Class Differentiation* (1987), *The Long Transition* (1999), *The Republic of Hunger (*2007) and, edited in two volumes, *The Agrarian Question in Marx and His Successors* (2007 and 2011). Her latest book, co-authored with Prabhat Patnaik, is *A Theory of Imperialism* (2016).

V.K. Ramachandran is currently Vice Chairperson, the Kerala State Planning Board; prior to this, he was Professor and Head, Economic Analysis Unit, Indian Statistical Institute, Bengaluru.

R. Ramakumar is an economist by training and is currently NABARD Chair Professor at the School of Development Studies, Tata Institute of Social Sciences (TISS), Mumbai. He has a Bachelor's and Master's degree in agricultural science and holds a PhD in quantitative economics from the Indian Statistical Institute, Kolkata. Before joining TISS, he was a Visiting Scholar at the Centre for Development Studies, Thiruvananthapuram. His areas of interest include agrarian studies, agricultural economics, rural banking and micro-credit, public finance and national identity schemes. His book *Note-Bandi: India's Elusive Chase for Black Money*, a comprehensive critique of India's demonetization exercise, was published in 2017.

Vikas Rawal is Professor of Economics, Centre for Economic Studies and Planning, Jawaharlal Nehru University, New Delhi. His research interests are in the areas of agrarian studies and development economics. He has been a part of field-based studies in many states of India, looking at agrarian relations and farm incomes. Over the last few years, he has also been looking at global issues in the area of food and agriculture. He has authored and edited several books, including *Ending Malnutrition* (2015, co-authored with Jomo Kwame Sundaram and Michael T. Clark), which was published by the Food and Agriculture Organization (FAO) as a follow-up of the Second International Conference on Nutrition.

U. Sankar received a PhD degree in economics from the University of Wisconsin–Madison in 1967. After serving as a faculty member at University of Wisconsin–Milwaukee for ten years, he joined the University of Madras as a Professor of Economics in 1977. He was president of the Indian Econometric Society in 1994, Director of the Madras School of Economics from 1994 to 1999, and is now Honorary Professor, Madras School of Economics. He coordinated the World Bank's Ministry of Environment and Forests Capacity Building Programme in Environmental Economics in India, 1998–2002. Sankar has also been an ICSSR National Fellow in 2003 and 2004, and was awarded UGC National Swami Pranavananda Saraswati Award in Economics in 2006. His publications include *Controlling Pollution: Incentives and Regulation* (1997, co-authored with Mehta and Mundle), *Environmental Economics* (2001), *Trade and Environment* (2006), *Economics of India's Space Programme* (2007), and *Ecotaxes on Polluting Inputs and Outputs* (2007, with Chelliah, Appasamy and Pandey).

R. Sujatha is Director of the Karupa Institute of Development Initiatives (KIDI), which works on socio-economic research and development. She is also an independent researcher with specialization in development economics, and has worked extensively with the government, multilateral agencies, academic institutions, corporates and NGOs. She is a consultant with the Tamil Nadu State Planning Commission and State Commission for Protection of Child Rights. Sujatha's specialization is in the areas of gender, children, health and social sectors; she works with government departments on cross-cutting issues and provides policy-level inputs for evidence-based decision-making. Her doctoral research was on women's empowerment. Sujatha's interest in health issues prompted her to focus on menstrual hygiene management in Tamil Nadu, an area in which she has done pioneering work. She has worked in this area with corporates as part of their corporate social responsibility (CSR), with Government of Tamil Nadu, UNICEF and the World Bank, to improve access and awareness of women at the grassroots level.

Meghna Sukumar is a freelance journalist in Chennai, committed to working on issues of labour and women's rights.

Madhura Swaminathan is Professor and Head, Economic Analysis Unit, Indian Statistical Institute, Bengaluru. She works on issues pertaining to food security, agriculture and rural development. She was a member of the Government of India's High Level Committee on Long Term Grain Policy, and the United Nations Committee for Development Policy. In 2018, she joined the Expert Group that prepared a report on Multi Stakeholder Partnerships to Finance and Improve Food Security for the High Level Panel of Experts of the Committee on Food Security of the Food and Agriculture Organization (FAO). Her most recent book is *How Do Small Farmers Fare? Evidence from Village Studies* (2017, co-edited with Sandipan Baksi). She is on the editorial team of the *Review of Agrarian Studies*.